ACTIVISTS SPEAK OUT

❑ ❑ ❑

ACTIVISTS SPEAK OUT

❑ ❑ ❑

REFLECTIONS ON THE PURSUIT
OF CHANGE IN AMERICA

Edited by
Marie Cieri
and
Claire Peeps

palgrave

ACTIVISTS SPEAK OUT

First published 2000 by
PALGRAVE
175 Fifth Avenue, New York, N.Y. 10010 and
Houndmills, Basingstoke, Hampshire RG21 6XS.
Companies and representatives throughout the world.

PALGRAVE is the new global publishing imprint of St. Martin's Press
LLC Scholarly and Reference Division and Palgrave Publishers Ltd
(formerly Macmillan Press Ltd).

ISBN 0-312-22978-X hardback
ISBN 0-312-23504-6 paperback

Library of Congress Cataloging-in-Publication Data
Activists speak out : reflections on the pursuit of change in America /
edited by Marie Cieri & Claire Peeps.
   p. cm.
   Includes index.
   ISBN 0-312-22978-X- ISBN 0-312-23504-6 (pbk.)
   1. Social movements—United States. 2. Social problems—United
States. 3. Social Reformers—United States—Interviews. I. Cieri,
Marie. II. Peeps, Claire.
HM881.A27 2000
303.48'4—dc21   00–062606

A catalogue record for this book is available
from the British Library.

Design by Letra Libre, Inc.

First edition: December, 2000
10 9 8 7 6 5 4 3 2 1

Printed in the United States of America.

CONTENTS

ACKNOWLEDGMENTS

IF YOU'RE VERY LUCKY IN LIFE, you might find someone—a friend, or colleague—whose wisdom and support sustains you. For this project, we have been fortunate to have two such allies whose interest and loyalty have been indispensable: Archibald Gillies and Pamela Clapp of The Andy Warhol Foundation for the Visual Arts. This book would not have been possible without their unwavering confidence and extraordinary generosity. We are grateful for the foundation's gift of time and financial support that allowed us to travel and meet with activists around the United States and to reflect on what we learned.

Thanks, also, to others at the Warhol Foundation: the board of directors for their support, Emily Todd for early encouragement, and Vivienne Barriffe for assistance throughout.

We are deeply indebted to the many activists who agreed to be interviewed for this project. Their candor, passion, and selfless dedication were constantly rejuvenating sources of inspiration throughout the many months of our research. We are privileged to have spent time with these leaders, from whom we have learned so much: Sue Anderson, Carl Anthony, José Artiga, Judy Baca, Teresa Caudill Bates and Carol Wright, Mary Ellen Beaver, Joe Begley, Father Gregory Boyle, Bob Brehm, Ann Brown, Jack Calhoun, Mel Chin, Tyree Coleman, Ola Cassadore Davis and Mike Davis, Pat and Tom Gish, James Green, Jan Hillegas, Judi Jennings, Hazel Johnson, Cleve Jones, Esther Kaplan, Maxine Kenney, Anne Lewis, Herb E. Smith, Stewart Kwoh, Abby Leibman, Iñigo Manglano-Ovalle, Joseph Marshall, Tim McFeeley, Pam McMichael, Amalia Mesa-Bains, John O'Neal, Angela Oh, Pepon Osorio, Rosanna Perez, Skipp Porteous, Bernice Johnson Reagon, Joan Robinett, Ada Sanchez, Peter Schumann, Pete Seeger, Joe Selvaggio, Gail Snowden, Kasha Songer, Lynne Sowder, Joe Szakos, Norma Swenson, Barbara Trent, Guida West and Lily Yeh. Special thanks to Jack Calhoun, Tyree Coleman, Ola Cassadore Davis, Mike Davis, and Rosanna Perez for their special efforts in guiding us; their insights informed the outcome of the book.

For their patience and meticulous attention to detail in transcribing the interviews, thanks to Laurel Kishi, Sara Wolf, Andrea Lazar, and Jean Moncrieff.

To the many individuals who shared their time, expertise and grassroots networks in referring us to dozens of activists: Andrew Griffiths, Hillary Smith, Caron Atlas, Peter Taub, Jack Calhoun, C. Carr, Walter Echo-Hawk, Carol Seajay, Kenneth Freed, Chip Berlet, Andrea Miller-Keller, James Green, Kathy Halbreich, Steve Durland, Norman Frisch, Elia Arce, Robert Dawson, Ellen Manchester, Bill Cleveland, Jennifer Dowley, Melanne Verveer, Karen Ito, Judith Luther, John Malpede, Branda Miller, Sandy Osawa, Kathie deNobriga, Mark Murphy, and Cynthia Mayeda.

To those good friends and colleagues who gave so generously of their time to read and reread the book through several drafts, offering vital feedback: Katy Kline, Neil Smith, Briavel Holcomb, and Cynthia Rallis. And to others who offered invaluable advice and other kinds of moral support: Torie Osborne, Robert Flynt, Joanne Rizzi, Jacki Ochs, Suzanne Sato, Steve Lewers, Katrina Kennison, Denny Griffith, Mas Masumoto, Mark Pendras, Katy Kennedy, and Julia Carnahan.

Special thanks to Susan Dowling, who not only shared her time and opinions in reviewing the manuscript, but also loaned a quiet space in Maine for writing; and to Nathan Birnbaum, for editorial help, intellectual challenge, and love.

To cultural workers Robbie McCauley and Peter Sellars, whose art shines bright as silver. We have been privileged to work alongside them for many years as they have created theater, opera, film, and festivals that are community-based and artist-driven. They have helped us to locate art in the center of community, not at its margins, and have taught us that spiritual searching, social justice, and personal and collective courage are basic to artistic practice. Their example, friendship, and counsel over the years have been a deep source of inspiration for this project.

Finally, to the wonderful staff at Palgrave: editor Karen Wolny for taking us on and for handling the material with sensitivity and respect, Rick Delaney and Amy McDermott for able production management, Enid Stubin for copyediting, and Ella Peirce for seeing it through.

—*Marie Cieri and Claire Peeps*

YOU CROSS THAT LINE

Marie Cieri

I just knew things weren't right.

It's not always what everybody is doing, and it's not what the spirit of the time is . . . it's more just looking at really what is needed.

In a way, I'm selfish. I'm doing what fulfills me. My life is made meaningful, I'm made more humane. . . .

You've got to keep in mind that none of us had ever done this before.

. . . the only way society is going to change is one person at a time.

. . . don't consider yourself a failure if you haven't changed the world, because you have no comprehension of what you've done with all the seeds you've planted.

I don't call them small victories, I call them big victories, because I know what we're up against.

. . . don't think it's going to be easy, don't think you're not going to risk your life. Sharpen all of your tools, including a few claws.

. . . I really, really feel the anger, but I also feel the importance of people taking the high road. . . . that you actually embody the principles of the kind of world you want to create. . . .

The thing is, so what, it's a challenge. You have to find a way to deal with it, whatever it is. You just don't sit down and say, 'Well, what's the use?' You don't belong in this job if you do.

. . . you cross that line, like Rosa Parks did. Like a lot of people.

You cross that line, and everything you do is different.[1]

THIS IS A BOOK ABOUT PEOPLE WHO HAVE changed themselves, and who struggle to change the face of America. They are scattered throughout this country, coming from different backgrounds, walks of life, and points of view. They are known within their own communities and activist networks, but most are not famous and do not aspire to be. But they are heroes nonetheless. They are part of a little-recognized subculture, operating on the belief that dramatic, progressive change is needed in our society and willing to pay the often formidable price of being an activist in America. Over the last several years, we visited and talked to many of these people and here present their voices and stories as springboards for reader reflection, analysis, and inspiration.

This book is the result of a research project co-editor Claire Peeps and I began in 1994. Both of us had worked in the arts, as producers, curators, writers, and administrators for many years, and we were trying to come to terms with the political, financial, and spiritual crisis that had overtaken the arts in the wake of the Serrano and Mapplethorpe funding controversies and subsequent challenges to the National Endowment for the Arts.[2] Two things quickly became apparent: that the art world, while outraged, was having great difficulty devising effective strategies against right-wing attacks (and in fact was divided on which battles to fight and on what grounds); and that, contrary to what was hoped, the general public, even its more progressive elements, was not leaping to defend the arts as an integral and valued aspect of everyday life. Among other things, the crisis shed a harsh light on the fact that a substantial gap existed between the art world and most other sectors of American society, and that the art world itself had played a leading role in creating this gap and widening it over time.

It became clear that artists and their supporters needed to address these issues, not just in terms of their immediate financial and political survival but also with regard to their long-term significance within the American cultural landscape. The questions were: how could they learn to fight effectively for what they believed in, and how could they best integrate the spectrum of their activities into the consciousness of people who actually shared their basic values and concerns but had been turned off by a media-driven understanding of art? How could they try to change the situations that imperiled artistic freedom and at the same time reverse the patterns and perceptions that had severed connections with the larger society?

These challenges are not so different from those faced by anyone who is disturbed by the path society is taking and wants it to change. But why turn to activism? Isn't the democratic system in this country sufficient means toward orderly change for the common good? Can't we rely on the various branches of government to sort out conflicting interests and come up with fair solutions to problems that arise? That would be only in an ideal world, not in the one where we actually live. To rely on elected officials, policy makers, or the judiciary to instigate social transformation can be tantamount to doing nothing.

Looking back through U.S. history, it seems clear that progressive social change most often is set in motion by ordinary citizens who are sufficiently dissatisfied with the status quo to upset it. Their strategies and tactics have taken a multitude of forms, from marching in the streets to boycotts and strikes to the disruption of public services to the collection and exposure of incriminating information and well beyond. What most of these activities have in common is the desire to bring to light the nature of injustices and the extent of public opposition to them. The idea is that if government officials or corporate executives see that it is not just one group of troublesome activists but a much broader swath of society that disagrees with current practice, they might perceive an actual *need* for change. This realization by people in power is a prerequisite for any official transformation, and the most effective means for provoking this has proven to be citizen-initiated, activist practice.

Most people will resign themselves to the situation as is, citing any number of reasons why they can't take action. But there are others who will not be able to rest until something is done. The question then becomes where to begin. Given the current cacophony of Americans "speaking their minds" through every public venue imaginable, what are the best routes to truly being heard and making a difference in society?

Our idea was to talk to people who have made progressive social change a focus of their lives, people who are "the real thing" as far as activism is concerned. We would ask them what events or conditions had motivated them to become activists in the first place, what methods they had developed for doing their work and why, how they achieved consensus among differing points of view, and whether they felt they had been able to affect public opinion and policy. We would ask them to speak about the personal as well as the collective. After hearing their answers to fundamental questions about being activists, we then would seek their perceptions about the role of arts and culture within contemporary American life and whether they saw the arts as a potential agent of social change.

This latter point grew out of a recognition that artists at times have played an important role in activist struggles. One need only think back to the singers who inspired civil rights marchers in the 1960s and the artists who created posters, performances, and other artistic rallying points for the Chicano rights movement in the 1960s and 1970s. More recently, the AIDS Coalition to Unleash Power (ACT UP) has relied on potent forms of graphic design and street theater to deliver angry messages about HIV and AIDS treatment to pharmaceutical companies, elected officials, and a complacent public. On a smaller scale, a number of artists have initiated community-based performances and visual arts productions to foster dialogues about such issues as race, class, gender, sexuality, the prison system, homelessness, ethnic dislocation, and social reintegration (Robbie McCauley, Pepon Osorio, Rhodessa Jones, Iñigo Manglano-Ovalle, Mierle

Laderman Ukeles, Rick Lowe, Mary Ellen Strom, and Krzysztof Wodiczko are just a few recent examples). Independent video and film artists have done much to heighten public awareness of issues ranging from domestic violence to the effects of globalization on workers to the impact of mass media on the national psyche. From our conversations with activists, we hoped ideas might even emerge for new collaborative approaches to change among activists and arts professionals. It seems, after all, that there could be a fruitful interplay between the political imagination needed to be a successful activist and the kind of creative thinking inherent in being an artist.

We scoured dozens of publications and tapped word-of-mouth resources, looking for people who fit the bill throughout the country, and came up with a list of more than 100 possible interviewees: people who worked in the fields of civil rights, the environment, women's issues, health, youth, education, immigration, gay and lesbian issues, crime prevention and community building, labor, land and religious rights, freedom of expression, and the arts. We then reduced the list to the 53 individuals we interviewed.[3] They came from diverse geographic regions, races, and ethnicities; urban, suburban, and rural environments; women and men from different classes and educational backgrounds, ranging in age from 17 to nearly 80, many of whom became activists as young adults or even children, while others took up progressive causes much later in life.

As we talked to more and more people, it became apparent that there were no stock answers to the questions we were asking. Each person's response was born of his or her specific life situation and cultivated set of values. What did come to the fore were remarkable personal stories of transformation, sacrifice, and dedication. As we continued to collect interviews, it seemed that the most important thing we could do was share as many of these inspirational stories as possible. In this way, readers interested in the processes of personal and societal change could hear directly from those closest to it and draw many of their own connections and conclusions.

The difficult task began of choosing which stories to include in this book. At that point, it seemed less important to focus on interviews that contained the most direct references to art than to choose ones that conveyed the most compelling messages about what it takes to be an activist, no matter what the field. Of the 15 interviews here, there are some that contain little or no content about the arts and culture, though there are others in which this topic is held under a particular spotlight. For us, the project quickly became one that transcended any single issue or cause, and our goal has been to provide material that can be used to address the crisis that progressives in general are experiencing, not just those affiliated with the arts.

The book starts with the broad perspectives of two veteran activists, independent filmmaker Barbara Trent and singer Bernice Johnson Reagon. In recent years, Trent has directed her activist work against U.S. interventionist policies in Latin America, while Reagon since the 1960s has used her artistic talents to further the cause of civil rights in this country. Following that is an interview with longtime women's health activist Norma Swenson, who, among other things, is one of the authors of the revolutionary, best-selling guide to women's health, *Our Bodies, Ourselves*.

Next is the story of Joseph Marshall, a man who has dedicated much of his life toward building better futures for young black men in the San Francisco Bay Area. Esther Kaplan talks about the galvanizing experience of being a member of the radical AIDS action group, ACT UP, as well her work on race relations and abortion rights in New York City. Gail Snowden and Lynne Sowder both tell remarkable stories about setting change in motion within the corporate system—Snowden as a Boston banker dedicated to providing equal financial opportunities to inner city neighborhoods and to women, and Lynne Sowder as a corporate art curator who transformed elitist art practices into populist ones at a Minneapolis bank headquarters.

In her interview, Lily Yeh talks about how art and a cooperative spirit have been key ingredients in her 14–year mission to revitalize a dangerous, economically depressed neighborhood in North Philadelphia. Mel Chin has not only integrated remediation of the environment into his artwork but also has collaborated with commercial producers to insert alternative social messages into the sets and props of a primetime television series. Carl Anthony talks about his innovative efforts to achieve socially just solutions to urban environmental problems in the San Francisco Bay Area.

Both Mary Ellen Beaver and Joan Robinett devote themselves to struggles in rural areas, Beaver in taking up the cause of migrant farm workers in the eastern and southern United States, and Robinett in battling sources of industrial pollution in the Appalachian coal fields. Artist and educator Amalia Mesa-Bains talks about some of the defining moments of the Chicano rights movement and her present efforts to stem racial discrimination within academic and arts institutions. In his interview, former fundamentalist minister Skipp Porteous speaks compellingly about the tactics he now uses as a First Amendment activist to counter arguments against free speech by the religious right. Finally, Cleve Jones tells how he developed the idea of the AIDS quilt and has worked to spread its grassroots production and inspirational message to people from all walks and persuasions.

Different thoughts well up in the reading and rereading of these interviews. Doing this project was like taking a journey from one world into another, to a real but rarefied place where people have been chiseled and honed by the extremes of their situations and actions. And yet, despite the dramatic moments, much of it seems so normal, grounded in what we all at one time or another know and experience as human beings. The difference is that these people have decided to "cross the line" and take action, motivated at times by what are clearly life-and-death situations but even more often by a well-developed sense of social justice and personal responsibility. (*It's really important that people don't do it only for the results, but because it's the right thing to do. How else are you going to explain how you spent your life?*—Barbara Trent)

It's interesting that for many, a key to their involvement was the example of their parents or various activist movements of the 1960s, especially the civil rights movement. For others, it was the legacy of their culture, or an outrage that sprang full blown from a specific instance of oppression directed against themselves or others. A common theme of conversation was that we're all in this together, that there's no real difference between "they" and "I" when it comes to the impact of—and responsibility for—injustice in society.

There are so many different personalities and approaches here. One activist speaks on the level of pure belief and emotion, while another reveals the deep thinking and analysis of a strategic planner. There are humility and arrogance, stubbornness, disappointment, dedication and faith, generosity, exhaustion, caring, and anger in these pages. There is a woman who never forgets anyone she meets, another woman who sees rich resources where others see only barrenness, a man who turned his own fear into courageous action. Many of these stories contain chapters about self-discovery and transformation in the course of doing things, about finding one's calling, and about then creating or discovering contexts in which one can best work for change.

There are people who labor primarily on the grassroots level but at times are drawn into a broader arena (Robinett, Yeh). Others work very much on a mass scale but sometimes make use of global perspectives to foster change in local situations (Snowden, Porteous, Trent). Most of the people interviewed have tried to promote change as outsiders, but some of the most interesting stories come from people who have entered the system and have found surprising ways to bend its direction for the benefit of the disenfranchised. There are examples of creativity and inventiveness, not solely among the artists interviewed, but also among people who work in the most impoverished and least visible of situations (Beaver, Marshall).

There is fear in various guises, and vestiges of trauma in some accounts, but also amazing, quiet courage in the face of real physical danger. There's also the strength to admit that you can't do things alone, or that you need to regroup when the pressures of pushing for change become too great.

There's the clarity associated with seeing beyond convention—for example, being able to accept extreme sacrifice as a process of receiving as well as giving. There is a strong current of faith and spirituality running through many of the conversations, even among the nonreligious.

One thing we learned most emphatically from these sessions is that there is no single formula for successful activism. Contrary to what some may hope, we have not written a handbook for change based on the research we've done. That said, there are a number of themes that emerge from these interviews that are important pieces of the puzzle and worth flagging for readers as they move through this book.

Almost all the activists spoke in one way or another about the need for self-education to the point of becoming an expert in one's field of concern and related areas. This was seen as absolutely essential in fighting forces that are resistant to change. Knowledge *is* power: it puts you on an equal playing field with your opponents. It protects you from being tripped up by "the authorities." It also enables you to identify the weak links in your opposition's arguments and to develop effective strategies to combat them. Sometimes you can even appropriate strategies from the other side because you've learned how and why they have been so effective against you. The more you know, the less vulnerable you are to being discounted by people in power, and the more leverage you have to act as an agent for people in need. (*The truth is the best weapon.*—Skipp Porteous. *The more you know, the more you owe.*—Joseph Marshall)

But learning what you need to know to be an effective activist can be demanding and difficult. Some activists spoke about how hard it can be to get pertinent information, and how long it took them to acquire working knowledge of a field that was completely alien to them, like the chemistry of ground water contaminants or laws relating to migrant labor. Artist Mel Chin pointed out how broad systems of power in the world conspire to keep most of us in ignorance, which very much works against the activist impulse. Joan Robinett, who is an activist in the mountains of eastern Kentucky, spoke about how many of her neighbors have internalized the designation "poor, dumb hillbillies" and resist becoming active because of it.

Knowledge can also be what you yourself know to be true rather than what the authorities say—a good example of this is found in the interview with Norma Swenson, who has worked for years to counter what the male-dominated medical establishment has had to say about women's health. Learning can come from unexpected sources in unexpected ways: sometimes from people who are younger, or less educated, or from a different socioeconomic background. Some are still learning, some have the knowledge and wisdom of elders; a few can provide the historic outline of an entire movement in one sitting.

Once the hard work of learning has been accomplished, it is essential to pass on what you know to your partners in activism and to younger generations. Many of the activists spoke about the importance of democratizing the activist struggle and guarding against the tendency for people in need to become so dependent on the largesse and authority of those in power that they won't work to change their situation. Some pointed out that "passing it on" is the way movements are built, one person at a time. It is also how you can create new communities or revitalize old ones over common needs. Others talked about democratization as an important counterweight to the tendency of some activists to take elitist positions in their work. (. . . *what you see is this mindless P.C. vocabulary, this endless mouthing of slogans that mean absolutely nothing to people who are struggling to support their kids.*—Cleve Jones).

The question of how to build consensus within activist groups or how to create coalitions between groups of different identity and focus generated complex and provocative responses. Some activists talked about the necessity of seeking out like-minded souls, sometimes in unlikely places, and then moving forward to address the opposition. Others spoke about the difficulties of reaching consensus in a group, even when there is general agreement about goals and process. These discussions ultimately brought up an array of thought-provoking perspectives on the nature of leadership and individual leadership styles.

There was general agreement that activism cannot be done well alone, and that sharing of power with other members of the group is key to the creation and sustenance of movements. (*You start with people's issues because your role is not to transform them into you. Your role is to empower them into who they want to be.*—Barbara Trent) But all of the people we interviewed are exceptional leaders, and the stories they told about discovering and developing their own leadership styles are some of the most fascinating in this book.

Some of the methodologies that these activists have developed are extremely subtle, so that they themselves are not necessarily perceived from the outside as leaders. They have chosen to submerge themselves within the group, where they have demonstrated their talent to impart a sense of worth, direction, and power to others. When it comes down to it, however, they pick up the work if others can't sustain it. They are dogged in their pursuit of change, and there is no question that they will continue in the struggle. There is a sense of confidence in their own commitment and capabilities, and this is something that draws other people to join them in working for a common cause. Certainly some activist leaders are more overtly charismatic figures, but the quiet Pied Piper is pivotal in many of the situations we studied.

After establishing one's identity and context as an activist in these many ways, the challenge then becomes that of moving the struggle outward and forward. There was disagreement among the activists we interviewed about how to do this, but a common topic of discussion was whether or not coalition building among different groups is feasible or even advisable at this moment in American social history. While a few of the activists downplayed this as a sustainable strategy, the majority felt that building coalitions is now absolutely key to fostering progressive social change. Some talked about the need for women of different races and sexualities to work together for the common good (Snowden, Swenson), while others spoke about forging alliances across class, race, and gender lines to deal with environmental problems, health issues, or bigotry (Anthony, Jones). Perhaps the process of differentiating among a gamut of personal and political identities has led to too much segmentation and social isolation on the left. Perhaps our definitions of who we are and what we need to survive are too narrow now to advance agendas that will be embraced by a critical mass of change-minded individuals. So the questions that must be confronted now are: What differences matter, and under what conditions? Do we understand difference sufficiently yet to discover what we might have in common? And can this commonality become the basis of working together?

This is not a call to give up identity-based communities in favor of a newly homogenized left but a push for change agents especially to embrace the many facets of their own identities in ways that connect them to larger society. In this sense, activists can become the glue among groups of different focus that want change to occur. There are a number of examples and projections of this in these pages, even among people who have disliked, distrusted, and attacked each other in the past. It's almost a cliché to say that working cooperatively can increase knowledge and understanding of what we fear or dismiss in others, but it's easy to forget this, especially when we find ourselves in a seemingly endless string of crisis situations. There's plenty of concrete testimony here about conceptual leaps that have produced successful partnerships in unlikely circumstances (for example, between African American and white environmentalists in the Carl Anthony interview; between television soap opera producers and activist artists in the Mel Chin section).

Effective activists need to be strong enough to read reality and to do what's required to maintain momentum. One of the most striking characteristics of all the activists we visited was the length and breadth of their commitment to change. Each one sees activism as a lifelong enterprise, whether he or she is young or has acquired decades of experience. This takes place in the face of the slowness of real change; while each saw specific events that signaled movement in desired directions, almost all said they did not expect to see truly significant change in their own lifetimes. This was true whether the goal was achieving broad-based equality for African Americans in this country or full acceptance of lesbians and gays here. Sometimes the struggle is more about holding onto ground gained than it is about advancement. A lot of the time it is about laying a foundation for the next generation. Despite this, and despite the toll that activist conflict can take on both individual psyches and interpersonal relationships, none of them said they would quit. (*I think always it's more than I can handle. It's always about to bust me. Yet, at the end of the day, the fulfillment was so deeply gratifying. . . . It's like the purifying process, it's like fire.*—Lily Yeh)

There is plenty of information in these interviews about specific tools used in activist struggle, such as person-to-person organizing, employment of mass media, economic pressuring, public actions, skillful oratory, legal weaponry, quiet persuasion, education, steady vigilance, even prayer. The tools very much depend on the type and scale of activism being undertaken, and more than one activist spoke of the need to develop ability in multiple techniques. But what of our second topic—what did these activists specifically have to say about the place of art in society and its role in social change?

Perspective and emphasis, of course, differed between activists working outside the arts and those working within, but there was a great deal of agreement on the main points of discussion. Some of the arts activists, in fact, were far more critical of art-world practices than were activists from other fields.

The perceived gap mentioned earlier between the art world and other sectors of American society was highly apparent in the conversations. It was clear that, for some, the arts play little or no role in their lives, and the questions we posed about the place of the arts in American society and potentially within progressive activism were ones they had not previously considered. While most were open to new ways of looking at the arts, it was often as a very pragmatic tool for other activism—for example, better poster designs or musical entertainment at rallies. Joseph Marshall was very straightforward in saying that art is utterly peripheral to his work with inner city youth, and that he never thinks about using it to advance his activist goals.

When the interviews that appear here do contain substantive content on the arts, they present something of a debate about what art is and what its role is or could be in our society. One of the most interesting aspects of what's presented is that it comes from environmental and human rights activists as well as from arts professionals working in community contexts. It is not the art world talking to itself about itself, nor is it the kind of politicized boilerplate that we have been receiving from national mass media.

These are dedicated, thoughtful people who have made it their habit to run counter to conventional ways of approaching the world.

That being said, there was general agreement that the problem of the arts can be traced to their social isolation in contemporary America. Even when we talk about "the arts," it is with a sense of their existing on a plane that's separate from other spheres of human activity. One of the biggest criticisms of the arts expressed by these activists, artists and nonartists alike, was that they have an elitist aura, that most arts practitioners view themselves as "special" and "better than" other people, and that their work is best when the majority can't afford to see or buy it or when it can only be understood by a select few. How much this perception mirrors reality is a moot point; it is how the arts are often perceived, even by progressive social thinkers.

A good way into the art content of this book is the story of Lynne Sowder, a former corporate art curator who tried to address how the arts are traditionally presented to and perceived by the public and how to change that. This interview, especially, speaks volumes to artists and administrators who have tried to grapple with similar issues. Admittedly idealistic and naive at first, Sowder, in rather dramatic fashion, turned over the reins of her professional art practice to the employees of the bank at which she worked. A rather unique "democracy of the arts" flourished for a while, in which workers on all levels of the corporate hierarchy made decisions about what art to buy, where to display it, and how to interpret it. This approach was eventually terminated by a reintroduction of corporate control, but Sowder's story in the meantime pulls the rug out from many of the art world's sacred cows in how art is mediated for the public.

A strong but sometimes subtle current that ran through the comments of many of the activists we interviewed was that the art they value is art that is of one piece with the broader culture. In this view, there isn't a big difference between art and such things as cooking or language or sport or religious ceremony, and the art they refer to isn't art of the art world but art that emerges within specific communities to which they belong. This is now widely categorized as a non-Western European attitude toward art, but it is interesting to notice how this plays itself out along class as well as ethnic lines in various sectors of American society. Some prime sources for this topic are the interviews with Cleve Jones, Joan Robinett, Mel Chin, and Gail Snowden.

Though the artists whose stories appear in this book have some connections to the art establishment, their focus lies outside of it, and they had much to say about the social isolation of the arts within this country. Along with many of the other activists represented here, they pointed to the emphasis on individual vision and to the inability of most artists to work collectively as prime factors in perpetuating separation. Several activists warned that artists should not then be surprised to find themselves estranged from others when crisis hits. (. . . *artists have to understand that when they allow themselves to go down certain paths, they will find themselves alone.*—Cleve Jones) If artists truly want to speak in concert with broader communities and, beyond that, work for social change, they must first do the hard work of transforming themselves, as any activist needs to do. (*You have to see the world not just as some material for a new song or a new sculpture. You have to validate that the pictures you see are life forces that have a story that you have an investment in.*—Bernice Johnson Reagon) Artists interested in working within communities must find those vital connections with people beyond the art world and be willing to reciprocate with their own knowledge and power in order to be effective.

This is not a call for all art to be targeted toward social change, but what these activists have to say and what they show by example cut through the rhetoric that often is associated with community-based art work. In the view of the activists who spoke on this topic, the "visiting artist" approach to community-based work, however well-funded, will do little to foster true social movement or a rapprochement between the arts and the rest of society. Change is a slow process and calls for immersion and continual exchange by artists in real-life situations (Yeh, Mesa-Bains).

Still, there is definite cause for hope expressed here. While activist Esther Kaplan is critical of artists who produce politically charged work but don't extend it beyond the safety of art-world audiences, she sees that art may contain something that is lacking but very much needed now within the activist enterprise. This value is echoed in the observations of Carl Anthony, Norma Swenson, and others: that art can be a way of letting others know who we are in all our complexity and can help us move beyond the superficiality of much social and political argument; that art can present controversial messages in ways that entice people to listen; that the practice of art can help people have a vision of what they are entitled to; that art can provide human messages within an increasingly technocratic and impersonal society; and that it can provide enjoyment while teaching us important lessons about ourselves and others. It is obvious that in the minds of these activists, art need not be employed in overt service to particular activist initiatives, but that it can work on a parallel plane to change subliminally the consciousness of society. Above all, the stories here of the activists who are artists are cause for hope: these are extraordinary individuals who do not think or act in conventional modes of making it in the art world. They are models of what it takes to be a truly effective agent of social change as well as an accomplished artist.

In reference to the controversies that continue to simmer around issues of freedom of expression and government funding of the arts, there is important and diverse material here. Some of the activists are able to speak from personal experience, because in their own struggles they have been confronted with threats of censorship. As a former fundamentalist minister, Skipp Porteous especially is able to provide valuable insight about the motivations and tactics of the right wing. He and others reiterate that the problem of the arts' isolation from the rest of community life must be addressed before there can be widespread support for what artists do in times of trouble. Others question whether issues of freedom of expression and government funding of the arts should be so strongly linked; artist Amalia Mesa-Bains in particular has provocative things to say in this regard. Bernice Johnson Reagon's comments also come to mind: that conflict is part and parcel of the process of change, that you learn who you are by living in the world and facing opposition, that you can't be slowed by questions of "Why me?" when you are attacked, and that the strength of any backlash is proof positive of how successful you've actually been.

This introduction is meant merely to scratch the surface of what can be drawn from these interviews, and readers are invited to dive in and experience the power of the activists' own words. In one of the interview sessions, environmental activist Carl Anthony observed, "If somebody could just tell us the story of who our neighbors are, that might help us find a way out of our problems." He was speaking about the challenge of forming coalitions among people of different racial and economic backgrounds who don't know and don't trust each other, but he might as well have been talking about any one of us who may want to embark on a path of genuine personal and social change but has no clear idea how to do it. Knowing who these activists are through this book is a start—and we wish every reader could sit down for a few hours with just one of these remarkable individuals. But going out, engaging with, and learning from activists and other members of our own communities is the next best step in bringing the lessons of this book into productive practice. It may well be the most important step we can take in crossing that line.

Notes

1. Quotes are from interviews in this book with Mary Ellen Beaver, Mel Chin, Lily Yeh, Joan Robinett, Skipp Porteous, Barbara Trent, Joseph Marshall, Bernice Johnson Reagon, Carl Anthony, Beaver, Trent, and Reagon respectively.
2. Serrano and Mapplethorpe made photographic art works with religious and sexual content that was objectionable to many conservatives.
3. See the Appendix for a list of the activists whose interviews do not appear in this book.

1

BARBARA TRENT

BARBARA TRENT'S EXPERIENCE AS AN ACTIVIST *spans 35 years and ranges from grassroots organizing in the Midwest related to the Vietnam War, poverty, and racism to the creation of highly controversial political documentaries that have been broadcast and screened in theaters throughout this country and abroad. In 1993, she and her filmmaking team won the Academy Award for Best Documentary Feature for* The Panama Deception, *an independently produced indictment of the 1989 U.S. invasion of Panama. Other award-winning feature-length documentaries she has directed and produced include* COVERUP: Behind the Iran-Contra Affair *and* Destination Nicaragua, *both of which are highly critical of recent U.S. foreign policy in Latin America.*

Currently based in Chapel Hill, North Carolina, Trent co-directs the Empowerment Project, a nonprofit organization that provides assistance to independent filmmakers and videographers from the Southeast region and beyond. She firmly believes that independents must take it upon themselves to counter the corporately motivated messages of mainstream media with alternative views that are aggressively researched, produced, and distributed to the public. "I think you are capable of intervening in history if you're able to move fast—you can save lives," she says. Knowing firsthand the personal, political, and professional challenges her objective poses, Trent is actively involved in lecturing and conducting workshops around the country on public and foreign policy, civic responsibility, censorship, and independent film production and distribution. In the pages that follow, she tells how she first became an activist, how she moved from grassroots organizing to international projects, and what she has learned about activism and the possibility of social change in the process.

Marie Cieri: I know you didn't start out as a documentary filmmaker but as a grassroots community activist. Why did you decide to become a filmmaker?

Barbara Trent: My work in activism of course started in the sixties. From the mid-seventies up through eighty-one, I was targeted several times by COINTELPRO, a counterintelligence program of the FBI. When Reagan came in they came right after me. Eventually the forces pursuing a conservative agenda brought an end to my job in Illinois as a trainer for VISTA [Volunteers in Service to America] under Jimmy Carter. My husband of ten years left me at the same time. Moved in with someone just a few blocks away in a town of 350 people. It was apparent that I had no life left there, no way to make a living. So I moved to California. I got a job as executive director of the Ocean Park Community Center, a big, octopuslike human service agency. I did that for awhile and wasn't very happy. It was more administrative than I'd hoped, although I have great admiration for the work they do. After the three-month trial period, the board of directors and I sat down and said, "Is it working for you, it's not working for me. Yeah, it's not working for me either *[laughter]*." We parted ways amicably.

I was living in Topanga [Canyon], and there were signs on the health food store that said this group was gonna do a caravan across the country to the United Nations Second Special Session on Disarmament. I called them and said, "I can't go, but if you need any connections east of the Mississippi River, I can give them to you," because I'd organized in six states when I worked for VISTA. So I got involved with those people and eventually actually got on the bus and did the trek, both my son and I.

Haskell Wexler, an Academy Award-winning filmmaker, decided to come along and make a film. It was such an eye opener to me because I had been going to each little town of 350, 500, 1,000 people, fighting poverty, racism, setting up programs. I thought, "Gosh, a film, what a concept." You could send this in with people who weren't natural-born organizers, weren't charismatic or really well spoken—they could show the film and the group would understand, be riled up, and something would happen.

David Kasper, who was on that crew with Haskell, and I hooked up and started making films. We went back to California and moved in together in Topanga Canyon. My son was 12, and the school he was supposed to attend was 14 miles away, down one stretch of road that had the highest fatality rate of any road in Los Angeles County. There was no school bus or public bus. You had to have a husband who supported you so you could stay home with a car and shuttle your kids. So I started talking to the people in the area, and they said, "Oh no, we've fought this for two, three years; we can't get school buses." I said, "Let me tell you something. I've been doing this since the sixties. This is what you call a sure shot—if we do all our homework, we will win it."

So we went about organizing and found buses that were sitting a mile away, waiting for handicapped students for three hours, that could be delivering our kids. We found out the number of people who lied and said they lived somewhere else so they could drop their kids off at a different school on their way to work. We added up what the school district lost in all those people illegally going to other schools: more than enough to pay for a school bus, a driver, and insurance. We got the sheriff department's information about the lethalness of that road. We did this great little video, David and I, of the organizing effort, and we got the buses. To this day, when a new school board comes in, they look at the budget, they say we can't afford these school buses in Topanga, and people drag out this 14-year-old video. The board takes one look and says, "We can afford it."

I learned all the aspects of making a video as we did this project. What was interesting was that the video didn't win the issue by playing on cable TV prior to the school board capitulating. The video worked because, from the get-go, people involved in the system understood that this wasn't going to be swept under a rug. We would have 100 people at a meeting (because I'm a good organizer), we'd drag in some poor school board member, the parents would rake him over the coals, and there's a broadcast camera running the entire time. They realize they might have to act on this one. That was the real impact.

MC: Do you find that's generally true when making documentary activist film?

BT: Yeah, I think you are capable of intervening in history if you're able to move fast. I think you can save lives.

MC: Do you feel that using film and video has been more effective in instigating change than other kinds of organizing?

BT: Well, gosh, if you work in a town with 350 people, it's easier to get the officials to come to grips with the problem and deal with it. You can do a lot in a small town. But if you're trying to impact the country or international policy . . . it's impossible to be in every town of 350 people or 1,000 people, let alone big cities.

MC: Was it your aim from the beginning to have a national, international impact?

BT: I don't think so; I don't know.

MC: How did you initially become an activist? What was the force behind it?

BT: There are a few things that are crystallized in my mind. They're such little things. . . . My parents were really good people. I wouldn't raise my kid the way they raised me, but they really loved us and did their best. There was no confusion for them between right and wrong. My dad ran a little wholesale food company, E. J. Byman & Company. My sister and I used to go in there on Saturdays and work with this black woman, Willie B.; she'd be in the back, checking eggs. She would reach her hands down and grab eight eggs, four in each hand, in this black room with a black box with a little hole and a light bulb in it. She'd look at one egg in front of that light and see if there was an embryo growing, which meant it was no good. She'd be flipping this egg, flipping this egg—she'd go through eight eggs like that. If she found a bad one, she would give it to us and let us smash it in this box, which of course made this small black room smell as putrid as you could imagine. But she loved us, and we loved her; we didn't realize the disservice we were doing to her [laughter]. We were young kids.

I remember one time this guy came in on a Saturday. Some restaurant had run out of chickens, and he needed a few cases to get him through the evening. There was nothing more fun than going back into the walk-in freezers, me and Willie B. with the hand truck, and we got two big crates of chickens and walked 'em out. Willie B. was a big woman—she's picking 'em up and putting 'em in the trunk of this guy's car, and this guy says to my dad, "Wally, ah, we've got a problem here." My dad says, "What's the problem?" He says, "I don't want a nigger touching my food."

MC: What did your father do?

BT: He didn't blink an eye. He never thought, "Let's see, this is the whatever chain of restaurants, it's in three states, there's 15 restaurants involved, it's so many thousands of dollars a month of business." He just said, "Well, gee, I don't know what to tell you. Willie B. pretty much does whatever she wants to around here, and if you've got a problem with that, you shouldn't be shopping here." Never blinked an eye. Never made that critical capitalist financial calculation. In a thousand ways he could've compromised it gracefully—"Ah Willie B., let me just do this for you." "Oh, John, don't be so silly." "Willie B., give me that crate." It wouldn't be a terrible way to solve it, but it would have been wrong.

There was another time when the teamsters went on strike. We lived outside Chicago in Lansing, Illinois. There were five or six drivers, that was all, who worked for this little company E. J. Byman, and they came in and met with my dad and said, "You know we're not strikers. You pay us good, you treat us fair, there's no money here that we're not gettin'." So they drove that day, and one of the trucks was shot at.

My dad called them all in, once again didn't blink an eye, just said, "You know there's not one of your lives worth this business. We'll manage, and none of that even matters. There's nothing we do here worth putting you at risk. When the strike's over, your jobs will be here."

MC: Sounds to me like you were destined to be an activist.

BT: *[Laughter]* No, but those images for me are so crystal clear. Isn't that funny, just those two *[laughter]*.

MC: What was the activism you first took up in the sixties? What were you impassioned about?

BT: The Vietnam War.

MC: You were in school then?

BT: In 1964, I went to college—Southern Illinois University. We closed down the university, we closed down I-55 and I-70 and the Illinois Central Railroad.

MC: When you say "we," were you one of the leaders?

BT: Yeah, I'd stand up on tables and talk.

MC: Did that come naturally to you?

BT: I think I have a healthy sense of outrage to the point where I don't consider the consequences, I just take the proper actions, like my dad did. I also had a great speech and debate coach in high school, and that didn't hurt either.

MC: What did you learn about organizing people in the sixties? What do you think are the key things about mobilizing people and getting them to work for something?

BT: The sixties was a little different in terms of the basic lessons of organizing because there was such a spontaneous uprising across the country, from Berkeley to Southern Illinois to Kent State. The hard thing in the sixties was to rein in a movement so that it wasn't just anarchy or bedlam. I learned more about what it takes to organize a community when, many years later, after several other organizing adventures, I became a trainer for VISTA, because I worked with all the other trainers in six states. Everybody but me was academy trained, from the Midwest Organizing Academy, or from the Industrial Area Foundation in Chicago, the Saul Alinsky place. I had only seat-of-the-pants, gut-level experience, rural experience, and they had all this educated experience. But I was able to take this graph, this "map," of all these things I was doing: how to recruit members, how to do this, how to do that. When I laid it over my experience, it fit perfectly over what I did. I just would not have been able to articulate the steps as well prior to that.

MC: There are real basic steps.

BT: Yeah. For instance, you go into a rural community with a liberal, progressive, college-educated set of values, and most people don't even have a high school degree. They don't know what's happening internationally, don't know how it affects their jobs or their unions or their wages or tax dollars. You kind of hunker down and learn from them for a while. That's where I learned to garden, raise chickens and pigs and turkeys and rabbits and butcher 'em, along with my neighbors. You adopt their lifestyle not just to pay respect but to learn what you can from them. You have to assume that they have an enormous amount to teach you because they are bright human beings, just educated different from you. And the trade-off is they allow you to give them your rap *[laughter]*. You're one of them, so now they'll listen to you.

MC: And one of your raps was about racism?

BT: It was different in every town, depending on what was going on there. The other important thing is you don't go into a town as an organizer and say, "Oh, this is the heart of the problem." You go into towns and get to know people and ask, "So what's the problem?" Then they'll say we got rats in the alleys, we've got this or we've got that. It may seem like, oh my God, put out a mousetrap! But you start with people's issues because your role is not to transform them into you. Your role is to empower them into who they want to be. If this is the issue they want to resolve, you help them learn the methods to do that. Who's in charge of vermin control? Who is on the town council? Where are the pressure points? How do you get it dealt with? Then they give you the next problem, and you help them analyze how to address and resolve it. And people win. You don't *give* people anything. You facilitate people in finding the taste of blood, the taste of success. Then you get into bigger and bigger issues. As it becomes a bigger arena, your knowledge of the larger picture starts to be an asset.

MC: Did you feel that over time some issues you felt really passionate about were being dealt with by these people, maybe their minds were changing about some things?

BT: Absolutely. And mostly they were feeling their own power, realizing they weren't a bunch of schmucks. Just because a few people were running the county didn't mean they knew more or were any better than them. They realized, too, that they were paying their salaries and that *they* themselves really had the power. That's what was the most inspiring for me. There was a woman in Ava, Illinois, named Dorothy. She worked at the drug store as a soda jerk. Everyone came in there every day and talked to her—the cop, the mailman, the other workers, the kids after school. She knew everybody's problems. I spent weeks telling her: "Don't you *realize* the role you play in this community? You have incredible power here." When she decided to use it, she was invincible, because everyone trusted her. She was one of them.

MC: In working in these small rural communities, what was your motivation?

BT: I just lived there. You're coming from a premise that I wanted to do this for them, but that's not where it came from. I was poor. I was a welfare mother.

MC: When was this?

BT: Nineteen-seventy. In the 1960s, I was fighting against the Vietnam War and getting into trouble for it, major trouble. In the late sixties I was involved, let's say, with the drug milieu, and in 1970 I opened a drug crisis intervention center with several other people in southern Illinois. We had trained with a guy in Chicago who was later jailed for running a hospital without a license, for pulling people who were blue off the street and saving their lives. I was one of the first two people in the state certified as a drug addiction specialist. We trained students, we trained parents, we trained cops how not to exacerbate an already delicate situation so people wouldn't be psychologically damaged forever. We trained doctors how to deal with multiple overdoses pharmaceutically because they didn't know. I did this because I had been involved in it, and one day somebody died. Completely unnecessarily. We said, "My God, doesn't anybody know how to deal with this stuff?"

When I had my son, I went to the welfare office. They treated me like white trash, and I was amazed. I was a little down on my luck. I just needed a year or two to finish my degree or get my act together. Their position was, "We're going to be supporting your little bastard for the next 18 years, and you're gonna regret every day of it." Nothing's changed, by the way, in how that system works.

So I started organizing welfare parents, started organizing indigenous poor people in communities around the county. Got a job at the mental health clinic as an outreach worker, started setting up youth diversion programs. I guess what drove me was that somebody would treat me in a certain way and I would say, "Nobody is ever going to be treated this way again *[laughter]*." That's how I've made these films. I turn the TV on: me and David Kasper are sitting there eating breakfast, and George Bush says he's sent 26,000 troops down to arrest one man [Noriega, in Panama], and we say we're not going to let him get by with this. How dare he stare me in the eyes in my living room like he's telling the truth when he and I both know he's lying. Then you cross that line, like Rosa Parks did. Like a lot of people. You have no idea how it's going to end up, what it's going to do to your life. Once you've crossed the line, you're on your way. Mission Impossible.

MC: Sounds like you crossed the line several times.

BT: Many times. . . . The first big international film was *Destination Nicaragua*. I was becoming more aware of what was happening in Central America—the contra war, how they were torturing children in front of their parents, things like that. I went through this profoundly disturbing period.

My son was 12, and we would wrestle on the living room floor. Sometimes he'd pin me and sometimes I'd pin him—we were still in a place where you never knew who was gonna win. I would occasionally win only because I let out these huge karate screams. He'd start laughing so hard he'd lose his power. I'd be pushing that last shoulder down to pin him, and he'd be laughing hysterically but trying to fight back at the same time. His face would be purple and the veins on his neck would be pulsed out and his face would be distorted. All of a sudden, he would look identical to a child whose balls were being cut off or whose eyes were being gouged out. I would jump up, he'd say "What's the matter?" and I'd tell him. He'd slap me on the shoulder and say, "No, Ma, we're just playing." But this happened consistently, and I could not roughhouse with my son for several months without all of a sudden this image flashing in front of my face.

One day I opened a *Sojourner* magazine that told about groups from around the country that would go down and create a presence in the rural areas of Nicaragua on the Honduran border which were under contra attack. While they were there building a day care center or doing healthcare work, there would be no attacks on that town, because if a U.S. Congress-funded or CIA-funded contra bullet pierced the heart of a Texas Baptist minister in his fifties, it would hit the fan in Congress. By their mere presence they stopped our country's mercenary military units (that's what they were using, not uniformed U.S. soldiers). And I said, as an organizer, what a concept! You go out and stand in front of bullets that your country is shooting at somebody else. So I said to Dave Kasper: "We've got to go down and document this. This is an incredible organizing strategy." I went through this real transformational period where I came to realize it didn't matter if it was this Nicaraguan mother's son or my son who was being tortured.

That was the first piece that sucked me into Central America and that kind of work. For every piece after that, we've simply been in the know. After *Destination Nicaragua,* we had a lot of trust, a lot of contacts from the former CIA officers and analysts and researchers. So with each thing that happened, Iran-Contra and then the Panama invasion, we were in the perfect place to make a film. In fact, now everybody expects us to be able to jump and do something on everything that happens. But we haven't done any of those. Mostly it's that something really makes us mad and we do it. For instance, MPI [a large video distributor in the Chicago area] came out with a positive video about Oliver North. I speak around the country a fair amount and had just been on a panel with a guy from MPI. I called him up and said, "How could you? Do you comprehend this is not a harmless video, that thousands of people are dying? You've just whitewashed it, and they're gonna go on dying."

MC: What'd he say?

BT: *[In a deep voice]* "Well, you know it wasn't my decision," blah, blah, blah. I said, "Listen, you tell these guys we'll give 'em a story so much hotter, so much more unbelievable, so much more juicy, so much more sexy, so much more violent, and it will be the absolute truth *[laughter]*. *Fund that!*" And MPI actually said, "Let's see how the sales go with this North piece." They called us up: the North sales were going well, so they gave us the first $40,000 of the royalties to launch the film *COVERUP: Behind the Iran-Contra Affair.*

MC: That's truly amazing.

BT: True capitalism.

MC: Did they think you were going to make money for them?

BT: We did! Oh yeah.

MC: That's sick, isn't it?

BT: It's just the way it is right now in this country. It's not sick that they funded our film. It's sick what they did to make Oliver North a hero. But you always gotta come back to "There but for the grace of God go I." Who knows who raised them, or what their trip is? If you asked any baby at birth what do they want to bring into the world, joy and happiness or pain and misery, I believe all would choose joy and happiness. We create an environment that says to please me, do this. Make this money or do this job. Little by little people conform, I guess.

MC: Obviously the media is a very powerful tool, and you've been able to get hold of this tool as an independent and create films that provide an alternative story to what the mainstream media is saying. But being an independent can be a very frustrating existence. To get projects funded and made. Beyond that, to get the films seen.

BT: Which is the bigger job? The bigger job is to get the films seen and used.

MC: Exactly. Can you talk about how you've attacked mainstream media, how you've been able to reach people in an alternative way?

BT: We've not had a lot of success impacting mainstream media. Well, we have and we haven't. We cover stories that should be on the front page because they're news items, but we're in the entertainment section as a movie review. We have language from newspapers like the *Chicago Tribune* and the *Washington Post:* "calm, cohesive, and coherent" or "meticulously researched." But these are the very papers that condone the rightness of the invasion. Obviously the right arm doesn't know what the left is doing. One arm is saying "don't believe any of this," and the other side is saying "this is the final truth." This is the real debate, and that propels the film into the world.

I'm a firm believer that if you want your film or video seen, one important way to do it is to make it mesh into the capitalist system, so that everybody who touches it, whether it's the publicist or the agent or the booker or the theater, makes money. If you just show it in church basements, as a service to the public, it never enters a machine that's self-propelling. It's been a very difficult message to convey to the left. The left wants you to give them the film for free so they can show it in a church basement even though that will then make it impossible to release it in the theater across the street with a free review in the newspaper because it's already been shown. We would get letters from people that would say, "I just want you to know this film changed my life. I made 200 video copies and sold them off the hood of my car in front of the theater." What do you do? *[laughter]*. You just say, "Good going guys. Nice job, nice dog-gone job." We're still in debt, living on $7,000, $8,000 a year, servicing the debt. The left doesn't seem to have an understanding of the power of money the way the right does, and of course that's because we don't want to believe in the power of money. I appreciate that, but we gotta find some middle ground.

MC: There's a key piece here in that, with some of your films, you've been able to get over a major distribution hurdle. How have you done that?

BT: By knowing that if we booked a theater, talked 'em into a one- or two-week run, we wouldn't get booked in the next theater if we didn't pack that theater every single night and blow their minds. And we had to do this consistently, before they realized it wasn't a fluke.

MC: Okay, the first theater you go to—what do you have to do to get people to see it?

BT: We have to fly one of us in, plus maybe a former CIA analyst or officer. We have a big opening night benefit for one or two community organizations, who do an enormous amount of PR in advance. We have to stay there and pitch for donations after every single screening, five times a day, seven days a week. Answer questions. Leave people with an "Action Alert" to go home with, because they raised their hands and promised to talk about the issues on talk radio. Call the newspapers. We also say it took us two years to make *The Panama Deception*—how many people will spend two hours between tonight and tomorrow telling people they've got to see the film? And they need to see it tomorrow because if we don't fill the theater every day, it won't be renewed for next week. You open on Friday night. Friday night, Saturday, and Sunday, all day long and the evenings are critical. On Monday morning, every distributor in the country is calling every theater in the country saying how much they made on their film in some other little town, trying to bump your film out.

We would explain that to the public in the theater. You can't wait and pass the word around. We can be sold out Wednesday and Thursday nights, but by Friday we'll be out of the theater because they will already have signed a contract for another film. We try to *train* people in how it works. We also try to give them things to do, so it isn't just an "ain't it a shame" film—we give 'em names, addresses, phone numbers for the people responsible for the injustices illuminated in the film. We also provide ways to contact the media, who are responsible for holding this information back from the public. We've gotten national coverage on CNN, MTV, and a few others on our work.

MC: It's a very different way of affecting people than when you were living in the rural community, talking with them every day.

BT: Well, that was more rewarding and more fun. This is much harder.

MC: Now you're trying to affect many more people. Do you feel you're able to activate some kind of intellectual and emotional change in people? How deep do you feel it is?

BT: I know we're making a *significant* change, which is just one more drop in the bucket. I also understand that, okay? I know the impact on enormous numbers of people is significant. A certain number of people see these films and redirect their lives. They quit jobs, quit schools, and dedicate themselves to these issues.

MC: Have you ever felt that the films themselves affect people in power?

BT: *[Long pause]* I don't know. When you figure that these people are comfortable with the genocide in East Timor, in Guatemala and Haiti—clearly it's a consciousness that I don't understand. What I wish is that those people could just be retired or driven out of office, live on a farm, raise their own food and heal.

MC: How do you rate things like the 1994 elections, when there was a pretty big sea change toward conservatism and a cutting back of programs that benefit people who aren't well off?

BT: I think the country is becoming unwittingly calloused as a result of the propaganda of the major media: "poor people are poor because they choose to be poor and lazy, welfare parents are having babies just to have more welfare money." People work a hard day at the office or the factory and come home, turn on the news, and that's all they know. There's a deterioration of people's understanding of their own neighbors, let alone how the world works. They've accepted the influence of the media, which is protecting corporate interests around the world, allowing them to rob resources out of other countries and to have cheap labor in those countries while we lose jobs here. The chickens are coming home to roost—our country is deteriorating in my eyes.

MC: Do you think independent media is the only way of countering what corporate media tells us?

BT: Independent newspapers, magazines, video and film, speeches, and community gatherings are all we have now. When we're able to get a film into the theaters, like we did with the last two, in 80 different cities—we ran for nine weeks in New York, seven weeks at a ten-plex in Seattle against major Hollywood films. That's powerful if you do a discussion after every one and people promise to go out and do things. You begin to turn people into activists.

MC: You've been a real model of success in getting the message out to people.

BT: Nobody's done it like we do it. It's too labor intensive, and most filmmakers are primarily filmmakers in the traditional sense of the word. Our great fortune is the combination of David Kasper, a long-time media activist and a brilliant filmmaker, and me, a filmmaker with a talent for the organizing needed to guarantee not only good distribution but also real change. However, combining film distribution and activism takes a significant toll. Nobody's ever had something so lucrative and been left in as much debt as we have. We turned over so much money flying organizers around the country to keep the film going. People think we must be rich because we ran for all these weeks, but every penny was used to fly in an organizer or make more flyers. It's a bizarre experience. I guess because we won an Oscar, people think we're on easy street.

MC: That changed things somewhat.

BT: Yeah. We stopped getting donations. We had all this international interest and no way to respond to it. All these phone calls, faxes, press kits. How are we going to fund that? We were just as poor as we were the day before we got the statue. We were living in a garage in Milt Wolpen's backyard for free.

MC: I was told you were a bit of an oddity at the Academy Awards ceremony.

BT: We tried to fit in, and people were very nice to us. Oh, they hissed during the speech at one point, but after that . . .

What happened was there was a commercial break and I came out in the hall—I was in tears because the whole thing had become such a hassle. Were all four of us gonna go on stage if we won even though I'd already promised the Academy only two of us would? The whole thing was real stressful. It's a process of exclusion. Only a few of our team can come to the awards ceremony, only two can go on the stage, but hundreds helped to bring this film to fruition. I was just in tears and said I can't deal with this anymore, I've had it. Then one of the producers, Joanne, said, "Come on, Barbara, you can do it, you're okay, wipe those tears away" *[laughter]*. I had in my purse this little two-and-a-half-inch receipt from buying a bottle of spring water on the way, she pulled out a pen and I wrote four words—that was the speech.

David and I already had decided that if we won I'd talk because I was the fast talker and they were cutting people off. So we dedicated the film to all the people around the world working on issues of peace and justice, to the four people associated with the film who died, to journalists who put their lives on the line and reversed the ban against the film in Panama, and to the hundreds and possibly thousands of Panamanians who lost their lives in this invasion whose stories might not otherwise be told because of the deceptive practices of the U.S. government and the major media. And they didn't like that. They started hissing. And it got louder and louder. So I threw up my hands and said, "Hey, I don't like it either. That's just the way it is." Then they all realized I was on their side. I don't hate America. So I was able to finish. We dedicated it to all the people in this country who may or may not see this film now that PBS had refused to broadcast it. At the end I challenged the audience. I said we here in the audience have a lot of power over how people think, and we can make a huge impact. Let's use that to reverse the legacy that we've created through our policies in the world and become the Americans that we are capable of being. Have this country reflect the goodness of all of us. Then, of course, everybody was really happy *[laughter]*. But it's true! It's what I believe.

What was interesting was that afterwards Ted Turner shook my hand and said "Good speech" *[laughter]*. Maybe he was just trying to whisk me away, but I think he meant it. However, Turner did not show the film. Cinemax did, Free Speech TV, Bravo, the Independent Film Channel, and some select PBS affiliates have chosen to show it. They all have had this phenomenally positive response, which means the country is dying to see this film. So why won't PBS broadcast it? There's no justification, other than in the film we discredit the major media including the "McNeil-Lehrer Report," [which was on PBS] because of the way they delivered the news prior to, during, and after the invasion.

MC: The film that I've seen is *The Panama Deception,* and it's clear you were in some danger while making it.

BT: It's true for all of them.

MC: When you're planning the production of a film, do you have a strategy for getting people to work with you and be interviewed for the film? And also how to get out of there . . .

BT: Alive.

MC: *[Laughter]* I'm sure you also have to strategize about the safety of people you're interviewing. Can you talk about that, about the process you go through when you decide to make one of these films? How do you make decisions about what you're going to do?

BT: When I make the first decision to do the project, I don't consider anything. Just like my dad, not blinkin' an eye. If I ever knew what it was going to take out of my life in advance, I'm ashamed to say, I would never do the project.

MC: Really?

BT: I don't think so. This one *[The Panama Deception]* cost me my relationship. They all cost a lot, but this cost everything. I think if I really comprehended what it was gonna involve, I could not face it in advance. I could not perceive how I would survive through it and would be afraid it was going to be more pain than I could absorb. The decision to do it is always out of a sense of healthy outrage and complete ignorance. I think that is the only way these decisions are made. Then day by day each obstacle and challenge hits you in the face, and you deal with it because you're already on the path, and you'll not quit until you get to the end. The challenges get progressively more difficult, strenuous, painful and sometimes dangerous, but you've come this far, what are you going to do, quit? *[laughter].*
This is a terrible thing to say, but the fear of being shot only crosses my mind on occasion. Fear of not meeting the UPS deadline, or not getting the money together to pay the bills—that's what keeps me awake at night and terrorizes me. Fear of failure. I remember the closer we got to the end

of making *The Panama Deception* the less functional we were, so it seemed like we'd become completely nonfunctional the day before we ended. It seemed like the train might stop before it got to the station. I remember driving from Milt Wolpen's backyard to the office, thinking if *I turned* the car *here* and ran off the road and into *this* ditch, big enough to put me in the hospital, nobody would blame me if I couldn't finish the film. That's what you call having a real tough time of it.

MC: That's after the really intense physical danger.

BT: Correct. During the times I'm in real physical danger, I'm really strong. I don't bat an eye. I'm real grounded and real calm and stand right up to guns—they don't even faze me. I just look in that person's eyes and, of course, they're usually the age of my son—that makes it a lot easier. I talk to them like a mother, or like a journalist if they're older, or like a committed activist: "We're going to do this shoot—if you have to come in here and stop me physically that's your business. I've got a job, you've got a job. You figure out how to handle your job, I'm going on with my job, 'bye." When I finished *The Panama Deception,* I went through some real post-traumatic syndrome for quite a while—weeks, maybe even months. I couldn't look people in the eyes. I would just look below their eyes. But the more bizarre thing was that every day for the first three days, I woke up not knowing where I was, not knowing what I was doing there and not knowing who I was. Then the next thought was, "And I'm in imminent danger." I was in a state of panic. I didn't know if something was gonna come through the window. I had no idea what the danger was, but I knew I was in physical danger. On the third day, I went through those three things, and all of a sudden the bedroom door opened and David Kasper, who I'd been living with for almost ten years, walked into the bedroom— I had no idea who he was. But I felt this immediate sense of safety. And the panic just washed away and never came back. Yeah, so I guess it's affected me sometimes *[laughter]*.

We do all these security things when we're on location in another country. We make a deal with the hotel—we'll clean our own room. No one can come in. Even in the room we hide all the tapes, dig them into things. When we leave the country we have letters from Congressmen saying to the customs official *[in an authoritative voice]:* "If you'd like to detain this woman, do so at your pleasure, but do not separate her from her videotapes at any time. Call my office. Her plane arrives at three AM, I have someone waiting in my office for your call." They take a look at that and say, "Okay, ma'am, just get out of here." They don't want to stay there until the next afternoon dealing with the FBI and the Congressional offices.

MC: Are you afraid of sabotage?

BT: No. Too many people close to me died whose deaths are all explainable but suspect and untimely. They all knew more than me. I don't see myself as a primary target because I'm not a primary witness. I can't stand in court and say I flew the cocaine. It doesn't hurt that I won an Oscar either. But when I'm in foreign countries, I know I'm in danger sometimes. The secret police picked up David for four hours in Costa Rica. Commandeered him in our car when we were doing *COVERUP: Behind the Iran-Contra Affair*. We had just done an interview with John Hull, the CIA asset in Costa Rica. All hell broke loose, and we had to literally get out of the country. I've had trouble in Argentina. I would have been deported in France because at a press conference I released information available through the Freedom of Information Act in the United States which was not yet public in France that had to do with their intelligence service. It was considered a crime against the government. Everyone came up to me at the end of the press conference and said, "You're in trouble. We will arrange a clandestine meeting with this man because they're gonna deport you," blah, blah, blah. But the next day we won the festival, the Prix du Publique, so it was like, "What are they going to do now?"

Whether it be in a foreign country, a car wreck, a drug overdose, or poisoning from eating raw oysters—come on, don't you think? There's no sense in being afraid. When they want you, they'll just come and take you. They'll take you down *in a heartbeat*. There's no way to protect yourself, and there's no need to worry about it. You just have to be responsible. I have occasionally said, "You idiot, Barbara, this is completely irresponsible considering the issues you stand for and the work you're doing." To be in the middle of a train station at one in the morning in some foreign country is completely unacceptable. So trying to be responsible is all I can do.

MC: You are going to make more of these films, aren't you?

BT: I don't know. I like talking at universities a great deal. I like the inquisitiveness and the learning process. I've been teaching at University of North Carolina, Chapel Hill. I may do that at other colleges for a semester at a time for a special class on political and activist filmmaking. I'm also very tempted to offer myself to one of these communities to set up and coordinate a drug treatment program.

MC: You're thinking of going back to a smaller scale.

BT: Not smaller scale, but direct organizing. Interaction with human be-ings as opposed to sitting behind a desk, corresponding, and taking phone calls. That has become the thing that rules my life. The moments I get to spend with students or filmmakers or other people are a joy, but I'm always feeling like, oh God, I'm going to get in trouble because this is late or not getting done. We've run such a successful organization we've become a magnet for people all over the world who want help, but nobody funds us to give it to them. I definitely have to come up with a new plan.

MC: There's no issue right now that you're really burning to take on.

BT: Oh, that's not true. But I try to be like a mule, grind my feet into the mud and not let myself go forward every time I get aroused. Because I'll be dead. I can't continue like this.

Three big films. David and I are done. We've kind of got it down, and it would be exciting now to do something that's a new craft. It might be uplifting for me.

MC: Do you feel any connection to the arts community or to what's going on in the arts right now?

BT: I hesitate to talk about that very much because I don't think some of my opinions are very progressive. I have a soft place in my heart for peo-ple who believe it's a right within the Constitution to bear arms in case our government turns against us—that's the whole purpose of it, not to protect ourselves from robbers. Similarly, I believe in the concept that the public that pays for art has a right to want it to enhance the planet. We've already got Hollywood making money, and there are a lot of cheap shots out there that make the world worse. As a Midwesterner and a mother, maybe I just don't have as much compassion for some of the stuff I see. On the other hand, I understand that if the funding isn't provided, it censors art in the same way that we're censored economically in our film work.

MC: Are you sympathetic to the argument that the arts should be funded because they need the money or because it's an issue of freedom of expression?

BT: I believe it should be funded because of freedom of expression, and the only way you develop a free culture is if you don't censor what you fund, in a sense. I appreciate people's anger with certain stuff that's funded, but we ought to be able to tolerate those things. If you don't want to see it, don't go look at it. Personally, I would like to see most tax dollars go to things that contribute to community development and children. I know that's a big problem in the art world, more funding going to arts education and not really to art. I'm just more of an activist than I am an artist. Except I do want money to go to that other artist who's stretching the limits. I think there's money for both. The government has suggested to us that we have to fight over this one bean, and that's not true—there are enough beans for everybody. I think what's important is above and beyond my psychic confusion over the issue—just don't even get into the debate. The issue is why are we scrapping with each other over this buck when we should be scrapping with the big guys over the fact that we need more bucks for all of this.

MC: I think a lot of people have ambivalent feelings about government funding and the arts, or the arts in general for that matter, largely because the arts are so set apart from everything else. They can seem rather elitist. There are attempts to bridge the gap, but it remains nonetheless.

BT: Where does really great art come from? From kids doing finger-painting in grade school or a mother raising three kids and taking an oil painting class once a week? Or does it come from eccentric, crazy weirdos who devote themselves and step over that line, not knowing that it's going to destroy their lives and turn out phenomenal art?

MC: It's kind of like being an activist.

BT: Right. We have to have both.

The lesson for me, which I've always taught other people, is that as soon as you take action, the pain doesn't disappear, but it diminishes. When we ran the drug intervention program, we would take people with drug problems and have them be counselors. I used to do workshops for shrinks with the Association for Humanistic Psychology on the fact that we can't just *fix* people. We have to respect that they're crazy because they're normal, living in a crazy world. We have to help them learn how to behave in a way that won't cause them problems, but also help them find ways to change the world. To make it a sane place for their sane beings to live in. I just wanted to make that point. Things that have moved me have usually not been by choice. They've been something I had to do.

MC: It sounds like you're at a point now where you'd like to teach other people what you've learned.

BT: Maybe I'm moving to something like that.

MC: If I were a college student sitting here, really incensed about certain issues or just generally wanting to change the world *[laughter],* what kind of advice would you give me?

BT: To do the work because it's worth it and needs to be done. Because it's the only thing that's right for you to do. But don't expect to always see the results in your lifetime. On little issues, yes, but, on the global issues, don't consider yourself a failure if you haven't changed the world, because you have no comprehension of what you've done with all the seeds you've planted. It's really important that people don't do it only for the results but because it's the right thing to do. How else are you gonna explain how you spent your life?

October 28, 1996
Chapel Hill, North Carolina

2

BERNICE JOHNSON REAGON

BERNICE JOHNSON REAGON WAS A COLLEGE STUDENT in Albany, Georgia, when she participated in Albany's first civil rights march in 1961. Reagon was known as a soloist in her church choir, so it was no surprise when other marchers turned to her to lead them in song. Carried by the moment, she adapted the words of a well-known spiritual and sang, "Over my head, I see freedom in the air." The song became a favored anthem of the civil rights movement.

Reagon became a member of the Student Nonviolent Coordinating Committee (SNCC) Freedom Singers, and throughout the sixties she was one of a group of musicians who used music as an organizing tool in the struggle for desegregation and civil rights. In 1973, she founded Sweet Honey in the Rock, an African American women's a cappella ensemble whose repertoire continues to be characterized by politically and socially progressive ideals. As Reagon says of Sweet Honey, "We plough the path forward with sound."

Reagon's own role as a warrior for change has been multifaceted—as activist, singer, composer, scholar and producer. She serves as a Professor of History at American University in Washington, DC, and Curator Emerita at the Smithsonian Institution's National Museum of American History. She has published numerous books and articles, and produced the radio series "Wade in the Water: African American Sacred Music Traditions" for National Public Radio and the Smithsonian. The series received the 1994 Peabody Award for Significant and Meritorious Achievement in Broadcasting.

In the following interview, Reagon reflects on four decades of civil rights activism— on the role of the organizer, strategies for sustaining focus and momentum, and making space for the next generation of leadership. She describes how collective action invites people to step across internalized, societal lines, and how "when you cross that line, you're free."

❐ ❐ ❐ ❐ ❐

Claire Peeps: Can recall when you first realized that singing could be a tool in social organizing?

Bernice Johnson Reagon: My sense is that I only came to realize it when I began to try to explain what I'd already been doing for more than 15 years. I don't think I had that kind of naming for music, it wasn't necessary to separate out music from anything else I was doing. I came up in Albany, Georgia, as a singer. I joined the church when I was eleven and by the time I was twelve the church got its first piano. My sister played the piano for the choir. I was a contralto, and I did a lot of the solo leads. Everybody in the family sang. There were three generations in that choir—teenagers, parents, and grandparents. You don't see that a lot now in choirs. It is an amazing thing, working across generations in singing.

When I was a senior in high school, at sixteen, I became secretary for the local youth chapter of the NAACP. Throughout that time and into my college years at Albany State, if there was singing in any of the meetings, people would turn to me and I would lead a song. It just happened naturally.

So when the civil rights movement started in Albany in 1961, I was one of the people in Albany known as a singer. There were a few of us: Rutha Harris was another. There were also other people who were solid singers who could lead almost anything but they'd never been in a choir, they could do a really great alto or tenor. It was a great singing culture, and there was a real freedom with people leading songs. There was no "I can't sing that well" attitude. Anybody could start a song. And in addition to the people who could sing, there were those like my mother who said, "I can't sing, but I love to sing," who sang all the time. There just didn't seem to be a lot of space where people weren't singing. That's the kind of culture I grew up with.

The first march in Albany happened in December of '61. Two students had been arrested for buying tickets at the white window of the Trailways bus station. Four others were also arrested for joining in, so there were six in all who were taken down to jail. The four others were from the NAACP youth chapter, which had a strategy to get people charged and booked so they could push cases into the legal system, things to court. So they bailed out the four NAACP students. The other two students, Bertha Goba and Blanton Hall, refused to post bail, saying that they had not done anything wrong. We did a sympathy support demonstration for them. We marched around the campus twice, and we knew we couldn't go back because the campus administration was very hostile to activism. So we went into the closest church, the Union Baptist Church. Charley Jones, a SNCC field secretary, said, "Bernice, lead a song." I began the spiritual "Over my head, I hear music in the air, over my head, I see trouble in the air, over my head,

I see shouting in the air, there must be a God somewhere." But I turned it into "Over my head, I see freedom in the air."

CP: Just at that moment?

BJR: Yeah. I started down the line of the song and I could see "trouble" coming at me—and I didn't see "trouble" then as a progressive term so I flipped it to "freedom." It was the first time I had, in public performance, experienced coming up with a song—an old song, a spiritual—and making it appropriate to the situation. It's something I've done many times since then, but I won't forget it. The interesting thing about "the trouble in the air" is that I have since come to understand trouble as a positive term in a lot of black songs. It's like "Wade in the water, God's gonna trouble the water," which was clearly saying, "Go ahead, don't worry, it's gonna be troubled." But I didn't know that in '61. I think I was about 18 then.

CP: Was that first march a frightening experience for you?

BJR: I think so, but not in terms of fear like you're scared to death. I already had a way of facing fear or walking through it, being scared but going ahead.

CP: Where had that come from?

BJR: I don't know. Lots of times, you know, you do things when everything is telling you, "Don't do it, it'll kill you," but you just do it anyway. I understood mastering fear and using it as a side mirror. Like one time, my biology teacher brought a snake into my high school. He said it was not poisonous, but everybody was running from that snake. I picked it up. I was clearly scared of it, but that snake curled around my arms and they named it Bernice *[laughter]*. My mother thought I was out of my mind. So I've had a few experiences where I've done things while inside my head there was a tape running, saying, "You're going to die if you do this." But I would do it anyway. And that was kind of what happened during the march. We went through several school buildings and into classes announcing to students what we were going to do. At this point, in '61, there'd been marches and sit-ins elsewhere, so there was already an accessible language and action to get students into the street. And that day in Albany it felt like the beginning of something very important. We started out and we had to go up a hill and across a bridge over the river to get downtown. When we started off the campus, there were very few people with us, and I can remember being disappointed. I decided not to look back after the first glance. When we got to the top of the hill, which was about three blocks from the campus, Annette Jones, my friend and marching partner, said, "Bernice, look back." I wasn't looking back because there was nobody there. But she said again, "Bernice, look back!" I looked back and as far as I could see there were people stretched all the way back to the campus. I realized then that SNCC field secretaries leading us were scared to death. This would be the first march in Albany, Georgia, and they were making it up as we went along. We marched two by two, and it was like, we won't sing, we'll be silent, we'll be dignified and respectful. They had to send somebody to find some place for us to go because they hadn't planned that far. So I found out things were operating on the cuff. Sometimes you find the people who are leading you are not a step ahead. You're pushing them and they're just trying to keep up so they can be in the front.

CP: Can I ask you about that? In another interview you said a wonderful thing about writing music that relates to that phenomenon. You said, "A living thing needs to be guided, it needs incredible work and discipline. You need to let it go, you don't need to always be in charge of what happens to it. If you're putting the work and discipline, commitment and integrity into the piece, then you can just watch it. You don't have to know what it's going to be and what it's going to do." In light of what you just said about the SNCC field secretaries leading the march, can talk about this notion of making art related to the process of organizing?

BJR: I don't think leadership is different, really. Take Ella Baker, for example. Her work, at its base, was about trying to let people have a chance to hear themselves talk out enough so they could get as clear as they could get about where they were. She reaffirmed everybody she could touch that they had a right to an opinion, and that their opinion needed to be heard before a decision was made, that everybody ought to speak. She believed that you don't trust a thing if you've not heard where everybody is. And you only do that by taking some downtime where you get to talk about what you're thinking inside. Then you can watch your words be woven into what becomes policy and what becomes action. That was the way she felt leaders were created, and that was the way she led. Her leadership style was basically a style of creating leaders. If you're unleashing power in people, you can't really lead those people. You can only create forums or situations, processes for them to go through. She always felt that a voice or a person who would be in the front would come out of those situations. We always felt she was therefore the master leader.

It was a new model, because in the black community we only saw the leaders who were in the front—the president or pastor, the soloist, or the whatever. The people who created the environment were almost invisible. They tended not to get the accolades. You sensed they were heavy hitters, and the leader never wanted to be anywhere without these people, but they were not considered the master leaders. Ella Baker taught me to trade in my understanding of leadership. In almost all of the work I've done with people, I've been often the person in front but my most important work has been creating and nurturing an environment where people had a chance to speak—to set policy and decide action and create another space in their lives to do something they weren't doing before.

CP: Was the civil rights movement trying to advance specific goals that you were working toward?

BJR: I don't know about specific goals. We'd say we were working for freedom, and that was a very specific goal. Anything we did on any given day was just a little piece of that. But we found that we were in a culture, especially in terms of sympathetic newspeople or people who wrote or talked about what we were doing, that seemed to need something more than "freedom" to understand our efforts. We felt sorry for them. We understood them as supporters and we did the best we could to give them what they needed, but when we read what they wrote or heard what they said, we always felt they didn't quite get it. The catalogue of specific targets was never it. If you list specific targets, you think you have a way of evaluating whether or not you have been successful or not. I found that very alien to anything I needed in my life. I understand it now as the Western scientific method. It's everywhere in our culture, but it's so flawed. If you picket in front of the drugstore to get them to hire somebody and they hire somebody, then it's a victory. If the next year that person is fired, then your victory has been short-lived or failed. But this system has no way of evaluating something that is changed that never goes back. That is what happens to the people who step across lines—lines that are not simply drawn in their communities but are drawn in their own lives, lines that are internalized in our racist society. When you cross that line, you're free. Now you may be in jail at that time, you may just have failed to successfully get the city commissioners to meet with you, but if you've stepped outside that line, you've broken it for yourself. And that's not seen to be concrete for many people trying to get a handle on what was happening in the movement.

CP: But does that suggest that picketing in itself is not a useful strategy or just that the end goal is not an appropriate one?

BJR: It has nothing to do with evaluating specific action. You cross the line and everything you do is different. You can walk the first time in a march, you can picket, you can go to city hall, you can go to jail. You can do all of these things and they become behaviors. They are crucial, because crossing a line inside of yourself means nothing if you don't manifest it in changed behavior. And so we started to act differently, and we were not the only ones. We structured organizations within the civil rights movement to focus in on changed behaviors, to make them have an impact on the overt organized lines. It was not just me walking into the library by myself one day, saying, "I want to check out a book" and getting put in jail. It was more like ten of us going and they closed the library. That's where the action is, for me.

CP: In the collective. Is that what you're suggesting?

BJR: Yeah. And the brilliance of it has something to do with timing. You can have people stepping across the line internally, but if there's not a collective effort, it's just isolated stuff. But if you can create structures that invite people to consider crossing the line, it becomes seductive. That's what organized action does. You're not by yourself. Somebody actually knocks on your door and says, "Will you go down to register to vote?" or " Will you come to the mass meeting?" or "Will you go on this march?" Whatever it is, the actions are really things that you use to get people to consider transforming who they are as human beings—trading in who they are for who they can become.

The civil rights movement pushed against the overt lines in the society. And when people saw black people pushing that line, then other people in the country were seduced to consider. There were people who looked at what they saw on their TV and said, "If this is going to happen in the country, it is not going to happen without me." That's a personal move. It's not a missionary move. There were some missionaries, but what I'm talking about is a more personal sort of saving yourself—understanding this was an opportunity for you to be different, to reorganize everything in your life. Seeing it like that means that everything you do becomes a skirmish that you can win or lose. It matters. Now, if you are also an organizer, you weigh the importance of what you're doing, because you really don't want to be in a society where you're the only one who's stepped across the line. So you really are transforming yourself as a piece of transforming your society. You see yourself as somebody who is responsible for the shape of the world. That in some ways may sound like you're going to change the world, but you don't have to play with that image. You have to just play with whether, with every breath you take, you actually manifest in some way that you exist in the world around a certain system, a certain kind of vision, a certain system of values. And that while you are here, you will not miss an opportunity to see that that comes into being. For me, the central thing is being changed yourself, and being conscious of that change so that you will always seek another opportunity. So you will never get to a point where you feel that the powers that be are stronger than you, and then you give up.

CP: In those skirmishes, you're going to have some victories, you're going to have some defeats, how do you sustain people's momentum?

BJR: You can't determine whether you're going to sustain people's momentum. The first momentum you have to sustain is your own. I'm an optimist. And I'm an activist, which means I not only became transformed myself, I became committed with practicing so that I'd be a marker. Anytime anybody looked at me they'd say, "There goes that lady. She does so and so, you'd better watch out," you know? They knew what I might be liable to do. That's what I have to sustain. I always have to look for ways to be a visible marker.

CP: So that you become the inspiration for others?

BJR: If I become it, I become it. It is not up to me that I become it. It is up to me that I'm there. And with that kind of line, I can be the marker longer. The presence of a Sweet Honey in the Rock as an important voice in this society is an important marker. I've had to pay particular attention to the impact we've had, I've had to pay attention to having the tension, the radical line some place in our voice when we speak. Sometimes people say to us, "Thank you for your work." And I look at them to try to understand what they are talking about. They're saying "Thank you for being in the world. I could look up from wherever I was and you were there, and then that made me think I could." So the important thing is to be the marker. For myself, I would prefer to be a marker within a large, organized structure like the civil rights movement, where you're operating in a time when there are coalitions and everybody's moving and pushing. You are a marker, but you have so much company. There is a safety there that I find you don't have now. Today, there are organizations on the grassroots level, and some national organizations, and they're all over the place. They call for you. You go, and you service (in my case, through singing in an organization that was little more than a cultural group). But it's not that time now. I don't bemoan that I'm not in that time; it's just not there.

CP: The political climate is so different today than 20–30 years ago. From your perspective as a long-time organizer and activist what do you make of the current crisis in the arts in this country?

BJR: What crisis in the arts?

CP: The sense of lack of public support that is reflected in the dismantling of the National Endowment for the Arts, and a groundswell of public sentiment toward the arts that ranges from apathy to antagonism.

BJR: I don't see it as that. What is happening to art is what is happening throughout the country, where the Republicans are basically saying, "We can deliver back to you some variance of the old America." I think you have to look back to 1895, which was a marker for the systematizing of segregation in the country. The North, which had been dominated by Republican business industries straight through the Civil War, basically said, "You can do with black people what you will, let us have the economic South." During Reconstruction, the line in some way was, "We can deliver the South back to the Union with the black vote." No state in the South would've been brought back into the Union without black people voting that those states come back in. I'm oversimplifying at this point, but in a way, the sixties' civil rights movement can be seen as a response to that earlier oppressive reduction of our freedom. The movement generated a drastic change of status of black people in America. It triggered a process by which this country validated its people and became a country of many peoples and many cultures. Group by group—women, gays, lesbians, Native Americans, Chicanos—everybody spinning out of the sixties said, "We are here, too, and we want to change our status." As this move started to unveil, you began to hear people missing their narrow view of America. You know, "If you let everybody in, the quality changes; it's not the same as it was." People began to worry about English, and all sorts of anxieties showed up. The Republican Party riding that line is what we are now looking at. It's almost like, "We can't put blacks in chains. Slavery has been dismantled, but we will leave them to you and you can do with them what you will." It's very much a states' rights argument.

And so inside the states all of these issues will be pushed, and the arts are a part of that. Women are a part of that, children, education, health, age are all a part of that. As a historian, I see these parallels. What bothers me about them is that if you look at 1895 as a marker, it's the 1950s before, with a string of unbroken efforts, we generate a collective response. The civil rights movement is the next massive collective step after the dismantling of slavery. Between the dismantling of slavery and the civil rights movement is a period of reaction to a struggle against race-based repression and terror. It began in 1895 with a number of organizations that were started in the black community, national organizations, coalitions coming together. The Niagara Movement took place in 1906—the first political protest activist group saying, "We have to stand." The NAACP came a few years after that, and then the Urban League. Step by step—legal, legislative action until it built into the civil rights movement.

I think what we tried to do with the civil rights movement has triggered a similar reaction, which we are currently experiencing. We have to look for the next step. There will be a price. My sense is, when you have a step the way you had with the civil rights movement, you're not going to be able to continue to work around a monocultural perspective without getting a reaction. There has to be a reaction.

We're in the reactive part. There is an effort to roll back the accomplishments of the civil rights movement. We have to respond to it. And responding, we are going to be split and shattered because of the stress of the reaction and how devastating it is going to be to the way we've restructured things from a point of some collective power. The fact that we have a president now who doesn't have to cross a line in himself to hire intelligent women or to think that Spanish-speaking people or blacks can be leaders is the result of this period. It's the first time we've had anybody like that in that leadership role. When you look at people like Dole and Gramm, on the Republican side, you're looking at people from another generation and—even though they have lived through it—it has been forced work for them. With a person like Clinton, it's like eating breakfast in the morning. It's supposed to be like that. For all of his drawbacks, and there are many, it's such a breath of fresh air to have that kind of space at the top. But what we are facing is a tremendous period of hardship. A tremendous period of hardship! We will lose a lot, I think. It will force us to fight, to find new ways to fight, to crawl back to each other, without the power of success.

We must understand now that when you lose, you are not lost. When you fall, you're not dead, but the ground is where you get up from. It's much more difficult to be vulnerable to people who don't know that you exist or don't think you should exist. But that's also a time for you to find a voice that you could not possibly find from a powerful position. There is incredible art to be created in this period. Maybe there aren't any grants for it, and we will lose a lot of things in this period, but energy does not disappear, really.

CP: I think there is a sense in certain sectors of the arts community that arts institutions and to some extent artists themselves haven't done a really good job at speaking outside their inner circle, at speaking to the general public. Do you think that artists have left their audiences behind along the way?

BJR: I think there are corridors in our culture where people collect to themselves. Intellectuals do it. People outside the academy think intellectuals live in their own world. And then when the isolated groups are attacked or their budgets cut—like in the state of Virginia where higher education ends up taking cuts 20 to 30 percent—and they find their lives threatened, they don't know how to articulate to the community how important they are. They find they have to work to explain who they are and why the community should have them in existence.

I think artist communities are similar to that. But rather than look back and say artists have been too much talking to themselves, I look at the fact that artists now are trying to define for the community who they are, trying to convince the community that the community needs them. That's a hard conversation to have, and it's a hard campaign to wage when you've lived through a period where you've not had to have the words. But I think it's a good thing. It will be problematic and it will not be wholly successful because the language is different. Artists who have been a part of an artist community that has not been in dialogue with the rest of society will have to learn a certain kind of language, and they will have to learn to service the society. They will have to learn the ways in which their work can help people in the community do what they need to do, which is stay alive and take care of some of the life-and-death issues that are threatening them. The same issues that are impacting artists are impacting everybody else. Artists will be forced by the crisis to structure a strategy across issues. And that will be interesting to watch.

CP: You've said that socially conscious artists are not born, that they are culturally oriented and trained. Where do people go to get that training?

BJR: You have to live in the wider world to get it. You have to see the world not just as some material for a new song or a new sculpture. You have to validate that the pictures you see are life forces that have a story that you have an investment in. You can really train yourself by looking at your community—not by going to a meeting to draw pictures but going to a meeting to see what the meeting is about.

CP: Can I ask you about that from our own experience? Some of your work has been within the context of the church, and the church has taken a conservative stance on certain kinds of issues. How do you live with that opposition? And how do you find the bridge when you're dealing with populations that may not always share the values that you have?

BJR: If you live in the world, you learn to be who you are with opposition. I found that the church made sense when it went into the street and when it went to jail. And I found that there were actually Bible stories I understood in jail. I found that I understood the crucifixion better from studying American lynching than anything else. You know, I felt like there's some people who've been lynched who can just sit down with Jesus and have a talk about that experience. And that leveling is just very important, was very important in terms of making accessible to me things you don't get if you're not in the world.

The idea is more one of letting go and trying to find a way of being who you are in the mix of everything. It's a dangerous kind of life and at various points you have to have a home to go to, where you pull together in your artists' colony, in your intellectual community or with women or with black people, or whatever. You have to have that safety zone where for a little while you're with people who know you exist and know who you are. But that's only your home and you don't live there all the time. That place gives you the support to be in the world.

The training is sort of a self-training. I don't know of any place that's organized that will teach people that. I think it runs in cycles. I believe there is a period of your life when most of your work is supposed to be in the world—contending with being who you are and putting your stuff out there in the mix of opposition and watching it. I think probably when you get older you become more of an elder and you become a little bit more of a teacher and a trainer, if I understand the Ella Baker model. So I think there are changes over time when you're out there and how you can put out in the face of opposition.

I operate strategically. I try to understand if I'm with more than three people the destruction of my work is with me. I have to watch the health of the work. If you have that kind of configuration in your mind, you're ready to be anywhere. You keep a conscious eye on taking care of yourself. It's almost like the sensibility that martial artists talk about, of being able to walk in the world but you can feel the air. Blind people also talk about it— you can feel the air change around and behind you and you know how to be mindful. It's the kind of thing they teach women to do when you walk in the street: Don't forget. You must always have these eyes. And that alertness wears you out. A lot of people think it's wrong, you know: "It's too bad we can't walk out of our houses and feel safe." But I don't know where that's really possible in the world. The thing is to break people out of this cocoon of "It can't happen in our community" and say to them, "Listen, the world has come to you now, and you need to learn to walk in it."

It requires an energy outflow. You need to be putting out in order to know when something counter is heading for you so you can dialogue with it. I believe very strongly that what's missing in the world is the sound of your voice. If you're feeling like things are not right, then maybe you need to check on how much you're putting out, and you need to increase or change where you're putting things out. At the same time, you need to understand protecting yourself. And you don't protect yourself always by getting behind a fortress. There's a way you can move in the world and protect yourself, and that's when that fear tape runs a lot.

The first time Sweet Honey decided to do something about AIDS and condoms in a black church, the fear tape was running. I can remember those early occasions, but now when we do it, the fear tape is not playing because we have broken through in some ways. That's the way I see it. You just step out there, and you stay out as long as you can.

The thing is, don't think it's going to be easy, don't think you're not going to risk your life. Sharpen all of your tools, including a few claws. You have a right to fight for your life. Just get out. You know, go out an inch at a time. I don't like martyrs. Jumping into the pool where the lions are so they eat you is just boring to me. The idea is to really try to be skilled around putting your message out and thinking you are worth protecting.

And no matter what message you put out today, if you can invest a little in being around tomorrow, the message might actually be more important. This may not be the last concert you sing. It's what I tell Sweet Honey about singing—you don't owe your voice to any concert. We don't have set keys, and so the key is set by the person who starts the song. So I say, "If the song is too high, change your part. You don't owe your voice to any song." It's a way of saying, "I have a right to exist. Since I'm alive part of my work is taking care of the life." And those two things allow you to go out and be in places where people will oppose you and attack you and walk out on you when you say things they don't like, which hurts your feelings. What people have to get used to is that the pain and the hurt is a part of normal, and that's what we're not socialized for. When we hurt, we think something's wrong and we need to change it. But if within the context of your life, you experience with the satisfaction and the joy, disappointment and trouble and difficulty and challenge, then probably you're doing all right.

CP: You've said you can't do something for 20 years and not lose your focus along the way. Sometimes you get lost. How do you find your way back?

BJR: Go back to the last time you knew what you were doing, and start again. When you get confused you just think of anything that's clear. When you are lost and you can't find any clarity, you need to be hospitalized. That's when it's too dark, when there's no light anyplace. Sometimes the only thing that's clear is washing your clothes; you know how to do that. Do it. Go to any corner that's clear and function, and from that place you will find other clarities. When you get lost in an organization, or your work just gets to a point and you do not know what to do next so you feel like you can't put in another cycle, it means you have to pull out. People will charge you with going for shelter, but what you're doing is going to clarity. Sometimes it's your child, sometimes it's writing a poem—anything you know how to do. You know how to type, so you can type something for somebody else who's clear. Any way to get near clarity is the way to find yourself back to light. You don't ever have to find yourself back to that other light. You don't ever have to go back to that organization, you never have to do that again in your life. If it was any good, somebody else will do it. But if you start from clarity, you will find your way to light, and you will again see a time when you can shine enough so somebody else can use what you're reflecting, which is the point.

I had a conversation with a guy who ran an organization, he was really the life force of it. He wanted to go to Africa for two or three years, but he didn't know how to leave. I said, "Why don't you put it on a schedule, tell yourself you're going to give yourself a year or two to get your resources together, and with one hand preparing for departure, the other hand will do the best you can. Set the date and go to Africa." He said, "What happens to the organization?" I said, " It may fall or it may go on, it depends upon whether you built it so that there is a possibility that other people might find a way to use it."

CP: Carry it forward.

BJR: The only reason they'll carry it forward is not because you did for yourself. It's because of something it does for them they don't want to be without. That's a test of how you organize. Think about how difficult it is now for you to leave this work, and if you've not put in those layers, the next time you do it, put in those layers. I do things for ten, twenty years, but you may really be a two-, three-year person on a project. You might have to change projects every three years. That's not a negative. Just know that that's who you are and try to do what you can.

CP: Within that framework.

BJR: And give whatever little light catalyst you shoot off a chance to continue. And that's about bringing people in who can sit you down. People who are more brilliant than you. They make you nervous because they are brilliant, and they're the people who fight with you. Maybe bring them in younger so they don't fight as much, but bring them in. Because you know that after your second year you'll start to itch, something else will come up for you, and therefore you need to get ready to go to a new place.

CP: In one of your recent interviews, you said that progressives in this country are the majority but they don't speak as the majority—that many of us who work for change also participate in denying the impact of our efforts. Why is that?

BJR: It may be in the culture. It's almost as if we don't believe that we're successful. The Republicans' control of Congress exists because of the success of our work. They backlashed against a very, very successful, broad-based initiative in this country. If you don't understand that, then you end up going, "Why are they picking on me?" It's almost like you turn yourself into a victim. We're not victims. We launched an offensive to change this society. The offensive has been very effective. We are all soldiers, we've been fighting, and we've been effective. That's why we're targets. If you fall to the position of "Oh, those mean people, they're taking all of our money," you are not acknowledging that they're shooting at you because you are out front. For me, I have always been mostly an offensive player. I always see my work as breaking through new ground. People shoot at me moving forward. The progressive people in this society move forward, and when they get hit they go—"Why'd you do that? I'm such a nice person. We're just going with what is right." It is such a naive way to deal with it. If you're pushing to rearrange the country, you are going to get hit at.

We're not telling ourselves we're actually rearranging the structure of our society. That's a power move. When you move in power, you're going to get a response in power. The more effective you are, the more powerful the response. We allow our work to be rewritten very quickly. The march on Washington, which was real, becomes taught as "I have a dream." And dreaming is what you do when you sleep. Focusing on the dream metaphor doesn't give you the picture you would get if you were actually taught the march on Washington—where you had 250,000 people gathered, most of them black, for the first time in these kinds of numbers. You had army personnel shooters all over the place, all the liquor stores in Washington, D.C., were closed. Children hear the "I have a dream" speech in place of something that was very real, that was happening, changing, being done by hundreds of thousands of people from all over the country.

The coalition between activists in the South and the labor union and the churches is what you should be teaching.

We allow our work to be rewritten so that it is palatable and much of the reality of it is lost. What gets transmitted is the polish, or some phrase to stand in for it. The next generation really has to learn the lesson that most change is brought about because people change, they step out of what they've been doing to do something different. Those are the pictures they need to see all the time.

CP: What will the next generation of leadership be like?

BJR: In the black community we have so many examples of loss. It's best demonstrated by how many children are being raised by grandparents because the parents are gone, either through drug epidemics or AIDS or whatever. When you have that phenomenon there is an immense drain on the system. It is not one we don't know about and it's not one that is not survivable—but we have both the fact that there will be new leaders and the fact that those of us who are moving into elder positions have to actually operate as a parent generation. That's a strain. I think it's going to be difficult. We still have to see. The sixties generation is a difficult one because we really don't get old, it's hard for us to think that anybody is younger than we are. So we haven't allowed for the training of the next leadership tier. The next level of leaders are really going to have a time dealing with these old sixties people, who should be moving into an elder position of training and supporting.

CP: But are trying to hang on?

BJR: Not even trying to hang on. We're the youngest people in the society, we think. We're not hanging on, we're just absolutely doing what we do. But when you move to the elder position you really can't see the way young people can see. You really can't size things up and come up with solutions. When Du Bois wrote *The Souls of Black Folk,* he was 35. He critiqued Booker T. Washington. Booker T. Washington was an elder. Booker T. Washington was the most famous black person in the country. And here's this little Turk who says, "Let's have an organization that criticizes him, because for all the good he's done, he's calling the shots wrong." So I think some of what you're going to see as we move forward is people speaking against solutions that older people are projecting. Some older people will be wise enough to listen, because when you get the new leadership, new leadership has to have the elder base, otherwise they really don't have enough sense to stay alive on their own.

CP: How does that rapport happen?

BJR: With the elders? During the civil rights movement, we didn't know how come our parents hadn't done this or that. There would happen to be parents and grandparents in the room who heard us saying that and heard our willingness to move forward, and they covered us best they could.

CP: Do you think the emerging leadership wants the elders in the room?

BJR: Yes.

CP: They do?

BJR: Oh, absolutely. Young people always want older people to support them. Always.

CP: Don't the young think they can do it all themselves and that their wisdom is wiser?

BJR: Of course, young people know everything. What you want is an old person who'll say, "You got sense." You don't want an old person to say, "Here's the plan. You carry my plan." The old people you let in the room are the ones who'll say "You've got the ball." That's the vision of Ella Baker.

CP: What is the role of the elder people after they've handed the ball to the young people?

BJR: They help create the forum where young people get a chance to process and work out and hear themselves think and talk and ask themselves questions. Sometimes you ask them questions. The model of Ella Baker and the civil rights movement is so important because you had the layers. You had young people—elementary school children, high school, college people—every age level was present in the community. The hottest line was pulled by young people in the civil rights movement. There was no line hotter than that. Everybody watched as best they could, and did the best they could with it. The young people were angry many times because even though they were taking the brunt of the initiative, the culture requires a leader and it didn't give the leadership to them, it gave it to somebody who was older.

CP: How do you become a longtimer in the movement? What gives you hope?

BJR: I don't think about it a lot. There were times when my children got me out of bed in the morning. There were years when I knew they needed breakfast, so I got up. I'm a self-starter now, but I think it's because I'm an optimist and I know what I'm doing and I know what my work is. I know what my contribution is to be in the world. It's like I know what Bernice Reagonism is, and I'm responsible for it. And I don't want the world to be without it. So everyday I do the best I can to put it out there. I also have an image of burning out every minute of my life. I don't want to relive it because there's nothing left when I finish with it.

CP: When you're a teenager, you think that if you work very hard, you can change the world in your lifetime. As you get older, how do you deal with the realization that you may not actually live to see everything that you're working and hoping for?

BJR: I'm not sure that's a teenage phenomenon, because I talk to people who are much older who don't like the notion that it's all right to do the best you can and die. They really feel that what they can do about a situation is never enough to change it; therefore, why does it matter to do anything at all? Of course, they are longing for a movement, they are longing for an organization, they are longing for a collective. I'm saying, "If you wake up and you're breathing, you have a chance to change the air you move through. And anybody who walks in your space can feel something different. Even if you're not in an organization you can do that. But I also believe that nobody should exist in the world without being part of an organization. The organization can be anything. I believe the idea of going through the world without being in a room with a group of people at least once a week is a dangerous thing for a human being. If you can think about something like Sweet Honey, that I've been doing now for more than 20 years, there have been very few weeks when I haven't been in this space with these other people. That's a check-in. Everybody should have it. If that organization is configured with a concern for your external environment, for your society, then it is not just something to keep you going, but it can also have an activist effect to help you know how to be in the world for somebody else. That's the other thing that is very strong in my life: make arrangements for somebody else while you're here. Little Brother Montgomery, a blues singer, said that. Occupy the space you're in in such a way that somebody else can share it. If you're only taking care of the space you need to exist, you are in fact not living. I think you should be pulling it on multiple levels. You should be making space with contemporaries. You should be working with other people trying to find a way for you to exist right then, but there should also be a way in which you are supporting people in generations below you. That's making arrangements for somebody else while you're here. Then when you're gone, somebody else can mess around and take a whack at a space you've dug out. It's theirs to mess up, but you at least dug it out. I think that's important.

November 10, 1995
Washington, D.C.

3

NORMA SWENSON

FOR THE LAST FOUR DECADES, NORMA SWENSON *has been one of the principal forces behind the definition and creation of a women's health care movement in this country and abroad. Swenson first became disillusioned with the male-dominated medical establishment as a young woman over the issue of childbirth, and since then her role as a health activist has spread to encompass the range of factors that specifically affect the well-being of women around the world. She was one of the founders and a senior staff member for more than 20 years of the Boston Women's Health Book Collective, the group of women who in the 1970s revolutionized the health care field by maintaining that women, not male doctors, were the experts about the nature and care of the female body. She is a co-author and co-editor of the collective's groundbreaking guide to women and their health,* Our Bodies, Ourselves, *which has sold more than four million copies worldwide and which National Black Women's Health Project founder Byllye Avery has called "the bible for women's health."*

As the collective's first director of international programs, Swenson helped oversee the translation and adaptation of Our Bodies, Ourselves *into 20 languages. She has visited and worked directly with women's and community groups in most regions of the world and has consulted for many NGOs and national governments. For the past 15 years, she has taught a course at the Harvard School of Public Health called "Women, Health and Development."*

In her interview, Swenson traces the origins and history of the women's health care movement as well as her role within it. As she says, by the early 1970s, "I knew a hell of a lot about medicine, medical education, and the institution's power in society," and she was more than ready to counter them with alternative messages. She also provides valuable insights on human rights and women's autonomy, freedom of speech, and the challenges that both the women's health movement and the arts have faced from political and religious conservatives.

❏ ❏ ❏ ❏ ❏

Norma Swenson: I have a little sleeper for you: when I was quite young, I never saw myself as anything but an artist, even though you could see the outlines of some kind of activism or social criticism. I was very interested in drawing and painting, and for a while I wanted to be a writer, but then I discovered dance and thought, "Well, now, this is really more like it." I was a dancer all through late high school and college years and even as a married woman. (In those days, a married woman was *not* a dancer!) Then I went through a major struggle around the birth of my child and discovered it was a watershed. You could not deviate, you could not ask questions, you could not have any control at all over what happened to you in the hospital.

Marie Cieri: That's when they used to knock you out.

NS: Oh, yeah. I was totally unprepared for my sense of outrage, the violation of my autonomy. I realized there was no mechanism built in for any exercise of rights whatsoever. And to be awake? Forget it. I had been influenced quite strongly in my senior year at college by the books that were emanating from Yale, which had started the first natural childbirth program in this country. From then on, I couldn't see why a perfectly natural, normal thing should require hospitalization and surgery and anesthesia. I was also concerned with the degree to which it became an alienating experience within the couple (couples were all we looked at in those days—there were no single mothers with any social identity). It certainly wasn't doing anything to cement their confidence as a family. All that was swirling in my head when in 1961 or 1962 I read an article about the tenth anniversary of an organization dedicated to trying to change all this—the Boston Association for Childbirth Education [BACE]. It's funny because the week previous I had been talking to a friend about wanting to do something about this situation, "Maybe I should start an organization," I said. I had no background for it; I had what I had, a BA in French and sociology. Anyhow, I called up the BACE, got this woman and said, kind of cocky, "How come I've never heard of you?" She was very smart and said, "How would you like to be the publicity chair?"

MC: *[Laughter]* She worked you.

NS: Exactly. I started going to meetings and became, in short order, not only the publicity chair but the vice-president of this struggling group. Within two years, I was president of the national organization. The whole childbirth movement is a thread in my activism that I've never let go of.

MC: How widespread was that movement nationally?

NS: It was quite a movement in those days. My analysis is that it was a "movement between the waves"—the first wave of feminism came to an end with the establishment of the vote, then they all went home and went to sleep; then they had a depression, and then there was a war . . .

MC: But World War II ultimately kicked off another wave, didn't it?

NS: I would say not. I would say there was a blip on the screen and, strictly due to the labor shortage, women were given a place in the work-force. But it was understood that they were substituting for men and not functioning in their own right. In fact, it was in that context that you could look at the childbirth education movement. It was a way of saying: "We are being very good girls. We are doing *exactly* what society expects of us—we are growing up to become dutiful wives and good mothers and having done all that, we find the system wanting. In order to carry out our motherhood function, we deserve to be treated better. Our babies deserve to be treated better." It's one of the reasons why sexuality was so muted in that movement.

MC: What kinds of things was the BACE doing in the sixties, and what was the reaction?

NS: We were doing extremely heretical things, and we were not alone. Some very powerful institutions across the country had already come to the conclusion that the norm of hospital birth, obstetrician/gynecologist-attended, was a true disaster for the society, for women, for the economy.

MC: Who were these groups?

NS: I'll give you an example. Maternity Center Association [MCA] in New York is the oldest maternal and child health nonprofit in the coun-try, and it's still breaking records and making waves. It was an incredible marriage of Park Avenue society women and the medical establishment in obstetrics and gynecology and their associated New York hospitals. Their idea was that because New York had endured such an influx of immigrants, [and] had a more or less permanent, if not growing, underclass, something needed to be done to address their needs. So they pioneered these things called "maternity centers," which were really the forerunners of neighbor-hood health centers. The birth control war was being fought elsewhere—this effort was about how to find women when they were pregnant, how to make sure they got proper care and were able to have their babies with a minimum of trauma and loss of life.

MC: Were all these activists women?

NS: Yes, but these were all elite women in the beginning—their husbands were bankers and industrialists.

MC: Poorer women were not involved in this?

NS: They were not participating at all in this organization. It took that level of social power to recruit a board of consultants from the leading academic posts in the New York medical circuit and keep them involved as long as they did.

Maternity Center also set the tone and the groundwork for what later became childbirth preparation classes. MCA pioneered the creation of midwifery schools along with Mary Breckenridge at the Frontier Nursing Service in Kentucky. Then came an enormous backlash from the obstetrical establishment. It was on the heels of it that I moved into the Boston organization. My first task, in fact, was to write a letter rebutting an article in *McCall's* or *Ladies Home Journal,* written by a Boston obstetrician, called "The Medical Case Against Natural Childbirth."

MC: I'm assuming that obstetricians at the time were primarily male.

NS: Yes. When we put together the first *Our Bodies, Ourselves* [1970], we got hold of figures that said only six percent of practicing physicians were women, and in the field of ob/gyn it was only three percent.

I'll give you an example of the backlash: a doctor here in Boston had hired two psychologists to run studies on the women who wanted natural childbirth in order to demonstrate their peculiarities. There were three diagnoses: one was character disorder (people who don't conform classically in the DMS [*Diagnostic and Statistical Manual of Mental Disorders*]); another was neurotic, extremely controlling people who had to run everything; and the third was plain psychotic—they denied their pain, denied the reality of birth, and that was what they wanted everybody else to do. The word quickly spread through the medical community because this guy was giving lectures and, after all, had hired some crackerjack psychologists to do the study.

For the natural childbirth advocates, it was not just about being awake. It was also about the condition of the babies after anesthetized births, and there was a big push for breastfeeding. It wasn't entirely La Leche

League—there were spontaneous groupings that occurred in conjunction with childbirth education groups. These groups were teaching the basics of the physiology of reproduction. I find it fascinating that you can't say it was sex education, because the sexual act through which conception took place was not explicitly discussed.

Maternity Center felt the scale of ignorance was so colossal that they should illustrate exactly how this worked—to show anatomy, conception, gestation, and birth. So a well-known physician named Dickinson and a famous European sculptor named Belsky were hired to create something called *The Birth Atlas*. It's a world-famous bas relief sculpture, and you can go to New York now and see it. This was in the twenties, and it was lambasted as pornographic. There were attempts to shut down the exhibit, but they persisted. They not only kept the sculpture on display, they created a book with black-and-white photographs of the sculpture you could use as a primary teaching tool.

There were other groups besides Maternity Center across the country. The autonomy of the cities and their own associations came ahead of any national linkage at first. But Maternity Center took the leadership and pulled together these groups of teachers and leaders from different cities across the United States to discuss whether or not they wanted to form a national organization. It was out of that that the International Childbirth Education Association was formed in 1960, of which I became president in 1966.

MC: What was the reason to link up nationally?

NS: The idea was that everybody would benefit from being part of a national organization. The credibility would help them in their local struggle, and there would be the possibility of exchanging ideas about how to organize, how to work with the medical profession, how to teach classes.

The other part of the struggle had to do with the alienation of the father from the process. We would have men telling the story of how they would go to St. Elizabeth's Hospital [in Brighton, Massachusetts]. They would check in their wives and wait for the bag of laundry that would come back—she had been stripped of her possessions and her clothing. He would take the bag, go home, and wait for the phone call. That was birth in the fifties and early sixties. Of course, an improvement over that was supposed to be the smoke-filled waiting room.

We started with labor. After all, if a woman wasn't going to be knocked out during labor, she deserved some companionship. But when the delivery came, he had to leave. Then we started talking about fathers in the delivery room. Well, for a surgeon, this is pure heresy—you cannot have awake and alert lay people standing around in surgery.

Boston became one of the places for that campaign. We brought people to Boston from across the country who were doing this, held public meetings, organized the media, and basically created a revolution. There were two or three doctors in Boston who would allow fathers in the delivery room. At the time, almost everybody who had insurance could move it around, so we would play one hospital against another in order to get other doctors to comply. We would basically say, "We'll take our business elsewhere."

MC: You used an economic tool.

NS: Absolutely. It was economic, it was psychological, it was political. And, not surprisingly, the major Boston teaching hospitals were the last to fall; we were able to pick off little local hospitals out in the suburbs first, then slowly worked our way into the center. By 1965, we had a fairly consistent possibility of offering this through our classes because we knew where the right doctors were.

The other thing we did was create a governing structure over these classes where lay people hired the teachers, organized the training of teachers, evaluated them, managed the evaluation of the feedback from the couples, and ran the classes. Parents who came to our organization would talk about how they felt about the instruction, how they felt about the labor and delivery experience, and would rate the hospitals and the doctors. The principle was one of citizenship, pure and simple. This became quite a weapon in the struggle to change obstetrical care in this town. That's what we did in the sixties while the rest of the country was in an uproar about other things.

MC: You mean about the Vietnam War and civil rights?

NS: Well, many things. I think they've identified now some 20 or 25 movements that were alive and flourishing in the sixties. You could say we were about civil rights in birthing. We were asserting our right to control this experience for which we paid so handsomely in institutions that were totally inaccessible. We eventually got consumers onto boards of hospitals.

MC: When you were working with this group in the sixties, would you say that your primary focus, as far as activism, was educating people?

NS: If you want to make a distinction, which I would, between educating and organizing, you have to say both. At first, a lot of us were disappointed when the majority of people simply went on with their lives at the end of their birthing experiences. They felt they had paid for the product, were satisfied with it, and went on about their business. What we wanted was for the majority of them to stand with us and try to topple this unholy system. They had escaped, but the average woman was not escaping. Looking back, I can tell you it was naive on our part—we were this little group of citizens, lay people primarily, even though we always had doctors with us. We couldn't have moved an inch without them.

It's interesting that this became a serious issue when some of the medical profession tried to stop the classes. Our response was: "This is an educational matter, not a medical matter. Therefore we provide this information as educators and not as medical [providers]." Their attempt to delegitimatize us was a continual battle throughout that decade. I don't think it stopped until the hospitals finally decided to co-opt us, which is what they did.

MC: They co-opted you?

NS: Oh, yeah, and I participated in it without understanding what I was doing. This was just before I came into the collective, about 1970 or '71.

We had been so successful that the Lying-In [Hospital] nurses invited us to teach their people what we did. We ran a whole set of classes at the hospital to explain to the nurses what to do during labor and delivery. They paid us, and at that time $1,000 was a lot of money. That was the beginning here in Boston, and to some extent nationwide, of hospitals deciding they had no choice but to prepare people for what to expect in labor and delivery. Co-optation went on wholesale during the seventies to the point where childbirth educational groups and their community-based services suffered because the hospitals at first made the classes free.

MC: In past decades, men were disconnected from the birth process, as you said. It is now more the norm that fathers are there when the babies are born. How do you think public opinion changed?

NS: The husbands were terrified because the medical profession was saying they were going to faint and crack their heads on the delivery room floor, or they would be so traumatized they would never be able to make love to their wives again. Nevertheless, we had male "survivors" who thought it was the most thrilling experience of their lives: "I have bonded with this child in a way I never could bond with any of my other children. I have such a profound and deep respect for my wife now because of what she's done." Interestingly enough, I do think there was a strong element of patriarchy and consumer entitlement fueling the whole thing: "A man has the right to see his child born."

MC: Once the hospitals co-opted you, how did you develop a broader-based initiative over women's health?

NS: In the early seventies, I knew a hell of a lot about medicine, medical education, and the institution's power in society. Because of the tremendous focus on abortion at that time, I could see that in a sense those of us in the childbirth movement had been trapped into an arena that was considered legitimate—it was legitimate to talk about motherhood and parenting and even the physical details of the birthing process, but it was not legitimate to talk about sexuality or abortion or birth control.

Suddenly, I had this realization that professional obstetrics and gynecology were indeed united. They had the capability to monitor and create social control around every single reproductive event of a woman's life in this culture. Most women could not get really effective birth control, could not manage an abortion, could not get a sterilization, could not give birth without passing through this system. I saw the whole panorama of women's lives being commissioned by this institution in a way that seemed not only unjust but tyrannical. So the appeal for me of what *Our Bodies, Ourselves* was trying to say was: "We are the most important experts on ourselves, and we should not be under the domination of this gang of men."

MC: How did you find the people you worked with on *Our Bodies, Ourselves?*

NS: I was in the throes of trying to dethrone the medical establishment, playing the economic game with these other people and training people to do the childbirth classes when the first paper-covered *Our Bodies, Ourselves* came across my desk. I was shocked by it because women were speaking about their own sexuality and sexual self-determination. And here was a whole bunch of Lamaze types who had written the childbirth section with what I thought were very poor insights. "How can women who are otherwise so smart . . ." A friend of mine from the childbirth movement called me up and told me one of these women was living in her neighborhood, and we should talk to her and others in the group. We had one meeting, and it was extremely tense; I had never had such a difficult meeting with a group of women in my life. It was clear they didn't think much of me either. We decided to have another meeting, and it was worse than the first. I remember vividly this woman saying to me, "You're not a feminist, you'll never be a feminist. What you need is to go to school." She was crying and slammed out of the house. I was very sobered by that because I had had this sense that I really understood what women wanted and needed and was so sympathetic to them compared to the medical profession.

At that time, "Our Bodies, Ourselves" courses were being taught in Cambridge. This was part of a whole wave of popular education going on then. It was never intended to be a book. But some people couldn't get to the course and found out that people were writing down some of it and asked for Xeroxes. The Xeroxing got to be too much, and the women giving the course thought maybe they could print it. They approached the New England Free Press, and the Free Press said, "It's not political," and refused to publish it. The women said they'd pay for the printing, so the Free Press printed it. It became a runaway bestseller on which all the Free Press's political tracts were able to move around the country. It was that process that produced the printed book that came across my desk.

MC: Can you explain a little more specifically what that woman meant by saying you weren't a feminist?

NS: She was understanding that I was playing what I call "pre-feminist politics;" in other words, take some guru figure, primarily male, and use his legitimacy and authority to promote women's entitlement to certain things. It's true! We had a number of gurus—the doctors who would accept natural childbirth patients, who would not routinely use anesthesia and might even finesse an episiotomy, and the pediatricians who were sympathetic to breast-feeding.

MC: She didn't feel you were hardcore enough?

NS: Uh huh. I think she was right. But there weren't any other ways in which women could assert their entitlement to have what they needed or do what they wanted. It was awareness of the abortion struggle that prepared me to see that if women were willing to confront the medical establishment on the *entire range* of issues it controlled in women's lives, it was a noble enterprise. By that time I was convinced the thing was sick and corrupt in every possible way.

So I took that woman at her word, and I went to those classes. But going to school wasn't enough. I have to say it was really the tutelage and role-modeling of a generation of women 10 to 15 years younger than I was that was my real education in feminism. That's how I came to the [Boston Women's Health Book] collective.

During the course, tiny pieces of tissue paper would come around the room saying, "Meetings to revise *Our Bodies, Ourselves,* go to this apartment" on the back side of Cambridge. I made my way there and met the women who had put the book together. Over the summer, we were all going to write a chapter, and I was given permission to rewrite the one on childbirth. We came back in September, and, lo and behold, I was the only one who had written a word. By that time, commercial publishers were clustering around the door, trying to get control of this thing.

MC: Because it was a bestseller in its first . . .

NS: . . . in its underground incarnation. It was listed in the *Whole Earth Catalog,* and that provoked an explosion of demand for it. We spent six months haggling over whether or not to even go with a commercial publisher. New England Free Press found out we were considering it and, without our knowledge, put an extra page in the back of the book lambasting us for selling out to the capitalist pigs. We insisted that a page of rebuttal be put into every book that was being shipped out.

MC: Were you trying to get a bigger circulation with a mainstream publisher?

NS: The decision we made was about how quickly and how cheaply we could get this book into the hands of every woman in the United States. The key piece was a Robin Hood arrangement whereby distribution through bookstores would produce the kinds of sales that would allow us to provide the book at a 70 percent discount to any women's group, community group, or health counseling center that wanted it. We knew New England Free Press didn't have the kind of distribution capability that was necessary. As a consequence, we decided it was an ethical decision to go with the commercial publisher [Simon & Schuster, in 1973], and we would produce a golden goose that would allow us to do other kinds of health work.

MC: What other kinds of health work did you do?

NS: When the book became a bestseller, we made so much money we had to give it away because our tax status then was as a private operating foundation. We had these challenges of where to give the money. We gave it to a mental health collective in Vermont, we gave it to a Lakota Indian group from the Midwest to translate the book onto tapes. We gave some of it to the film *Taking Our Bodies Back.* We contributed to the 1975 Conference on Women and Health. That really set the stage for the launching of the women's health movement in this country, because the National Women's Health Network was founded that year.

MC: How many members were then in the collective?

NS: We were 11 meeting once a week for 13 years.

MC: That's real longevity.

NS: We're not now. I think that experience is difficult to match, and it's difficult to describe what happens as a consequence of it. Some family therapists who do organizational work take the family as their model, but I would say this was beyond family. The group and its activities were pretty nearly divided between women whose primary interest was the work and women whose primary interest was support and personal sharing. There were strong women on both sides of that pole, yet no one who was truly opposed to the other activities. It was just a question of keeping that tension and balance going through those years and through all the money and all the fame that followed.

MC: Over time, were there significant disagreements about what projects to do or what alliances to form?

NS: I think it was more about how our leadership would be managed and what our process would be.

MC: I'm curious how you reached consensus on things.

NS: We believed so much in consensus that one woman really had the power to block something if she wanted to. One of the things that has colored my perception of this was the fact that we were all pretty much lay women. (I had gone to the Harvard School of Public Health in 1972, but had decided there was no future for me in public health because of the way it was organized then.) That was our strength, in my opinion, because we were able to explain to ourselves—and therefore to other women—what women's health was all about. Until that time, only experts in medicine were writing books telling women what they should know, what they should think, what they should believe, what they should do. Ours was really a groundbreaking experience.

MC: Did each woman, or team of women, start by discussing the topic and then looking for information as needed?

NS: Right from the beginning we did that, and we'd pull it all together into a paper. Those papers were given from the earliest moments of the class. One of the campaigns we got involved in was around unnecessary surgery. Hysterectomy was the earliest and most spectacular example, but equally spectacular was mastectomy—by wading into the medical literature and discovering there were controversies behind all the dogma surrounding us. We pulled them out into the light of day and said, "There really is controversy in medicine about whether or not a quick-frozen section of breast tissue is accurate enough to make the kind of diagnosis that would justify a mastectomy," particularly a Halsted radical (which was the norm in those days). Then I did more research on the Halsted radical and saw that making this the norm on millions of American women was based entirely on a sample of 147 women. I realized this was something we had to work on. When I say "we," I mean the movement that by this time consisted not only of the collective but the National Women's Health Network and many other women's groups. People would jump up all over the country, get hold of something issue by issue, and we would support them. That's when we made certain we'd keep documentation of every single sentence in the book, because everything we were saying was so radical it just scared the wits out of everybody.

We were involved in all kinds of campaigns. Let's go to sexually transmitted diseases. We would interview the heretics within that community and find out what they were saying, what they were doing. We would correspond with people in Europe who had different approaches to things. We spent a lot of our money putting out the first six-sided leaflet I know of on sexually transmitted diseases and the unique ways in which women were affected by them. Military wives, at the end of World War II, had brought all VD education to a halt, saying, "It isn't seemly for the U.S. military to be involved in these sordid activities." Stopped condom distribution, stopped teaching men how to tell whether or not somebody was at risk for disease and what the symptoms were. There was a brief period when condoms again were available until the pill landed about 1962, and then zero teaching in the general public about sexually transmitted diseases, practically until the age of HIV. But we were doing this very early. All of it was in the service of the book, but there were also many opportunities to speak. We went all over the country to tiny women's groups in small towns, Planned Parenthoods, and YWCAs.

MC: I bet you were really in demand because of the large circulation of the book.

NS: We were. But you've got to keep in mind it was really in the counterculture circuit, though I can show you a photograph circa 1974 of the then-president of the American Association of Medical Colleges holding a copy of our book saying, "This should be required reading for every medical student." But that was because in the sixties there was a brief climate of openness in medical schools associated with something called "community medicine" that involved such things as Model Cities programs with Neighborhood Health Center components. As part of that movement, we would be invited to talk about the women's health piece.

We published the next edition of the book in 1976, and it was selected by the American Library Association as the best book of the year for young adults. The following year, one of the ten best all-time for young adults. That set off a right-wing backlash campaign—Phyllis Schlafly, Jerry Falwell, all those people started to circle around us saying, "No public money should be spent for a book like this." In spite of our discounts, it had a chilling effect.

MC: They have a lot of media power.

NS: Oh, yes. What they also had was a peculiar kind of authority that still obtains in politics: local communities can control library budgets and public school budgets and are relatively immune from the vagaries of federal or even state politics. By stacking those entities with their people, they were able to get our book out of the public schools and to threaten to cut off money for Planned Parenthoods and YWCAs if our book was used. There were more than 42 communities across the United States that attempted, in one way or another, to ban or remove our book from circulation. They weren't all successful, but the chilling effect was quite widespread.

MC: They felt it was immoral?

NS: Well, what they selected was childish in a way. I remember going to a radio station in Oregon or someplace, and the questions the announcer asked were the same ones I had been asked in St. Louis, so I knew they were working from cookie-cutter challenges about the medical profession, which they saw as socialist, or things about communal living and communal child care, which they also saw as socialist. They focused as well on some of the more straightforward excerpts from our chapters on sexuality. As you probably know, "immorality" is not always entirely about sexuality; for the right wing it's often also about economic systems. The most prudish sexuality is usually linked to the most conservative economic policies. Now that's *extremely* simplistic and very dangerous, but it seemed to hold through all our struggles.

The bestseller provoked a rash of European editions of our book and ultimately dragged us into the international arena. Our understanding was not only of how the medical enterprise works but also how the medical industrial enterprise, the drug industries, the device industries and the hospital systems work as a global enterprise.

MC: By then you must have seemed dangerous.

NS: We were certainly on the list. We had seen the written material on us, along with a lot of other groups in this country that were being targeted by right-wing forces for de-funding by philanthropies. Also, the economic climate at that time was getting so bad that most of the foundations in this country felt duty-bound to try to fill in the gaps for social programs that had been slashed by the Republican administration. In any case, foundation giving to women's groups in this country had never been more than half of one percent of the total.

That's when the question of how we were going to survive long-term became critical. We had to develop more aggressive fundraising programs than we had before. That's also when we came to the conclusion we had no choice but to put out another book. By that time, a good two-thirds of the people in the collective had moved on to do other things, but in 1984 we published *The New Our Bodies, Ourselves.*

MC: It's interesting when you talk about Phyllis Schlafly and the right-wing opposition, because the attacks you are describing are similar to those that have been made on the arts.

NS: I know that and have followed a lot of it. Those people never sleep, and I think, if anything, they have grown in strength over the last 20 years. My understanding is that the worldwide economic contraction of capitalism began somewhere after 1974 or 1975. It is directly parallel with this kind of sleeping, substrate morality that exists in the American psyche that wakes up in economic hard times and begins to think that racism wasn't such a bad idea after all, that women are really the cause of a lot of these problems, and that sex is really a mistake *[laughter]* or is such a dangerous force that enormous amounts of energy and public activity have to be focused on trying to control it. It's really about speech. When people talked about free speech, I said, "Sure, of course," but I now understand it in a visceral way. The freedom to speak and to represent ideas—anything that chills, that is really the problem. It's so interesting when you talk to Europeans and understand the differences. You just take the profiles of what we do around abortions and teenage pregnancies and we stick out like sore thumbs. It's clear that whatever of that they had to deal with has long since been buried, and we still haven't come to terms with it.

MC: I want to talk a little more about conflicts within feminism you've encountered. When you've been forming coalitions with other feminist groups around the country or internationally, what have been the key issues, and how have you been able to resolve them?

NS: That's a marvelous question, and I think it's just as alive right now as it was *almost* from the beginning. Even though there is no question that the women's health movement came out of the second wave of feminism, we diverged from mainstream feminism. We had our own thesis, our own agenda, our own leadership, our own analysis, and our own constituencies almost from the beginning. Mainstream feminism was really focused on women's rights, women's equality, and women's entitlement to be economic, social, and legal actors. When I say "we," I'm thinking of the nexus between the collective and the National Women's Health Network. Of course, the women's health movement in this country is much broader than that; now there are groups of women of color like the National Black Women's Health Project, the Native American Women's Community Board, and the National Latina Health Organization with which we collaborate. The nub of the split is that mainstream American feminism has been about women getting their share of the pie, and we are about changing the pie. In other words, social justice has dominated the women's health movement.

The other difference that's become quite large and is moving toward open conflict is the question of technology. A lot of progressive feminists had bought much of the socialist/Marxist line, derived from the writings of Marx, about how technology will save us. That, I think, has spilled over into notions that technology is essentially value-neutral—it depends on who's controlling the technology whether it's good or bad. There's another school of thought that says technology has ideology imbedded in it, and our first task is to identify that ideology and learn it; to ask questions about who's benefiting and who isn't; and to question the use of technology in terms of how things could be done in less wasteful, less destructive, less costly ways.

As far as women's health goes, the collective and the National Women's Health Network have taken what I say is the truly scientific stance of skepticism toward the onrushing technology. The other piece tied to that is a continuous process of demystifying corporate power—how corporations manipulate public imagination, how they design technologies that benefit certain groups of people at the expense of the rest of us. These two things have characterized what we've done from the beginning, whereas I think mainstream feminism has increasingly embraced technology as something to which women are entitled and without which women are getting something called second-class care.

MC: Traditionally there's been much less medical research done on health issues specifically related to or manifest in women than in men. Would more mainstream feminists argue that women-specific research should be done?

NS: Yes, but I'll be nastier than that and say that's the Republican way of packaging women's health issues. It's no accident that Bernadine Healey, under the Republicans, got to be the head of NIH. It's no accident that mainstream feminism hailed this as progress because she was an honest-to-God biological woman heading up the male establishment called the National Institutes of Health. Her way of defining women's health would be to focus on primarily chronic diseases, primarily affecting white women, and attempt to demonstrate (which was correct) that the NIH had not done its job to include more women, and that it had, indeed, generalized the research it had done on men to apply to women. But that was her way, and *their* way, of creating an idea about women's health that would focus off the abuses inherent in the system—the continual subjecting of perfectly normal, healthy women to high technology experiments, to institutionalization and hospitalization when it's not appropriate, to drugs and pharmaceuticals that are inadequately researched and inappropriately prescribed and which are far too profitable.

MC: You've been touching on issues of class and race as we've been talking. I know that the women's health movement, as you described it, pretty much started as a white, upper-middle-class, then middle-class movement.

NS: Middle class, yes. The upper-class women became doctors.

MC: Could you talk more about racially or ethnically based groups like the National Black Women's Health Project and their relationship to the collective and the National Women's Health Network? It seems that some people felt they couldn't work within existing structures and had to create their own.

NS: Ultimately, it is the best possible expression of what the women's health movement is about that groups of women with specific identities should form their own organizations and say, "This is our experience, this is what it looks like, and this is what it feels like from where we are." It's obvious that no white woman alive can ever really know what it feels like to come as a black woman into an entirely white institution and be handled by the people there. We can listen to what women of color say and incorporate that into our message, which we do all the time, but we can't speak for them.

I think the question of where that puts primarily white women depends on which white women you're talking about. The majority of the women in the collective already knew a lot about discrimination and civil rights. Every woman in the collective was involved in some kind of activist movement before she ever came into the collective. The feeling that it was critical for us to maintain our *stability* for as long as we could was occasioned by seeing how much like a balsa chip other organizations had become. That was why we clung to our impenetrable, if you will, identity, which was the case for such a long time. Very gingerly in the eighties, we brought in two women who had already been working with us for a number of years, and they became part of the core group.

MC: Were they white women?

NS: Yes. In the last four or five years, we've started to hire people from the outside who have zero history with us and to whom we've offered full-time jobs. They have been women of color. But that doesn't change the mix very much, given that four of us from the original group are still on staff. It's a leadership that's still white, predominantly baby boomers, and a staff that is multicultural but sitting on the bottom of the totem pole. It's a set-up for problems. [Swenson has since reported that the collective's staff and board of directors have become more diverse and that its current advisory board is very multicultural.]

MC: When the collective had been doing new editions of *Our Bodies, Ourselves* and other books, were there attempts to bring in more issues of concern to women of color?

NS: We had a whole system. By the time we came to the 1984 edition, there were so many new women's health movements out there in which we hadn't been able to participate. They had lives of their own, literature of their own, political constituencies and interests of their own. Not only were they based on ethnic and racial identities, but also on specific women's health issues. It more and more became our job to identify them, locate them and give them as much of a voice as we could in our book. We made sure the leadership of all of those constituencies were involved in the book in some way. So we had a black pencil, a gray pencil, a lavender pencil, a disability pencil—different kinds of women were given the whole manuscript to look over to answer, "How does this strike you? Is there something inadvertently racist or insensitive to lesbians or insensitive to women with disabilities?" We couldn't do any more than that because we weren't any more than that. But that worked extremely well.

The original National Women's Health Network was really much more multicultural than the collective by the late eighties, and Byllye Avery was part of that before she moved on to create the National Black Women's Health Project. Then, in the middle years, the network developed a constituency of primarily white older women, which was very disturbing because it became a question of whether the tail was going to wag the dog; the interests of the membership were more about cancer and osteoporosis than about social justice issues, women's rights, abortion/fetal medicine, the drug industry, dangerous contraceptives. At a critical moment in the late eighties, the network decided it no longer wanted to pursue its mission without a sense it was representing the whole spectrum of concerns in women's health. The network held a two-day retreat and invited the leadership of all the ethnic and racial women's groups we knew of with an interest in health. As a consequence, the network was able to produce a multicultural board which it has to this day. It's one of the best single examples in the women's movement of a functioning multicultural alliance in the leadership of a national organization. It's not a perfect alliance—I'm sure there are tensions and frustrations going on there—but it has been sustained since that period.

MC: Has there been as much tension about lesbian issues within women's health as there has been about race or class?

NS: No, not that I was aware of. Lesbians were on the stage and having their place from the very beginning. Primarily I think it's because sexuality went hand in hand with health from the very start, and it now seems so absurd to me that medicine and public health have tried so hard to promote health without much discourse about sexuality. But you could say that of all of medicine in terms of social and economic forces that impinge on people's health. It's the best-kept secret of the Western world that health is a consequence of the work you do, the income you have, the education you have, the habits you've formed, the relationships and networks you're in, the air you breathe, the food you eat. It's not about throwing money at medical care, but we still don't believe that in this culture.

MC: I'd like now to talk about culture and the arts with you. We spoke a little about similar things that have happened—right-wing attacks, for example—but the questions I have for you now have to do with your overall perceptions of culture and the arts in this society.

NS: I've been thinking about this for years because I came out of that world.

The culture and condition of people in this country are changing. The literacy level is going down. The volume of people coming from other cultures with other languages is going up. The public education system is going down. Television as a medium of information-sharing is going up. We recognize there is still a very influential segment of the upper middle class (the magazine readers of this country) that holds the greatest disenchantment with the medical system as it is. On the other hand, there are other ways of communicating these issues that may be more effective within other segments of the population. In the past, we produced a Spanish-language edition of our book, but we pulled it about four years ago because it was out of date—there's nothing in it about AIDS, for example. We now have a group of Latinas in the Boston area who have been vigorously involved in creating alternative theater and media productions to communicate health issues. What I see coming is the absolute necessity for us to throw resources behind other methods of communicating these messages that will be more visual, more accessible to the mainstream, and more powerful than the enemies' messages, which are having an enormous impact in terms of socializing people into fantasies about what medicine can really do for them.

MC: In the arts, some people are very worried about a gap that's been growing wider and wider between the arts and other spheres of life. I'm wondering what you think the reasons are for that, and if you see ways to try to close that gap.

NS: I don't know. I'm a little pessimistic, and I do think that what I just said is an illustration of the utilitarian way in which mainstream society now might think about relating to the arts—you have something we could use in our work, rather than your work is valuable in its own right. I think it is because of a decline in what I'll call a European sensibility; to the extent that the arts had a life in this culture, it came with an understanding of what in the broadest sense a humanistic education would consist of. That has been declining in the face of the technocratic onslaught, the notion that human problems can be reduced to technical problems that industry and the scientific enterprise can solve. Somehow, that kind of imagination suggests you can delete the human element and make it work better, rather than enhancing the human element and putting it in charge of technology to serve us. This has been fueled by the fact that we have a conservative administration that is able to make a target of the arts and show them as either irrelevant or immoral or both. It doesn't matter if it's true or not; the distancing becomes greater. That, plus the cutting of arts programs in public education has served to make it feel like the arts are an alien culture.

I don't see any easy road back. The only way I see that anything is going to swing around has to do with the degree to which we understand and value what other cultures have been able to build into their daily lives and how that contributes to their ability to compete successfully against us. Those are the doors through which I see these insights coming, but not in terms of what they can do for the human spirit.

Then I would say, too, that when I was a young woman growing up in this city, it was possible to buy reasonably cheap tickets to see an opera or a symphony performance. That's not possible anymore. That fact created the notion for people at the bottom of the system that the arts are for somebody else and not for them.

MC: Which in a practical sense is true, and not just for people at the bottom of the system. One last question: what do you see for the future?

NS: Mostly I feel that the enterprise that's bearing down on us will not succeed, primarily because it's too expensive to ever be made popular. Other times I feel it doesn't matter whether or not it's ever going to permeate the whole culture—the fact that it's held up as an ideal is going to permeate the whole culture, so people who can't get access will feel deprived. I worry a lot about that. I dream of a post-technocratic age when technology will have been put in its place and the idea that we control it, we evaluate it, will be the way. But I think I will not live to see it.

It is finally about speech, it's about reading and writing, it's about the ability to articulate ideas and make them your fruit—that's my idea of what freedom is about, and, if people don't experience that they can't value it. I was thinking of how I spent the first 20 to 25 years of my life. It's probably because of that that I have been able to have some vision of what people are entitled to. If I had been a pre-med or an MIT type, I probably wouldn't have that vision. I think there's an important crossover that I may not have thought about until just now. When you look around the collective, close to half of the people have had some connection with the arts, either as artists or in some other role. It's almost as if that immersion in the humanities made us feel this was important to do.

MC: The collective takes a humanistic approach to health, so having that kind of background makes a lot of sense.

NS: Between the psychologists and the artists [in the collective], I would say it's inevitable. I hope we can keep that purity. I fear we can't. I fear we'll start to bring on doctors, and we'll get more invested in the big struggle to overwhelm the technocratic system using its tools. The only other insight I have had is that the artistic enterprise, as best practiced, is much less about the kind of collaborating and daily, weekly, hourly sharing that's integral to the business of political organizing and movement life. One of the things that's unique about our work, by the way, is that our manuscripts were put on the table and ripped apart. It was kind of a systematic destruction of individuality in the service of some greater whole. That's where I see the minimum of crossover between community organizing and the artistic enterprise. In a sense, the core of art is a Western heightening of the individual and using the stuff of self to produce something for the world.

MC: That's true in most cases, but there are some artists who focus on a collective process.

NS: Oh, yes. And apart from the soloists, certainly the dance enterprise and the music enterprise are about exquisite cooperation and collaboration, but many fights happen over this. I read about them all the time.

MC: Yeah, they do. Did you fight over the manuscripts?

NS: Oh, yeah, terrible fights *[laughter]*. But we managed to resolve them.

August 22, 1994
Watertown, Massachusetts

4

JOSEPH MARSHALL

JOSEPH MARSHALL HAD BEEN AN EDUCATOR for the San Francisco Unified School District for more than two decades when he decided that classroom teaching wasn't enough. Promising young students whom he'd seen in his math class weren't making it. Instead, they were being lost to drugs, gang violence, prison, or teen pregnancy. In 1987, Marshall founded the Omega Boys Club to provide after-school tutorial, mentorship, and violence prevention programs for the predominantly African American youth of the Potrero Hill neighborhood. The club emphasizes academic achievement, nonviolence, and noninvolvement with drugs, and it provides college scholarship support to its participants.

The Omega programs began at a relatively intimate scale, but when Marshall got access to radio airwaves in 1991, he was suddenly able to take his message to a much larger youth audience. He founded what is now a syndicated violence-prevention radio talk show called Street Soldiers, *a youth call-in program that reaches more than 50,000 weekly. Because callers may remain anonymous, the show's format has created an unprecedented space for public dialogue around the highly charged issues that face young people today.*

In the following pages, Marshall speaks about the genesis of Street Soldiers, *why he has given his life to this work, and what he has learned. His most important lesson is a simple one: "Extend yourself."*

❑ ❑ ❑ ❑ ❑

Claire Peeps: What was the origin of the Omega Boys Club?

Joseph Marshall: Jack Jacqua and I started the club February 27, 1987. Both of us were longtime employees of the San Francisco Unified School District. Jack was a peer counseling professional. I had been an educator for 25 years, with about 15 years of that spent as a middle school math teacher. The club started just because of the failure of our own students to have successful lives.

CP: What led you into teaching initially?

JM: I was born in St. Louis, raised in Los Angeles. I came to San Francisco to go to college. One of the reasons I chose the University of San Francisco was because I wanted to get away from home, being the oldest of nine. But that wasn't the only reason. I had attended Loyola High School in Los Angeles. What I had missed there was black people. It was a good school, a very traditional Greek/Latin education. But culturally it was bereft. I came to USF thinking that I was going to be around a lot of black people because I saw the basketball team on TV and it was all black. So I thought the school was black. I got up here and found out that the only black people in the school *were* the athletes and me. So I was back in the same situation again.

That was the late sixties which was, of course, a consciousness-raising time for the entire country, particularly for black people, and I was no exception. I became the founder of the Black Student Union and an activist on campus. I was what some people would call "militant," and what I would call "socially conscious." People will tell you that I was pretty much instrumental through the BSU in bringing black faculty and ethnic studies to the school—in making the campus for us. There was a burgeoning number of black students at the time because we got a lot of students to come to the school. We created a home for ourselves, from the food we ate to the music we heard in the jukebox. But what we were particularly happy about was bringing ethnic studies to the school. We felt that knowledge was important. I thought if kids knew what I knew it would lead them on to great heights. I was pretty charged up to become a teacher. I started teaching high school seniors when I was 22. I would walk into school with a dashiki on and Malcolm in my briefcase. I was pretty fiery. I led a student walk-out over certain demands the kids had. I also had African festivals, huge events that we started in my first year of teaching, and plays. It really did a lot for the school. But I was too much for the faculty, I guess, young militant that I was. They moved me out after one year *[laughter]*. I went into Special Education for the next four years, and ended up teaching junior high school math.

CP: And from there into the Boys Club?

JM: Well, from there to the club. I was always involved with my students at school. I wrote curriculum, I was the Student Activities Director for most of those 15 years. I put on talent shows, plays, dances. I ran the student government. Mr. Marshall was it! I felt that if the kids could survive me, as rigorous as I was—and I was pretty demanding as a teacher—that they would have decent lives. Certainly get a good job, hopefully go into college if that was what they wanted. The only thing that mattered to me was whether they could pass my exam. A kid could come in every day, turn in all of his homework, but if he couldn't pass my test, I'd flunk him.

When the kids left, I figured everything was going to be okay, but I got horror stories when they entered high school: getting a letter from a kid in prison, where he'd been incarcerated for selling drugs, instead of from a dormitory; a girl coming back to visit me, knocking on the door with one hand and she's got a baby in the other. She's maybe 15 or 16 now, when she left me she was 13. Walking in the streets of the Tenderloin in San Francisco, a kid once walked up to me and said, "Mr. Marshall, don't you remember me? You're the best teacher I ever had." I couldn't figure out who he was because he was cracked-out. Jack would come to me saying that we had to take the day off to go to a funeral because one of the kids got shot in some sort of gang violence. That led me to realize that the fact that they're with us 180 days a year, 55 minutes a day wasn't producing the results that we wanted, that they wanted. So we felt that we had to go beyond the school. Instead of 8:00 to 3:00, it needed to be 8:00 to 8:00. We became an extended family to the kids. We felt that if we kept them around us, we could guide them.

CP: What were the first programs and goals of the Omega Boys Club?

JM: The first programs were modeled on the Continental of Omega Boys and Girls Club of Vallejo, California, which has been in existence for about 25 years. Filmore Graham runs that club; he's a fraternity brother of mine. I went to him and said, "Filmore, I want to do this in the Bay Area." He said, "Fine. I was waiting for you to ask me." He had a facility, and he did sports. We did a little bit of that but we designed our own programs, too. One of the programs that we started early on was a Peer Counseling Program in which we took young people from the club to do counseling with the incarcerated youths in juvenile halls. A lot of our kids used to be in detention. We thought that they could aid the incarcerated kids in getting out and staying out, since they'd done the same thing.

Our first meetings were held at the Potrero Hill Neighborhood House, three blocks from the middle school. We asked the executive director, Enola Maxwell, if we could meet there, and she said, "Sure, no charge." About 25 guys attended our first informal meeting.

CP: What age range were you working with?

JM: Then it was primarily 11 to 18. We told them that we wanted them to belong to an academic, drug-free Boys Club. We knew most of them— a lot of them were former students, some were kids Jack knew from the neighborhood. We scheduled meetings on a regular basis and we told them that we'd be there with them every step of the way.

CP: What does that mean?

JM: Well, that means whatever they needed we'd try to help them with. Period. Anything. We were their extended family. We were going to be the fathers that maybe they didn't have. The specific commitment was to college, but the general commitment was to being involved with their lives. I think that out of the 25 at the first meeting, 15 came back to form the core membership of the club. A lot of the emphasis in those days was on field trips. Our first one was to Wrestlemania 1. We took the kids out to see Hulk Hogan with the giant screen. We gave awards for everything from school attendance to improved grades.

CP: Did you have trouble recruiting those first 25 kids?

JM: No. I talked to kids in my class, and Jack talked to other kids from the neighborhood. We told them if they were interested in going to college, we would help them identify schools, complete financial aid forms, study for the SATs, we would even try to raise some money for their tuition and expenses.

CP: So this was initially just you and Jack, on a volunteer basis?

JM: Exactly. We met twice a month, on Thursdays.

CP: Were the 15 kids who emerged as core members pretty solid academically?

JM: Oh, no. Our kids have never necessarily been good students. Just about all of them were dealing drugs or involved in some sort of neighborhood rivalries. In San Francisco, we don't have gangs; we have what we call "turf." So they were all involved in some sort of turf. We talked about teenage fatherhood, because that was also a big issue.

We found that meeting twice a month was not enough, so we came up with the concept of having a weekly study hall, a tutorial, on Tuesdays. Jack said to me, "Well, if we're going to have them there, let's feed them." And I said, "No way, Jack! These kids are coming to study, they're not coming to eat." But finally I agreed to try it his way. It turned out to be really good. The parents would come in and cook, and the kids would study. That brought this sense of family closer together. So that's kind of the way it went. Some sports, some field trips, the tutoring, and some serious discussion.

CP: What was the incentive for kids to keep coming back?

JM: I don't know, you've got to ask them *[laughter]*. I would say that kids want a way out. I think they came back because, at the base of it, they just wanted a way away from the streets. We didn't give them any money, we didn't have a building. We didn't have much of what the traditional Boys Clubs offer in the area of activities or recreation. But I think the kids knew Jack and me pretty well, and believed that we were genuinely concerned about them. With new kids, we had to break down their initial cynicism and skepticism. You know, "Why are you doing this for us? What's your angle?" Most of these kids live in a predator's world where somebody's always trying to get something out of them very early in life. So of course they were cynical about us.

CP: What did you say to those kids?

JM: We told them we were doing this just because we wanted them to have a decent life. That simple. They didn't believe us at first, but after a while they'd say, "You guys are for real." New kids would hear about us from their friends and they'd come here. In early '88, we got a lot of publicity. The local ABC affiliate in San Francisco did some stories on the club and actually asked people to send in money. Strangers just started sending us money!

CP: How had you been supporting the Club up until that point?

JM: Jack and I did it out of our own pocket until people began to hear about us. One lady saw me on TV. She called me up to her office in Marin County and said, "I like what you're doing." She gave me a check for $10,000. We got about $30,000 from on-air solicitations. That was our first real money. Then foundations began to hear about us. They didn't quite understand it because we didn't fit the models that they were used to. But they sort of believed in the spirit and started making small grants, which turned into larger grants. In May of 1988, when the club was about a year old, we had eight kids who had finished high school. We made a pitch on

TV and raised $8,000 to send these kids on a tour of Southern black colleges. The news stations covered their trips—their leaving, their coming back, and the meeting at the club when they returned. In September, we sent all those kids off to college.

CP: Did you solicit that media coverage?

JM: No. That coverage occurred because there had just been a big story about black kids throwing rocks at the buses. Some reporter went to his news director and said, "We're always doing negative stories. There must be some positive stories out there." He went to one of the San Francisco city supervisors and asked her to find some programs, and she directed him to us. The station was so enamored by what we were doing—the whole bit, these two teachers sort of picking these kids up on their back—that they did almost two weeks of full stories on us.

CP: How have the programs at the club evolved since that time?

JM: First there were the two academic programs—tutoring and sending kids to college—along with the Peer Counseling Program in Juvenile Hall. That actually developed because a lot of the kids in the Boys Club wanted to visit their friends, kids from the neighborhood, locked up in Juvenile Hall. At first they were denied access because they weren't relatives. So we went back as the club, and the hall administration eventually changes their minds. It was a small start, but we still do that program today.

The academic programs grew fast. The number of kids from the club going on to college grew from eight to 20 to 32 to 64—just like that! *[snaps fingers].* So I spent most of my time raising money for scholarships. The next program to be developed was the Street Soldiers Violence Prevention Program, which came as an outgrowth of our working with these violent kids. At first we didn't know exactly what we were doing other than giving them our own personal help. But we came to realize what steps we had to take them through. At that time, in November 1991, we happened to have a chance to take the No Drugs/Stop the Violence message on the radio. Instead of speaking to 40 kids or 60 kids weekly at the Boys Club, we were suddenly able to speak to 50,000 or 60,000.

CP: How did you get access to the airwaves?

JM: The artist Hammer went into KMEL-FM radio to host a two-night call-in, "Let's hear what it's like out there in the community." There was such a huge response that the station wanted to continue it periodically.

They brought me in as a guest host and liked what I had to say. All kinds of stuff came out over the air: "My friend got shot. What should I do?" I sort of knew what to say because I had been working with the same issues with kids for four years. They asked me to become the permanent host in January of 1992. I brought in Ms. Margaret Norris as co-host about three months later. She's a mother who used to call in a lot [laughter]. After a while I said, "Why don't you just come into the studio?" She and I continue to be the permanent hosts of the show today. That's how we got access to the airwaves!

CP: How does the nature of your discussion change when you're reaching 50,000 or 60,000 kids instead of 40?

JM: It doesn't, really. Radio is just as intimate, but it's a different intimacy, that's all. Radio lends itself to anonymity, it's a personal phone call, it's us and them. As long as we really know what we're talking about, there's not much difference: face to face, phone to phone. Even at the club, a lot of my work is done over the phone because I'm working with kids all over California and outside the state.

CP: Do you ever work with the kids you've talked to on the radio?

JM: Yeah. A lot of them join the Boys Club or we continue to correspond over the phone. But they don't have to come in here and meet me, they just have to understand what we're saying: if they're doing something wrong, change it, and if they're not doing something wrong, continue to do it right. You see, we're trying to convince people to be Street Soldiers and to do the right thing. People have told me that they do it just because we're able to show them that it's the right thing to do. We validate kids' behavior and strengthen their resolve, or we give them reasons for change. Many kids have never met us, but everybody feels like they know us. Kids tell us that Ms. Norris and I are like their mother and father. In fact, one journalist even called us the "Electronic Parents."

CP: What are the basic principles that underlie the Street Soldiers Violence Prevention Program?

JM: It's a three-step process. The first step is identifying risk-taking behaviors for the kids, some of which they may not even be aware of. The obvious ones are things like carrying a gun, or using or selling drugs. But something like the language they use may actually predispose them to violence, or the fact that material values for them predominate over family values. These are things that are intertwined but not as obvious to them. So we spend time identifying those things.

The second step—and this is the longest and hardest—is dealing with the anger, fear, and pain that has built up over time because of their lifestyles. It's the hardest step because it depends how much scar tissue is there. Thirdly, we give them what we call the Rules for Living Nonviolently, which substitute for their old behaviors and allow them to get where they really wanted to get to all along. One of the rules is that you can never kill an enemy. A lot of these kids think you can. A lot of them use military terms: enemy territory, preemptive strike, defensive strike. These gang members have been watching Jimmy Cagney movies, war pictures. They sound like military men because that's their model. They think you have to get revenge for a recent problem and then it will all be solved. Except it doesn't work for them, all it does is get them killed. I have to explain to them that the Crips and Bloods have been fighting for 25 years. Every fight has been to solve a recent problem, but it's never been solved. The first time a kid hears this, "You can never kill an enemy," it goes against what he's been taught since he was about six: kill or be killed, do or die. You can never kill an enemy because he has a brother or sister, or buddy, or partner, or homeboy—there will always be another one. I said to one guy, "You know, right across the street, there's a guy just like you—just as strong, quick, fast, black, as smart as you—he's a mirror-image of you, you can't beat him. And his son will become your enemy, too." Just taking the time to sit down and beginning to explain this to them helps, because they're tired of it. They want a way out but they don't know how. What is really needed is a change in their thinking.

Along with "You can never kill an enemy" is the rule, "The most precious thing is life." Their most precious thing is funerals. So I can show these guys, "Well, all you got is prisons." It's a powerful argument.

CP: Do you meet resistance?

JM: Yeah, sure you do. Because you're going against what they've learned.

CP: How do you cope with that? Why are you able to walk in and get the attention of gang members when others have been unsuccessful?

JM: I don't know. I can only talk about me. I don't know why they don't listen to others. I think they listen to us because we're telling it straight. Like this kid against whom we were diametrically opposed. I knew if this kid didn't change, he'd kill somebody, he'd endanger the entire neighborhood that he claims he's trying to protect, he'd go to jail, his mother would be going to a funeral. I'm not going to let that happen. And I'm willing to risk my life not to let that happen. Technically, we're risking our lives every time we go to gang meetings, which we are doing frequently now, because we don't have any guns, we don't have anything. A lot of these guys are killers. But we're not afraid of them and we're willing to risk our lives to save them. I told this kid, "If I see you doing something wrong, I will stop you, or you're going to have to kill me. You'll have to kill me, Ms. Norris, and Jack." That's true. And by the way, this is not a kid, he's 29 years old. The L.A. gang members we've been talking to recently are not kids, they're men. It's hard for them to understand what we tell them, because they don't get that sort of genuine caring about them anywhere, except maybe from their mothers or grandmothers. Very few of them have fathers. Not even the guys in their own gang feel that way about them. Gang friendships come with conditions. You can't say no. You can't disagree. We don't put those conditions on our love or friendship for them. And that's *powerful*.

CP: How do you handle a situation in which a kid does the wrong thing?

JM: We just tell him that he did something wrong.

CP: Does it change your relationship with him? Does it carry sanctions?

JM: What sanction would I use?

CP: Would you ban somebody from the club, for instance, if you knew he was doing something like killing people?

JM: Would you ban your daughter or your son from your home? You might kick them out of your house for a while, but you'd say, "When you get it right come back," or "The door's always open." It's no different. These kids are our family. We're always pushing them to do the right thing. I've got kids locked up in prison right now who didn't follow our advice. We're continually telling them, "When are you going to learn? When are you going to learn?" The door is always open, but their behavior dictates how much mouth they're going to get from us. That's pretty much how it works.

CP: Do you think your work could be replicated in other places?

JM: I can't say that either. All I can say is that this is what we do, this is what has worked for us. I think anybody can do something like this. I think anybody could care for kids other than their own biological children. And they'd probably have to figure out how best to do that. That's all we did. This is the way that we've seen that's best to achieve the goals we want. It would be difficult for me to say that you can do this in Boston. If I was in Boston, I would be doing this. If I was in Miami, I'd be doing this. I think it's just a matter of figuring out the way you like to do things to get the kind of results you want.

CP: Do you think the arts could be part of this work?

JM: You're asking the wrong person. I never think about it. Never.

CP: You spoke earlier about how you had involved the kids at school in plays and festivals.

JM: I'll borrow any source out there to explain to the kids why they shouldn't be doing what they're doing. We've eliminated a lot of things in our programs because we don't feel they are essential or the core of changing the kids' lives. We don't do sports anymore, we don't do art, we don't do plays. We don't even take kids to see that stuff. It's not that it's not valuable. We just feel that what we're really attacking is a way of thinking, a mind-set. So we draw on anything that can help us attack that mind-set.

CP: What about Hammer, what about rap music?

JM: We deal with anybody, whether it be rap artists, or films, or books— anyone who has something to say that can attack that mind-set. It really doesn't matter where they come from. I mean, it could be a guy on the street.

CP: If someone who shared your concerns about the welfare and future of kids came to you and said, "What can I do to help? How can I approach these kids?," what would you say? Is there a starting point?

JM: I'd communicate the same message to the artists as I would to the sports figures as I would to anybody else, and that would be to try and be extended family to the kids in the best way that you can. Try to look out for them, try to give them the right messages, extend yourself as a person—whether your person is art, or sports, but mostly it's just you as a person—because kids need people to lead them through the land mines of life. That's the message I would give to anybody. If your art can help you do that, great. If your sports can help you do that, great. If your music can help you do that, great. But the key is your relationship with the kid and what you can do for that kid. To me it's not about art, it's about relationships with kids. It's not about sports but relationships with kids.

CP: Is there a limit to your capacity? Can you be family to an infinite number of kids?

JM: I don't know. I don't think about that. I'm only doing what I'm capable of.

CP: Do you have kids of your own?

JM: I've got three kids—a 23-year-old, a 15-year-old, and a 7-year-old.

CP: How do you find time for your own family?

JM: I just do it all. You know, kids here, kids there.

CP: Where do you draw the line? Do kids in the club ask you to extend yourself in terms of financial loans, a place to stay?

JM: Well, I can't take them home because I've got kids at home! *[laughter].* I tell them, just like I tell my own kids, "This is what I can do, this is what I can't."

CP: What gives you hope?

JM: My hope is that the kids will change. That they will stop going to prison, that they'll stop using drugs, that they'll use their talents to do things constructively rather than destructively, that they'll stop destroying themselves and their communities and the people in their communities. That's what I hope.

I don't have a lot of choice, really. I owe a lot of people. I owe King and Malcolm and Jariet and Robeson and Jackie Robinson and Martin Delaney and Medgar Evers and Frederick Douglass. I owe them all. If I don't do this, then it's like—and I'm thinking particularly of Martin, Medgar and Malcolm—their assassins succeeded. They really succeeded if the spirit dies. This is my own way of carrying it on. I ain't got much choice. The more you know, the more you owe.

CP: Do you mark small victories along the way?

JM: Let's put it like this: that guy in Long Island, what did he kill—ten people, eleven people? If we hadn't gotten to some of these kids, I don't know how many people they'd have whacked out, or how many funerals their mothers would have had to go to, or how many families would be without fathers. I don't call them small victories, I call them *big* victories because I know what we're up against. For us to achieve anything, given the history of what black people have faced in this country, is not insignificant at all.

August 5, 1994
San Francisco, California

5

ESTHER KAPLAN

ESTHER KAPLAN IS A YOUNG ACTIVIST LIVING IN NEW YORK CITY who has worked on a number of issues, including gay and lesbian rights, abortion rights, anti-racism work within the Jewish community, Palestinian rights, and police brutality. But as she herself says, her involvement since 1988 with the radical anti-AIDS group, ACT UP, has provided both the defining context and methodological foundation for her work as an activist.

Within ACT UP, Kaplan participated in many of the large, highly visible direct actions that have made the organization famous, not only within activist circles but also among the general public. These included "Target City Hall" in 1989, protesting the AIDS policies of then-New York City Mayor Ed Koch; "Stop the Church" in 1989, decrying the Catholic Church's opposition to safer sex education, the use of condoms, and legal abortion; and blocking the entrances to Hoffman-LaRoche's New Jersey offices in 1993 to demand faster AIDS drug testing. She also has been involved in many of ACT UP's long-term campaigns, especially against the U.S. immigration ban on HIV-positive individuals; the struggle to have women included in both the government definition of AIDS and in experimental drug trials; and the effort to institute HIV education and condom distribution in New York City schools.

In her interview, Kaplan makes especially strong observations about the role of clearly defined self-interest in the activist process; about the difficult internal politics of race, class, and gender that often accompany activist struggles; and about how, in her view, politically minded artists have largely failed to translate their work into a true political practice, though she feels the potential for this still exists. Since her interview, Kaplan has continued to be highly involved in a number of activist causes, including AIDS (she is currently features editor of the national AIDS magazine POZ); anti-racism and educational work through the New York-based nonprofit Jews for Racial and Economic Justice (she was director from 1995 to 1997 and continues to serve as a board member); and police brutality and homelessness (in 1995, *she helped orchestrate a rush-hour shutdown of four bridges and tunnels in New York City to protest the budget cuts and "quality of life" policies of Mayor Rudolph Guiliani). Citing a "notorious record of brutality and racial profiling," Kaplan is currently working with a coalition of youth, parent, and teacher organizations to remove the New York City Police Department from its role as safety supervisor in the city's public schools.*

Marie Cieri: I understand you've been involved with several different groups as an activist.

Esther Kaplan: Yes. The main things I've done during the last seven years are abortion rights activism; AIDS activism through ACT UP; and now I'm involved with Jews for Racial and Economic Justice, which is a group that focuses on anti-racist work within the Jewish community as well as trying to pull Jews into multiracial coalition work. I entered that via getting involved in anti-occupation work around Israel and landed in this beleaguered community of progressive Jews in New York.

MC: I'd like to hear more about what that particular community is up against, but could you tell me, did you start doing activist work before you moved to New York?

EK: Sure. Even in high school, I was always involved as an activist in the sense of doing student empowerment stuff. I came here right after college.

MC: Are your parents pretty progressive? People who tend to act on their beliefs?

EK: I think they're people who act on their beliefs, definitely. I grew up in rural Oregon. It's not like my father was involved as an activist, but he would talk about what was going on. He had a very critical analysis of the world, one that was sympathetic toward power movements. I can remember at a pretty young age my dad trying to explain to me about J. Edgar Hoover and his repression of the Panthers.

My first activism was around antinuclear stuff. I worked with SANE/FREEZE for a while, pretty much as soon as I arrived at Yale for college. I was lobbying and organizing on a statewide basis, getting students from different campuses working. Then I became a feminist and also started getting involved with women. I was editing the campus feminist publication and doing gay and lesbian campus activism, which was really blooming at the time that I was there, from '83 to '87.

I feel that walking into ACT UP one day is the thing that really radicalized me. ACT UP was just about a year old at the time, at the very beginning of 1988. I don't think that I really identified as an activist until I got seriously involved in ACT UP. That was when I finally realized how serious people could be about organizing and how much experience and planning and work and risk and commitment a lot of people put into it.

AIDS hadn't even remotely impacted on my life then compared to how it has now, where I feel like it's a controlling factor. In the early years, people still didn't really know that much about how the disease was transmitted, and everyone was paranoid and flipped out. I think I got involved in ACT UP almost because of the theoretical basis of it—the whole idea that this illness was not being researched, the way it was being talked about, the kind of language that was being used about it—you know, of quarantine and tattooing and the way that people wanted to use AIDS to systematically marginalize gay people. That was the way it really pulled me in.

MC: What was your focus within the organization?

EK: It changed a lot. In a lot of ways, I've been like a soldier in ACT UP. Even when I've been working hard on a particular project, I've tried to put a lot of energy into working on just organizing the big actions that we do.

MC: You're still in ACT UP?

EK: Yes. At various points, I've gotten intensely involved in a particular aspect; one of those is the HIV immigration ban and one was the campaign to change the Centers for Disease Control and Prevention [CDC] definition of AIDS so that it included illnesses that women get and die of. Also, I've worked a lot on the school board issues around condom distribution and HIV education here in New York, which has been a really pitched battle.

MC: Most people associate ACT UP with being out in the streets, the signage (which I think has been very effective), the angry, in-your-face direct action. From your observations from within the organization, how would you describe the methodology? What do you think has been successful, what hasn't, and why?

EK: I think in the original years what ACT UP really did was politicize this illness, number one, and take it out of the world of nature and put it into the world of politics. More than anything else in recent years, it put images of empowered gay people into the media, saying "Our lives matter, the life of our community matters, and all of these policies that are congealing around AIDS to stigmatize us are not going to be tolerated." ACT UP completely transformed the way people were responding both to AIDS and to this stigmatized population—at that time, it was thought to be exclusively afflicting gay people.

Since then, the perception of who AIDS is hitting, and the reality of it, has changed too. I also think ACT UP promoted the idea that you can put the brakes on the rights of corporations to make a profit over anyone's dead body.

One of the early actions at the Stock Exchange really brought out the idea that not only governments can be targets of activism, but that corporations can too. We're in an age when corporations are really determining what's happening to a great degree. We've also struggled to establish the Catholic Church as a political target. So ACT UP is saying that there are all these players shaping our political reality, deciding whether or not we live or die, whether or not we get ill, and they are now open for targeting—and for vilification if they claim not to be political players. I think in those ways ACT UP's been extraordinarily successful and has won lots of small battles around the price of AZT and around expanded access to experimental drugs. ACT UP really transformed the way drug-approval processes work. I think ACT UP has probably stemmed the tide around mandatory testing and stigmatization efforts, although there are still a lot of problems in different states around the country about contact tracing, testing for state health care workers, and the loss of anonymous testing sites.

What ACT UP's done around needle exchange has made one of the few inroads into this "war on drugs" mentality, where the only answer is to get people to get off drugs. ACT UP took a completely different position, which was that we want to make sure people don't also transmit HIV when they're doing drugs. The needle exchange battle was transformative. It was done in a manner that's the opposite of how people *think* ACT UP works, which is out with its flashy signs or chaining itself to corporate headquarters. It was done mainly by a group of people who went down to the Lower East Side every Saturday for years. When they were finally arrested they stood a big, public trial, they didn't take a compromise deal, they really fought for it.

In fact, ACT UP has used a much broader range of tactics than people think, and a lot of that gets lost. There's an organization in New York, Housing Works, which provides housing for people with AIDS—better than any other organization by far. It was an ACT UP committee once. Despite the fact that its active membership remains very much white, gay male, and middle class, the issues it's taken up and the tactics it's used have been much broader than that.

MC: Why do you think ACT UP's remained that way demographically? And how do you fit in?

EK: It's hard to be there as a woman, and I think it's hard to be there as a person of color. There are ways in which the culture just doesn't speak to you. Gay male culture in this city is pretty segregated, socially speaking, so that's reflected in activism.

MC: By race or class? Both?

EK: I was thinking race, though I imagine it is by class, too. In ACT UP's heyday, the room looked very different than it does now; there were all these beautiful boys in the room, cruising each other. At the time, it was not only producing a lot of political energy, but it was also a social space for people. Now I feel it's much more the people hunkered down in the trenches who are left. I still think that there's some of that social stuff going on, though, and I'm sure if you're a man of color, and you walk in there, you're very aware that you're not a player. We had a lot of problems organizing around the schools because the media kept portraying a split between the white gay activists and the conservative, family-loving, working class communities of people of color. There was a lot of debate on the floor of ACT UP about how we weren't going to exacerbate this so-called split, what our strategies were going to be. Whenever ACT UP has had to try to directly take on the question of race, a lot of racist stuff has come out of people's mouths. Still, I think that it's possible to hear that, deal with it, and move along, the same way I sit in there and listen to misogyny a lot. It's a very conscious choice that I've made.

MC: And you've made it because you feel that, on this particular issue, this is the most effective venue for your activism?

EK: Certainly on this issue. There are not a lot of other ways to do direct action.

MC: Given the populations that AIDS is affecting now, has there been much discussion in the group about coalition-building with people of color, women, and straight people, or is the focus still one that relates, as you were saying, to the fact that AIDS has been used as a tool to marginalize gay people?

EK: That is a constant topic of discussion, and it takes a lot of different forms. There's a committee called ACT UP Americas that works to try to support AIDS organizing throughout Central and South America and the Caribbean. Another model that's been used, which has potential but also is problematic, is hooking in with service and community organizations that serve poor people with AIDS to get their clients involved in actions. But there's a kind of disequilibrium there because chances are the clients themselves are not necessarily organizers, so then there are these predominantly black and Latino people involved in an action that's been organized by highly trained organizers who are almost all white. One thing ACT UP hasn't done is pay much attention to cultivating new activists. Entering into ACT UP is like a trial by fire; it's not a welcoming place—it's got this intense pace at the meetings, the language is highly technical, it's very business-oriented (which is great because a lot of stuff gets done), but there's not a lot of talk, there's not a lot of normal human stuff going on, at least through the public airwaves. What that means is that a lot of people come into contact with ACT UP, but they can't quite feel like they know how to participate in it.

MC: How do decisions get made? Is it by consensus or is there a hierarchy?

EK: Majority vote, oh yes, not consensus. ACT UP would not be getting so much done if things had to work by consensus because there are real disagreements inside the group.

MC: Is there any pattern to the disagreements? Do they center on certain issues or certain kinds of actions?

EK: One is the split between the scientific and the social approaches, which aren't necessarily contradictory but can be in conflict in terms of allocation of resources. The other is in tactics. An example was the campaign to stop a trial of AZT in pregnant women, which was set up unethically: some people in ACT UP were really critical of a group of women fighting on this because they took over the AIDS Clinical Trial Group [ACTG] meeting and disrupted it. The treatment-oriented men in ACT UP, who wanted to maintain their relationships with the ACTG, were appalled. "Oh, don't pay attention to them, they're crazy," was what they said privately.

MC: How did ACT UP come up with its very identifiable methodology? I mean, people *know* when ACT UP is protesting something.

EK: Again, I think that ACT UP functions in a wider variety of forms than people acknowledge. I don't think people would walk by the needle exchange and recognize that as ACT UP. I think that the particular strain of activism you're talking about came mostly from the group of people who formed it—people with a lot of class privilege, access to media (much more than most activist groups), access to high-tech, expensive graphic equipment, computers. White, middle-, or even upper-middle-class people were involved—that's kind of unusual. People who could manage, through inside connections, to get onto the set of *CBS News* or get those little blue jackets you have to wear to get into the Stock Exchange. That's not something that Latino and Asian teenagers from Queens could do; it's just not.

These men had a sense of entitlement at the beginning. I think that's faded, but at first they had been able to lead very safe and privileged lives, and all of a sudden they were facing the reality of this virus. It was not only in their bodies but in the bodies of *all* these people in their community, and that challenged many ideas about how that community was functioning, and how sex could function, and how long they were going to live. Those men felt a kind of rage and urgency that I think people who have been systematically disrespected from birth, like women and people of color, may not necessarily feel. On the whole, these white men were people leading somewhat closeted lives, or they somehow had found places to work or live where they could be respectable "out" people. Their sense of entitlement and demand for immediate action, I think, is really unusual. In a way it's sick, but in another way it's amazing and great. It's really what's kept ACT UP so forceful, this idea that people are dying all the time, people are dying right now, that we have to stop it *in my lifetime* and that lifetime is being defined by someone who's HIV-positive. I think that ACT UP's in crisis now partly because most people have stopped believing it's going to happen in their lifetime. All of a sudden, it's much more like any other political movement where you're fighting for something, but you may not see the end.

MC: Could you talk a little bit about your involvement with women's issues through ACT UP and WHAM [Women's Health Action and Mobilization]?

EK: I'm actually working on a women's action right now at the FDA [Food and Drug Administration] about women's exclusion from experimental drug trials. Most women can be excluded from trials if they're in their fertility years and don't agree to be sterilized. We're trying to pull together different women's health activists to launch a real campaign this year. I think the exclusion of women from drug trials is an interesting illustration of the place of women in this culture, because it's about the total lack of concern for women's lives and women's bodies—they don't even exist. Especially in the wake of Clinton's election and the Casey decision, I feel that abortion rights activism fell apart and, with it, women's street activism—at least in this city. So much of what women have been working on got encapsulated in the abortion struggle. Even in the midst of that, I felt frustrated with it.

MC: Why?

EK: Well, no one says anything about poor women. Abortion rights had already been heavily traded away for poor women. It was like the unifying ability of abortion had its limits or something. Abortion is a really intense issue for women at a certain time in their lives, particularly straight women or women who are raped, but it's not something that spans the whole range of female experience.

WHAM basically stopped existing two months ago. But there was a great moment when ACT UP and WHAM were working together, particularly around HIV education and the Catholic Church's position against abortion, the use of condoms and sex education. Through that union, women with a lot of feminist health experience brought a new perspective into ACT UP. Women outside the AIDS movement have not considered it a women's issue. At the Dyke March that was part of Stonewall in June of '94, I was marching with a small group of ACT UP women with a banner that said, "Lesbians fight AIDS" or "Women Fight AIDS," or something like that, and people expressed a lot of anger toward us.

MC: Other women?

EK: Yeah, like we weren't really dealing with women's issues or something. It's weird. Why WHAM, as a women's health group, never took up the issue of women and AIDS except when it collaborated with ACT UP is a real question. When you work on AIDS activism, you understand how gendered it is: how differently it functions in men's and women's bodies, how different men's and women's access is to experimental treatments or even information about the treatments, how much more quickly women die, how much harder it's been, especially before the CDC change, for women to get access to services. From the outside, though, people don't think of it as a particularly gendered issue. They think AIDS activists are taking care of it. But I think many community-based women's health service organizations are now in touch with the fact that it's a women's issue.

MC: Because they're seeing women who are HIV positive.

EK: Yeah. To exist in ACT UP as a woman, as a feminist, is sort of a bizarre dichotomy. You end up applying your feminist analysis to these issues, but just to survive there and be part of the debate you have to throw away your feminist yearnings. It's not a feminist space, and it's not a space that's very filled with women. If you really needed to be working with women, you wouldn't be there. I think that's why all the attempts to have a women's caucus, a lesbian caucus, a women's issues caucus, and so on have all come and gone.

MC: There's a broader question, too, of whether, as an individual, you're going to choose to be a coalition-building force, or if you're going to choose to work with like-minded people.

EK: I've been thinking a lot lately about this question of coalitions. The term is used in a fast and loose way. Coalitions come together around particular battles, around HIV education, around the cuts to the Division of AIDS Services or whatever, and then they evaporate. That's the general pattern. Even for them to come together for a short time takes a lot of effort. People aren't necessarily looking at the work they're doing as trying to build a movement. They aren't always acknowledging to themselves how serious the changes that they're trying to fight for are, how fundamental they are.

MC: Things that don't seem connected on the surface may, in fact, be connected.

EK: Yes. I've had some really interesting coalition experiences as part of ACT UP, the most recent of which was an effort to close a U.S. detention center in Guantanamo Bay, Cuba. A couple of years ago it was opened to detain HIV-positive Haitian refugees. It was the first time that there had been systematic detention of people because of their HIV status; these people had passed their political asylum screening but were being kept there. I got involved with a coalition of predominantly white, leftist solidarity-type groups, and then a lot of Haitian organizations and Haitian political groups, ACT UP, and Black AIDS Mobilization joined together. What was really interesting was that it was two groups coming together that had a lot of power—both ACT UP and the pro-Aristide Haitian community have a lot of power and the ability to turn out people. It wasn't just a bunch of people sitting around, hammering out their disagreements. These were people who had the ability to make a lot of actions happen over a year's time. What happened with that, once the case was won? I have some connections in that community now. ACT UP is probably a lot more in tune with the idea of the Haitian community as an activist community and that AIDS is present there. But then what? I think the models we are all working with are not what they need to be.

MC: Do you feel that activism works best when there's a clearly definable self-interest?

EK: Yes.

MC: Maybe that's why coalitions come together only around certain issues.

EK: I think that's true, based on my experience with certain kinds of Central American activism or political prisoner solidarity work. I think there are a lot of white activist patterns expressed in, "I don't have any self-interest in this, I'm a radical and this is an important issue." That may be true, but that's hard for people to trust. When you have that kind of feeling about an issue, it's easy to get mired in political discussion, side-taking, principle-oriented, "This is the position we have to take." You aren't attuned to the problem in an urgent way that relates to your ability to live your life.

Working with Jews for Racial and Economic Justice [JFREJ] is almost at the opposite spectrum from AIDS activism. It's not like Jews get involved in this kind of work because they're about to die. It's much more subtle. Part of the process of mobilizing people in this case is to get them attuned to their self-interest. We do anti-racism workshops in synagogues, and a lot of it is about trying to wake people to the questions: "What are the ways in which racism is destroying my life; what are the things about my daily life that I hate, that demoralize me, that isolate me, that are the product of living in a racist city?" It's not about: "I am now in a position of privilege, so I will reach my hand down below to help those trailing behind me." It's trying to get people to think about and acknowledge the ways in which they're affected by this.

I've long been involved in Middle East peace work. I was initially interested in it in the same way that I was interested in Nicaragua or El Salvador, in terms of the general question of U.S. intervention in supporting repressive governments. Despite the fact that I have about half of my family in Israel, I have never particularly identified with Israel. But once I got involved in peace work, it became very clear that there were two angles from which I was approaching this question: one was as an American, feeling responsible for U.S. government military support of Israel and the Occupation; the other was from the way in which the fate of Israel has become the analogy for Jewish politics. Unless you resist it, particularly as a Jew in New York, you're seen to represent a pro-Israel, pro-Occupation, pro-U.S. support-of-military-action position. That's *the* Jewish lobby and *the* Jewish politics. JFREJ is trying to address how the racist and very hermetic views of a number of the city's Jewish communities have come to represent all Jews in the city.

The conflict in Crown Heights is an example. Things were so polarized, it was as if the Hasidic Jews couldn't acknowledge the race relations going on in that community but could only worry about this one death [the stabbing of Yankel Rosenbaum]. It's very important here, as a Jew, to position yourself against that viewpoint. Also, having Ed Koch as a mayor was really a drag. When I started getting involved with ACT UP, we were having all these demos against Koch. Meanwhile, he, of course, claims to represent the voice of the Jews.

JFREJ has given me an opportunity to directly do the anti-racist work that has been implicit in a lot of my white, feminist, gay/lesbian, or AIDS work. In all of that, I have been part of predominantly white groups whose ethos, I felt, was racist on some level. It was hard to wheedle through that weird form of white progressive racism, which they won't acknowledge, and which they therefore really cannot be challenged on. It's nice now to be part of a group that's really taking that on as one of its tasks.

MC: What does Jews for Racial and Economic Justice do?

EK: One goal is to bring Jews into multiracial coalition work; another is to strengthen the progressive Jewish community in the city. Many progressive, activist Jews in the city are doing basically what I have done: working in other movements, pretty invisible as Jews, maybe having a radical analysis, but one that's never consolidated into any kind of radical Jewish voice. The only consolidated Jewish opinion is the conservative one. JFREJ is trying to strengthen progressive Jews as a community, to nurture them as activists who are not invisible as Jews—which implies all kinds of things about how people relate to anti-Semitism among the movements they're part of. In the process, we hope to be able to funnel Jews into coalition work, making Jews much more of a substantive ally to different communities who struggle.

MC: This particular part of your activism seems a little different from the others.

EK: It's profoundly different *[laughter]*. I don't think I'd have the tolerance for it if I hadn't been around ACT UP long enough to really understand what some of its failings are. I like ACT UP's urgency and focus.

I'm really bored with groups that don't have focus, and I think that JFREJ could become one of those if we aren't careful. What I really like about JFREJ is the concern with the creation and taking care of a political community. I want to figure out how to apply that to ACT UP. That's no easy task. JFREJ is dealing with people who are very, very isolated. There's much more explicit acknowledgment and discussion about the malaise that people are in, the cynicism and the isolation, and that these are fundamental issues that we have to grapple with.

We are involved in education and activist work where the goal is to not allow Jewishness and anti-Semitism to be used in politically damaging ways. Of course, it constantly raises the question of, "Well, who are you?," but it's like, "Well, who are *you?*" A lot of times, people from the outside say, "Why aren't you in there dealing with the Hasidic community?" Wow, it's going to take us a while before we make strong inroads into the Hasidic community, you know? *[laughter]*. It's slow going.

MC: What is your perception right now of what's happening with the arts? [In addition to her work with ACT UP and JFREG, Kaplan in the late 1980s and early 1990s was involved with a number of alternative arts organizations in New York City, including Cheap Art, a street art collective, and Movement Research, an experimental dance organization.]

EK: What is my perception? I think the arts are beleaguered, obviously. I think people are really underfunded. In this city there's no support for space for artists to work in. The financial obstacles to creating any kind of experimental work, meaning any work by anyone who's not already established, are extraordinary. I think a lot of the struggles around trying to create a support community for experimental performance and dance are similar to what we're trying to do with Jews for Racial and Economic Justice. Starting from a point where people don't have the resources they need to make their art, how can an organization provide space and other kinds of support, like criticism, years before the artist's ever going to get a review? How can we get these experimental performers in situations where they can teach, so what they're doing gets disseminated? The situations of trying to be an activist right now and trying to be an artist are similar: there's just so little support for what you're doing. Of course, it manifests itself differently in the arts and in activism, but, in either case, I think it's easy to become demoralized.

Identity-based or issue-based organizing, which is the way that activism works on the whole right now, doesn't really acknowledge people like me—people who have multiple identities and therefore end up being involved simultaneously in three or four different groups and fall apart out of exhaustion. I think this is more characteristic than exceptional. I feel this issue is being taken up more in the world of art than in the world of activism.

MC: Can you talk about that a little more?

EK: One of the characteristics of postmodern performing is the way people are exploring different aspects of their identities and exploring the contradictions between who they're presumed to be and who they are, their history versus their current social and cultural situation, what it means to be biracial, or to be someone who can identify as an American but has another country of origin, how you sort out issues around race and gender and sexuality.

MC: The issues that you are articulating within yourself, then, are being articulated in a public way in the arts, so you feel a sense of resonance?

EK: Yes. I am frustrated, though, by the fact that all the political art that's being done—like Anna Deavere Smith's piece about Crown Heights *[Fires in the Mirror]*—doesn't really have a political practice that's associated with it. When I saw that piece, it blew my mind. She was talking about the huge rift that happened in this city. It just came rushing back. This was important and extensive work she had done, a distillation of community conflict, but it was only being shown to art audiences. It should have been in every public school in New York. Why isn't that happening?

Somehow these artists—with rare exceptions—don't seem to consider that end of it part of their artistic practice. The question is not only how to make this work, but how to gather certain communities together to see it and respond to it. That doesn't seem like a central question to most artists, whereas the question of marketing yourself is considered essential.

MC: From your vantage point as an activist, do you see ways that artists can make their relevance more apparent?

EK: I think there are countless ways. The starting point for answering that question is that activism is in crisis, too. Everyone doing activism right now is having extraordinary difficulty sustaining their movement. There's a lot of hopelessness and frustration with certain established methods and no clear vision about other methods that would work better. Activists have become more sophisticated in relating to the media in recent years, but an understanding of what community organizing really means has been a little lost because of that. If more artists were actively trying to apply what they know to activism, then activism would be a lot better. The things that artmaking nurtures are really good counterpoints to what activism nurtures. Artmaking nurtures reflection and the ability to acknowledge contradiction and to make more sophisticated political presentations. Activism's struggle is ultimately to make some issue into one of huge public concern; or alternately, in a more guerrilla fashion, to make the lives of particular politicians miserable until they give in. For anything bigger it takes a really concerted public campaign. Obviously, there are elements of that campaign that are artistic in the sense that they're about representation and communication. Activism often has an almost journalistic approach. It's very direct. People are so tired of coming together for a picket line, or for a rally where there are some people standing at a mike. There have got to be ways that artists could organize public spectacles.

What does it take to sustain a community of activists? What does it take to nurture them enough to keep going, to keep taking risks that are incredibly draining—spending time in jail, spending hours in agonizing meetings and phone calls? All that stupid hard work of organizing that can be deadening sometimes.

MC: Some of the activists I've spoken to have said they are so focused on their issue that they don't have time for the arts, that it doesn't really enter their consciousness.

EK: Sure, of course you don't have time [laughter]. Activism takes up *all* your time because there's just not enough people doing it. Once you're willing to take on responsibility, it's extraordinary how much responsibility there is. The only thing that's ever going to release any of that pressure from you is a stronger movement around whatever it is you're organizing—legions of people around you who are equally skilled and responsible and who are going to take on some of the work. That is the only thing that's ever going to make your life more livable while you are in this struggle, right? So the question is, what is that going to take? I think there are certain people who are willing to give over their lives to activism. But I think there are a lot of people who aren't going to do that work unless it is giving them something back. The first flush of empowerment that people get from being in a group isn't what keeps them in for the long haul. What keeps you there is a much more complex combination of decisions and commitments. You have to think about how to make it possible for non-masochistic people to make a commitment—how is your movement going to create a situation where people are not sacrificing their lives in order to be part of this struggle? That is where culture comes in. There have got to be pieces of what you are doing that take care of your members, your comrades. The revolution is happening tomorrow *[laughter]*.

MC: It sounds like you feel that activism has lost a lot of energy in recent years. What are the reasons for that?

EK: It's hard to say. I think that it's easy to be movement-centric. A lot of my sense of the ebb and flow of activism relates to the dramatic shift, for instance, between a massive abortion rights movement and then nothing happening, between ACT UP at its peak and ACT UP now. Clearly the Reagan/Bush years played a key part in all this. It's hard to estimate the countless ways in which the political and economic shifts that have come about in this country are absorbing us. All the energy that went into the abortion rights movement was because the right wing was strong enough to seriously challenge abortion rights. All of that energy could have gone somewhere else. So much of what we're doing is scrambling to hold back the onslaught. There was this huge struggle to get condoms distributed in the high schools, and a year later there has to be another fight to keep them in because there's a right-wing attack and, in fact, they're back out.

MC: Every time you win this little victory, the opposition comes back.

EK: Yeah. Who can underestimate that? I also think people feel they learned hard lessons from the civil rights movement, that activism doesn't really work—you get something, but then you lose it; you have this really powerful movement, and then everyone gets jailed, or whatever.

MC: Co-opted.

EK: Co-opted—well, that's a big one. That's another whole topic around activism—the co-opted "national leadership." So people continue to be hopeful for a minute, then are quick to say, "Oh, we can't do anything." They feel disempowered.

MC: Because things don't really change, or they don't change much.

EK: You can look at other parts of the globe and realize that things change as the result of social movements; it's just hard to feel it in this country. We're in the center of world domination, we're right here in the belly of the beast, and the systems of disempowerment and social control are so insidious and strong here. Historically, people used to get their information by coming to a political rally, whereas now people are atomized in relationship to their televisions and their computers. I think people still need community, but I don't know how much people realize it.

MC: I'm assuming that you're in activism for the long haul.

EK: I assume so, too.

MC: Do you have hope?

EK: Well, I've been pretty depressed lately, as an activist. Working around AIDS right now is a really, really hard thing. Having your comrades and the people you get your inspiration from die all the time does really bad things to you, as I'm sure it does in other movements where people get jailed or killed by police. I think that is part of why I've started doing other forms of activism, because the culture of anger in ACT UP has become increasingly difficult to maintain in the face of total grief. I'm actively in search of hope right now, but I don't necessarily have it. At the same time, I'm not at all interested in just doing activism as a point of principle. I'm really interested in doing it if it can change things. Otherwise, I'm sorry, there are much better things to do than go to meetings every night of the week. I feel like I can only continue to the extent that it becomes clear to me what the hopes are. I have met longtime activists who don't have any hope and who just do it because it's become their way of life. I have no interest in that.

MC: It must be incredible to keep organizing and not have hope. It seems to me that everybody I've talked to has . . .

EK: . . . tiny fragments. A grain of hope.

September 7, 1994
New York, New York

6

GAIL SNOWDEN

THE DAUGHTER OF OTTO AND MURIEL SNOWDEN, two of Boston's leading black community organizers of the post–World War II period, Gail Snowden initially wanted nothing to do with activism, becoming a banker instead after her graduation from Radcliffe College in 1968. But, as she says, "I found that the values learned in a socially activist family came to the fore," and over time she has become a major force for progressive change within the conservative, profit-oriented banking industry.

In the 1980s, after working her way up Bank of Boston's corporate ladder to the position of lender, Snowden initiated a transfer so she could begin recruiting and overseeing the training of people of color and women for the bank. At the same time, she embarked on a broader campaign to influence the bank's thinking about the communities it serves, especially in light of changing demographics. In 1990, Bank of Boston created First Community Bank, a unique "bank within a bank" that specifically serves inner city neighborhoods. Appointed its president, Snowden invested the bank's resources into innovative products designed to meet the needs of low-income individuals as well as minority and women-owned businesses. There are now 45 First Community Bank branches in 12 New England cities, and the program has become a national model for progressive banking practice that fosters community development in poor areas while still generating profits for the parent corporation. In 1998, Bank of Boston won the Ron Brown Award, the only presidential award that recognizes corporations for their community efforts.

Bank merger activity in the late 1990s involving Bank of Boston led to Fleet-Boston Financial Corporation, the eighth-largest financial holding company in the U.S. Snowden is now executive vice-president and managing director of the corporation's Community Banking Group, covering the states of Massachusetts, Connecticut, Maine, New Hampshire, Rhode Island, New York, New Jersey, and Florida. As such, she continues to oversee inner city banking operations, but also is *working on new approaches to economic development as part of the bank's Community Reinvestment Act commitment to other urban, suburban, and rural communities whose populations have been underserved. As she explains in her interview, fighting for the interests of women, people of color, immigrants, and low- and moderate-income groups within a corporate environment is laden with risks, but she has been successful because she has seen ways to fuse the bank's competitive drive to open new markets with a more equitable approach toward meeting the needs of historically underserved and culturally diverse communities.*

Marie Cieri: I'm really interested in talking to someone who works in a business environment who's trying to change some things from within. The supposition is that change is not going to happen within the establishment, that it will only happen on a grassroots level. But it seems more and more essential that people on the inside work for change.

Gail Snowden: Well, I've been doing this for a long time.

MC: How long have you been at Bank of Boston?

GS: Twenty-eight years. My activism followed several things I did in the early eighties. Until then, I was just earning my stripes. I had become a lender, which is the thing to be in this bank. But then I asked myself why I didn't feel the same way as the other people. I realized what I really liked was the part of our job where we interview candidates who want to become lenders. I couldn't help but notice that there were very few women and almost no people of color interviewing. So I created an internal consultancy by going to the head of human resources and saying, "I'm sitting on the lending floor, and there's no one else that looks like me. I think I can do something here because of my background." The whole weight of the bank was against it. People couldn't believe I was leaving lending to work in human resources *[laughter]*. But I think I discovered at that time that you have to follow your own internal drummer.

For about a year and a half I did what is now called "focus recruiting." I went to visit all the black colleges and programs for students of color at colleges here in the Boston area. I was able to impact the bank by bringing in much higher numbers of people of color. But then I realized they weren't making it. So I decided the solution had to be an organizational one. I went to the head of the training program and asked if I could work there someday. About three months later he asked me to join the program, and I ended up there six years. This is where I could really work from the inside in terms of changing a lot of things.

You can bring line lenders into teaching positions, but they are not necessarily teachers. So I developed a whole piece around not just diversity of people but diversity of learning styles. You had to be careful if only the white men were speaking in the class—you had to call on people of color. You had to be much more thoughtful about what you were doing, much more conscious of issues. Then I brought in consultants to work with the managers around diversity and brought in people from different cultures to work with all the students in the training program. In the end, I was promoted to head up the program, and that was a first—my break through the glass ceiling.

MC: That happened how long ago?

GS: That was in '86. I worked as head from '86 to '88. When I left, everything I had put in place fell apart in about three months. I realized it couldn't just be me; you had to have multiple leadership and a much broader support base than just one person.

MC: But what you found was that if there *is* one person, that person can set changes in motion.

GS: Oh, absolutely. A corporation looks monolithic, but it isn't. Bank of Boston is made up of a lot of little cultures, and it is also very entrepreneurial. But you have to have some kind of credibility—you have to have gotten your stripes at whatever the corporation views as important. You have to understand how to play the game. Then you have to assess how risky it is.

MC: Risky in what way?

GS: Personal risk. Are you going to be viewed as so far out that you won't be able to move? It depends on what the issue is. Sometimes it's better to take the longer route, try to get more people involved so it's not just you going in on a certain issue. For example, the gay issue, which is one I'm working on now. You have to assess whether you're going to be viewed as "Oh, that's just her bringing up that idea." If you don't have a business framework, don't still do your job well, you can be viewed as some kind of radical that nobody's going to pay attention to. You constantly have to assess how you're impacting the culture. At a certain point, you also have to ask how important this issue is to you personally, and if you are going to risk everything on it.

MC: Did you get to a point like that at the bank?

GS: The only time that happened was when we did not have paid maternity leave. I felt so strongly that I went to the top of the bank about it. I was a bank officer and felt that if someone like me didn't bring it up, nobody else would. I felt so strongly I was willing to risk everything.

MC: Also, since you were an officer, it was conceivable that you would be heard.

GS: Right. I didn't have a lot to lose either, because I was fairly new in the bank. I wasn't making a lot of money, so I wasn't as tied into the corporation as I am now. I stood up, and because of it the bank did change its policies.

MC: But for a while you thought you might lose your job?

GS: Yes.

MC: What was your goal in trying to recruit people of color into the bank? Was it to create opportunities for them within the corporation, or was it ultimately to affect the broader community?

GS: Both. I think even in the early eighties I could sense that there were untapped business opportunities. But because there were no women or people of color at the table, those voices were not being heard. For example, I was trying to place a black trainee in Atlanta, and the head of the program told me he did not think a black lending officer could make it there. I said, "You've got to be kidding! If you are thinking this, you are missing the whole change in Atlanta." Another example is when we had just gotten back into small business banking, and I was sitting there listening to the ad agency pitch, which was to men ages 25 to 50. I said, "Wait a minute, the fastest growing segment of small business is women." They totally ignored what I had to say even though I had all the statistics. A year later, I went back and said, "Okay, please ask the agency to do research on this issue." When the agency did the research, and I did some work in the library here, we presented a package, and they said, "Whoops, we're missing a whole segment." So we changed—we started putting women in the ads and being much more conscious about what we were doing.

I constantly have opportunities to shift the thinking on any number of issues. Not just about women and people of color, but about gays and lesbians and management issues. I've done a lot in terms of starting groups within the bank. But it all comes back to my parents and a social activist background. [Otto and Muriel Snowden founded Freedom House in the Roxbury section of Boston in 1949 and worked for years to promote racial harmony, urban renewal, and public school integration in the city.]

MC: I wanted to go into that a little with you. One of the things you've said is that your parents were not very happy about your choice of becoming a banker.

GS: They thought they had failed. But actually, my father got me this job at the bank. My husband was just coming out of the army, and I needed a job. I think my father thought it might be very short term, plus there were no black branch managers in the bank, so he could see it as being sort of activist. But when I got into banking, I didn't do any community stuff, nothing, and my parents sort of wondered what happened to me. I was in a rebellious stage because during my childhood the community always came first. My parents would make commitments to take me to the movies, and something would happen and they would say, "Sorry." I was determined to be more of a traditional person. But then I found racism and sexism everywhere.

MC: There must have been a lot of things you absorbed from your parents. I'm wondering if, in retrospect, things they did, things they went through have come back to you now that you yourself are an activist.

GS: Well, part of it was my parents' ability to be bicultural, to relate to both the white and black world. At the time Roxbury still had a heavy Jewish component. My parents were very much integrationists. I grew up in that and watched my parents work with people of various backgrounds. Also my mother was very interested in international education. She put pressure on the Boston School Committee, and that's why the Snowden International High School is named after her. So I grew up with this "change agent" kind of belief system. I never questioned it in the early days, and now I know for myself that one person can make a difference.

MC: In the in-between stage, did you feel that activism just didn't work or wasn't worth the effort?

GS: No, it wasn't about that. It was about not being what my parents were. Also fighting being a leader, because being a leader can be lonely. And my husband was a very traditional person, and he wanted me to play the traditional wife role. But I began to think that I have all these talents and gifts that I'm not able to put to use, and I'm extremely frustrated as a woman. Then I began to think maybe this marriage isn't going to work. It was a whole bunch of things. I also think in terms of passages—that there are points in your life where you can do different things. So I got it together in my life and began to explore on the nonprofit side. I became the first woman president of the Black Urban Bankers Association here in Boston. I had to motivate people—you have to be a charismatic leader to get people to do things. I learned how to do it on the nonprofit front and then thought, if I can do it there, I can do it in the bank, too. I also got ambitious. I knew if I wanted to have a major impact I would have to be higher than I was. I had to have some kind of power. That's when I began to speak up for myself in terms of creating the consultancy to bring more people of color in, going to the training program and being made head of it, then breaking through the glass ceiling and becoming head of First Community Bank, where I am now. I went and said I want to do this.

MC: This was an idea that was floating?

GS: Yes, but it was very amorphous. Immediately I knew this was something I could do. I went to senior management and said I'd like to stop being a senior credit officer, which is very traditional, to start this new little entrepreneurial business in the bank. My background fit, and they knew my energy was high. I had been a lender, I had done human resources, I had been in retail. I had all the components to pull this together.

MC: So the original idea of First Community Bank was . . .

GS: . . . very simplistic—seven branches and one product, which was a mortgage product. They had no idea, although I did at the time, where you could take this. There was a huge business opportunity here.

MC: It's so interesting to hear you talk about these human advances as being business opportunities.

GS: To say it's the right thing, it's the moral thing, doesn't cut it. You've got to translate it into the "business competitive advantage."

MC: What was the business competitive advantage for the bank to establish First Community?

GS: There was a whole untapped market segment. We could have come at it from a compliance perspective, because the Community Reinvestment Act [CRA] says you must meet the needs of the communities where you branch and do business. Or we could come at it as a business opportunity. Fortunately, we took the business opportunity approach. We could have done it very simply; we didn't even have to create a market identity and a bank within a bank with attitude, access, and accountability. But the management of this bank is rather forward thinking, or at least willing to innovate and explore. You have to have that; you can't be the sole little voice out there if you don't have support at the top.

A big part of it was attracting like souls—people who had not told anybody in the bank they'd been in the Peace Corps. There was a fellow who did a white paper for us in 1990 on the importance of lending to small businesses and inner cities. It turned out he had worked for the Center for Community Change in Washington and had written part of the CRA regulations. He had never told anybody in the bank. He had actually been doing acquisition finance here, which is breaking up companies. He wanted to do something more meaningful, so he wrote the paper. Then I convinced him this was what he wanted to do for the next part of his career. I've done that all along. I've gone after great people who have some interest in community.

MC: How do you find those people?

GS: I'm a magnet for it. I'll speak someplace, somebody'll come up to me, and I'll say, "Hmm, you'd make a good intern." I'm always looking for those opportunities. I love this work.

MC: It's interesting that First Community started out with mortgages. They are a real hot button in terms of how people perceive banks, positively or negatively. Up to that point, how would you characterize the banking community vis à vis inner city communities within Boston?

GS: I think there was activity but not as much as there is now.

MC: Were there branches there?

GS: Oh yeah. Bank of Boston was the only one that had never left the community. But once the Home Mortgage Disclosure Act said that what you do is going to be published, people started taking more of an interest. Then some banks got into trouble with second mortgage scams. Once that began to hit the newspapers, people in our bank said we have to take this more seriously. The president of the bank convened a task force that pledged we would do a better job. A lot has to do with the CEO's leadership in saying this is important, and you will report to me quarterly on how we're doing.

MC: Who is the CEO of Bank of Boston?

GS: Chad Gifford. He was president and just became CEO. There was recently a piece in the *Boston Globe* about a speech he gave on diversity. The work of getting the statistics together for that speech started with me. A year ago I said, "We're focusing on the affluent, but the population statistics tell me we've got to pay attention to the growing Hispanic population, the growing Asian population." There's a whole bunch of what we call "emerging markets" (they're not really emerging, they've always been there). I subscribed to something called *American Demographics* that publishes this kind of information. I did a tiny piece for my boss, and he asked me to present it to his boss. Then the marketing department took it over and created a whole study on emerging markets. Then the bank's strategic planner took it over to talk about both diversity and emerging markets. My position is that I don't have to get credit for it if I can get the germ of an idea going. To get that piece in the newspaper was the culmination of how you accomplish change. If you're going to be in this work, you may not always get the credit for it, but if you get the results there's some kind of internal, intrinsic satisfaction from that.

MC: How has First Community developed in its five years of existence?

GS: We're up to 29 branches in Massachusetts, Connecticut, and Rhode Island. We're in 14 cities. We've got six long platforms. So we've grown very fast.

Everything starts with analysis, so we did an analytical piece that showed where the top 25 communities were that had small business, had people of color, and were urban. First Community can't be everywhere. It's very expensive to create a branch from scratch. We know how to reach the affluent and how to model what we're doing, but there had to be a model for emerging cities. The analytical piece showed us where we needed to be—Providence, Hartford, New Haven, Lawrence, Lynn, Revere, Boston, Waterbury, Springfield, Holyoke, Worcester. In the places where we had branches existing, the major task was to convince the people running them that we could do a better job. It was a whole internal negotiation. We did that, and we grew from the seven branches.

We've worked hard and have been successful in traditional terms, which is in the sales programs. My branches had never won any kind of incentive program, because my people were demoralized and felt they couldn't win. In my branches, I have many people of color and many white people who have been written off by the system. They were sent to molder in the inner city. Then Dudley Street, which is a true inner-city branch, won its first award in 1992, a trip to Disney. All of a sudden everybody was a believer. My people began to say, "We can do this." Once they realized they could win, that they were smart and analytical, there was a complete turnaround.

MC: When you say sales, you mean new accounts?

GS: Certificates of deposit. We have all kinds of campaigns, because we're a retail organization. In 1993, we were number one in sales in New England, and in 1995 we were number one in sales and service.

MC: That's great. Okay, mortgages, CDs—what other things have you done?

GS: We created new products. The Community Reinvestment Act says you don't have to do stupid things, but you've got to look and see if you are unfairly screening out people. Our loans had a $3,000 minimum, so we worked with marketing to create a product that had a $500 minimum.

MC: That's small for a bank, isn't it?

GS: That's small. You don't make money at it; it has to be a volume business. Another thing that really made an impact was changing the advertising. In 1990, I was told we advertise in the *Boston Globe* and the language in which we do business is English. Now we advertise in all the little local newspapers, like the *Bay State Banner* or the *Jamaica Plain Gazette.* I had to show that, yes, people read the *Boston Globe,* but what makes them buy is seeing it in their local newspaper. Then I had all those stats on the growth of Hispanic populations, which meant you had to do things in Spanish. And if you are in Chinatown, wouldn't it be nice if you had something in Chinese? The Vietnamese are moving into Fields Corner, so you need to be in the Vietnamese newspaper. Then it would be nice if you had people of color in your ads. It's been a whole transformation in terms of advertising and marketing. Now they own it, but the first two years were kind of tough.

MC: Do you have stories about some of the loans made to small businesses in the communities where you lend?

GS: We did a loan to two women who had a cleaning company, Sparkle Cleaning in Natick. Two black women with about five employees, home-based business, first loan, no collateral. We figured out a way to pull in another group that would guarantee the loan, called the Business Consortium. The consortium will guarantee loans for minority vendors who get contracts with majority companies. Sparkle Cleaning has since grown to 50 employees and got the small business award for small company of the year.

That's a great story. At another point, the woman who runs Massachusetts Lending and I had a chance to meet the two entrepreneurs who were starting the Center for Women in Enterprise. We were very impressed and went to the committee that makes grants and asked them to give this little group $50,000. But the committee members said they didn't understand why we wanted to work with low income women. We felt this was really important, and as two women who control budgets, why don't we split the funding? We'll do the $50,000, and we know that they're going to be so fabulous that they will get the next two years of funding that they want. Then we asked Chad Gifford to come to the kick-off event and present the check. Chad came out and saw all these people and all the press and he got it. That's the importance of having people at the table who have an understanding of the issues. When you have women there, and people of color, and men who have a broader understanding of communities and social responsibility, you really can get things done.

MC: It seems really important for a bank or any kind of corporation to have employees who are of the community.

GS: But the corporation can't work against it. People can have those values, but if the corporate culture is not supportive, they're not going to step out and allow themselves to be seen differently. So you can have people working in investment banks in New York who will be too scared to be their "real" selves because the culture will not support it.

MC: Do you think the situation here at Bank of Boston is unusual, or are you seeing other instances of people in the corporate world creating change?

GS: There are really neat companies like Reebok and Levi Strauss and Lotus. I'm running into individuals from these companies at Business and

Social Responsibility [BSR] and seeing their successes in moving the companies. I don't know exactly what makes them different, but it must have something to do with corporate values.

MC: Is having a bank within a bank unusual?

GS: We're the only one. The bank that's most like us is South Shore Bank on the South Side of Chicago, but it's totally different. It's a small bank, started by a group of liberals. We're the only big money center, regional bank doing it this way. However, within most banks there are people like my guys who are doing community development and having an impact. We have an informal bond with those people across the country. Community development usually is created because of government regulation, but the people doing the work in those banks really believe in it. They're using the law to push the edge of the envelope and push institutions.

MC: Your parents were essentially in community development.

GS: They were in community development, and so am I.

MC: Later on in their lives, was there a better meeting of the minds?

GS: Oh, yeah. When I became president of Urban Bankers, my mother saw I was pushing the role of women forward, and she was very, very pleased. She died in '88, so she really never had a chance to see what I would be doing at Bank of Boston, but my father came out when we opened up a branch in Grove Hall [a Boston inner city neighborhood] and realized I was carrying on the work in a different way.

To me the biggest challenge right now is not the work, but driving it into the infrastructure and building the leadership and support. I've learned some tough lessons about how hard it is to keep the gains that have been made when everything rides on one person. When I look at the country as a whole, I see we're losing all of those gains we made on diversity issues. I see women not speaking up enough, and if it can happen to people of color it will happen on women's issues too.

MC: One of the things I've heard you talk about is the role of women in corporations and how you see white women, especially, colluding with the system instead of trying to change it. And that that's discouraging.

GS: I'm working on that now with this new group I've started of women across lines of color and sexual orientation. That group is going really well.

MC: Is this what you call "the Ark," like Noah's Ark?

GS: *[Laughter]* Two of everything. We're getting together for dinner on Friday because we've all seen [the film] *Waiting to Exhale,* and we're going to talk about it. And there'll be other things. I'm reading a book called *Sisters Divided,* and it talks about black women and white women. This is one of the most exciting things I've been involved with for a long time, that you could get a group of women to really sit down and work on these issues. I ought to do something about black men and black women, but I don't have time right now. Black guys have been very intransigent about feminist issues, and they recognize that I'm a feminist. Their position is race first and, by the way, black male issues first.

MC: It's interesting because many activists feel you should stay very focused on one issue. Then other people feel that the only way significant change is going to happen is by forming coalitions.

GS: I believe that if you go after your issue alone it's divisive, and people in power will cut up one tiny piece of the pie in smaller and smaller slices as opposed to broadening who's there. I think you can set groups up against each other. I saw that happen in Boston with the schools. South Boston and Roxbury were fighting each other around busing, but the school system as a whole was poor. I'm much more into coalition-building. I think there is power in more than one voice.

MC: Have you been criticized for staying within the corporate environment while trying to make change happen?

GS: Only by my daughter *[laughter]*. She just started Simmons School of Social Work and was doing this piece on radical Marxist social workers. We got into a discussion about working within the corporation or within social work agencies as opposed to whatever these radical Marxist social workers did. That's when I began to realize that I had taken this within the corporate role. I've been very happy with it because my corporation is one in which I could be successful doing what I do. If I had been in a different kind of a culture, I would have been long gone.

I have to admit this has been fun. To see that impact has been an enormous pay-off. However, at age 50, and after 28 years here . . . *[laughter]*. There are other things I want to do now, maybe be a consultant along these lines.

MC: Do you feel that what's happening with Bank of Boston and First Community Bank would continue?

GS: Uh-huh. At this point, First Community Bank is a national model. Bank of Boston is merging with BayBank soon, and that's a wonderful opportunity to grow. I can still work until I'm age 65 and stay in the bank, but there's a piece of me that says it would be nice to explore.

MC: In terms of social change, are there specific things you want to move on?

GS: I don't know. At one point, I wanted to be mayor of Boston *[laughter]*. There's a whole bunch of things I'd like to be able to impact, but I'm doing it in different ways. For example, BSR has just totally opened up my eyes, and I've met so many neat people. I'm on the board of the Calvert Fund, which is also socially responsible. I'm going down this path because it sustains me.

MC: You sound very optimistic, very energetic . . .

GS: I'm an optimist.

MC: . . . and . . . you have hope about change in the future.

GS: Absolutely. But I don't think my daughter's generation is as hopeful.

MC: What's the difference, do you think?

GS: Well, they have AIDS and nuclear power to deal with. It's a different world. I grew up in the sixties. We believed that anything could happen.

MC: But most people who grew up in the sixties don't have your optimism at this point.

GS: I keep asking myself what makes me different, and I can't figure that out.

MC: One of the things I've heard you speak about that I really like is "transforming the soul of business . . . putting our power to work." Beyond Bank of Boston, do you truly believe that business will transform its soul? *[laughter]*. And put its power to work for this country?

GS: I don't know, because there are some things that I *am* pessimistic about. One is the nature of technology. The changes that are coming are going to radically impact large numbers of workers. AT&T is laying off— what is it, 40,000 workers?

It seems to me that at some point businesses have to understand that there is going to be a cost to the country. It may be great for stockholders, but in the long run it is not good for the country to have all these people unemployed. I don't know if business will change, or if there are enough voices out there saying we've got to figure out a different way, but I think there are beginning to be *some* voices out there.

MC: You believe that businesses can be profitable, but at the same time . . .

GS: . . . provide a reasonable standard of living. The guys from Stonyfield Farms—I love that company, what they're doing for their people. Ben and Jerry's, even though they've had to get a little bit of grip on reality *[laughter]*. Rosa Beth Moss Canners. There are some good thinkers out there. Tom Peters, Peter Drucker. But you gotta read *[chuckle]*. You gotta spend more time focusing on these issues.

MC: It also seems that those people need to be in touch with each other . . .

GS: . . . to have a voice. Well, that's why I'm so interested in BSR and its ability to play a role in bringing people together. I don't know whether businesses can actually transform themselves, but I look at Bank of Boston, with Chad Gifford saying, "One of our core values is going to be diversity." So that to me is like, yes! I started working on Chad in 1985, when we brought him to his first diversity workshop. Ten years later, there's payoff. Gotta be patient! *[laughter]*.

MC: Well, that's another thing about change, isn't it?

As I mentioned to you, my partner in this project and I work in the cultural field, and we're trying to address the gap that exists between the arts and many other spheres of social activity. Can you see there might be ways that cultural activities can be brought into closer affinity with other kinds of progressive action pointed toward change in our society?

GS: The group called Facing History and Ourselves [in Boston] is doing the same thing around history issues, around the Holocaust, and making sure people talk about those issues. But again, it's dedicated individuals.

MC: Your feeling is that's really the key.

GS: But it's also building at least a cadre of support, so that it's not just two individuals. It's incremental.

MC: For example, you were talking about the Ark. Are there any analogies between that and what I'm talking about in terms of the arts? From what I can tell, a lot of people feel very alienated from the arts in part because the arts have often worked to make themselves separate.

GS: All I know is that the article in the *Boston Globe* talked about there not being enough diversity in the arts, and since then I have seen some positive movement by some of the larger cultural organizations. But I'm not seeing a way to draw all the people who are interested in that kind of change together. Maybe you can figure that out.

MC: *[Laughter]* Well, I'm trying.

GS: To draw like-minded folks together, because then you could really have a major impact.

MC: I think what's important is to break down categories, which can be barriers. When you say the arts, it's immediately off-putting to many people because there are so many elitist connotations. That's *true* in a lot of cases, but not always. I personally feel that there are a lot of things contained within the arts that are important to people.

GS: See, the thing that hits me immediately when people say the arts is Western culture. And to me that's not welcoming, per se. I was listening to David Brudnoy [a Boston radio show host] talk about the Western cultural tradition, and I thought, "My God, I don't understand how he can say this." You know, "the greatest traditions." That doesn't embrace all the other things out there.

MC: No, not at all. Do you go to cultural events?

GS: I generally don't. I go to things the bank sponsors, and I do some work for the Wang [Celebrity] Series, but on my own I tend to want to do things that are meaningful to *my* background, like Alvin Ailey [a black dance company]. I joined the board of one organization, which shall remain nameless, and when they started talking about "those people," and that they only like jazz, it was like, "I've got to get out of this." So it's been difficult for me emotionally to hook up to the arts because it feels too white, too Western-oriented, and I haven't been willing to explore. I only have so much energy. I read a lot, but I haven't really focused on the arts. As an individual, I'm concerned when I see what happened with the Mapplethorpe exhibit. I do get upset when people want to censor the arts or take money away, maybe because it's more political.

MC: Is there anything in closing that you want to say about First Community Bank, its role in the community, or what you hope to see in the future?

GS: I'd like it to be a model, not only of community development but of people from very different backgrounds coming together. I think we're beginning to do that. For us, it's not about hiring, it's about managing the expectations of a lot of different groups. You have Asian, and within Asian you have Vietnamese and Chinese and Japanese and Koreans, so you've got historical issues there. You've got within the African American community the Caribbean communities, saying we were never slaves. It is not easy managing all of this diversity. Managing, so that white people feel they can be part of the process, they are part of diversity. Helping the gay folks within our culture, even within First Community, feel they are as empowered. It's fine at the senior officer level, but where the rubber meets the road is in the branches. If you have a branch manager who's homophobic, you're not going to come out. Even within First Community, there's a lot of work to be done on that issue. I'd like First Community to be a twenty-first century model for a lot of people coming together and being empowered.

January 29, 1996
Boston, Massachusetts

7

LYNNE SOWDER

DURING THE 1980S, LYNNE SOWDER ALSO WORKED at a bank, but the opportunities for her to set change in motion were quite different from Gail Snowden's. A trained art historian, Sowder was hired by First Bank of Minneapolis in 1980 to build an art collection for the institution. With the backing of the bank chairman, she proceeded to buy contemporary art that she felt was not only of the highest caliber but also would focus employees' attention on important social issues of the time. Her hope was that the art would stimulate dialogue and foster connections among people who were working within what she perceived to be a strict and often hostile corporate environment. She soon had to admit, however, that precisely the opposite was happening. Hostility escalated, and much of it was directed at her and at the arts themselves as an elitist and alienating enterprise invading the workplace.

The gulf between the art world and its concerns, and everyday people and their concerns, was thrown into strong relief for Sowder, and she vowed to address the problem head on. In the following interview, she tells the story of how she and her art program collaborator, Nathan Braulick, handed over all aspects of acquiring, maintaining, and displaying the collection to the bank's employees. As Sowder puts it, "We began to build a democracy based on a one-person, one-vote process that didn't exist anyplace else in the bank." Not only was the corporate hierarchy softened, but also the arts were brought down from their pedestal and integrated into the workday activities of the bank.

Sowder stayed with First Bank until the art program was dismantled in 1990. Since then, she and Braulick have continued to address the gap between the arts and other areas of social activity through Y-Core, a company they founded in Chicago that advises corporations, public arts agencies, and museums on how they might integrate the arts and related social issues more fully into their dealings with customers and constituents.

❏ ❏ ❏ ❏ ❏

Lynne Sowder: First Bank's art program began in 1980. I was hired to build an art collection for the company. The impetus was the creation of a new headquarters in downtown Minneapolis. I'm an art historian, and I began my work in the usual fashion: you begin with a theme or idea, you establish your goals and agenda—whether it's essentially decorating, building an "investment-based" collection, supporting the arts in your community, or so on—and you present material to a committee of people from senior management. First Bank was trying to support culture in the community they were in. Most of the art came from the surrounding community.

From 1980 to 1985, we went through three different chairmen, which was typical of the banking business in the eighties. In the course of the changes in senior management, there arose an opportunity for us to think differently about the art program. Corporate collecting at that time was very commodities-driven.

Marie Cieri: Were you dissatisfied with that?

LS: I was very dissatisfied. But when Dennis Evans became chairman in the early eighties, he and I sat down, and we began to really talk about another way to think about the bank's art activity. That was right at the point when banking was being deregulated, and banking was about to become a very competitive enterprise. So the art program became an opportunity to talk about this changing phenomenon, to signal change within the organization and to, in a sense, be a visual metaphor for a whole kind of "reorging" of the business, as they say.

So I began, with very modest money, to buy avant-garde work of American and European artists and to take down the more conventional kinds of things that I had been buying before that, replacing them with Cindy Sherman, Barbara Kruger, Louise Lawler, Joseph Beuys, Gilbert & George, and others. In Minneapolis at that point, there was really no context for understanding that material. The Walker Art Center under Martin Friedman's leadership was still absorbed in the work of the sixties. So we were really out on a limb. Needless to say, the employee response to this activity was intense. People had violent reactions to it, really.

MC: They didn't like to be shaken up?

LS: No. So along with Nathan Braulick, an artist and art historian whom I had recently hired and who was to be my collaborator on all projects from '85 on, we beefed up all kinds of educational strategies that are typically done in museums. We installed wall labels written from a very lay-oriented point of view. We sponsored lectures by curators and other arts professionals, brown bag lunches, symposia, tours, films, created support libraries for the employees. Over the course of a several-year period, what we discovered was that the same percentage of people who probably belonged to the Art Institute of Minneapolis and the Walker Art Center and went to the Guthrie Theater had become fans of our program within the institution. In other words, we were preaching to the converted. The only people whom we had engaged, in spite of all our efforts to the contrary, were the same people who were essentially engaged in a cultural activity outside the institution—only some 12 percent to 20 percent of the entire employee base. So we really had a crisis.

My own sense about the business arena within First Bank was that it was a pretty hostile environment, period, especially for women, and that it was not a very nurturing and generous kind of place. My fantasy about the presence of art in a place like that was that it would encourage connections between people, that it would encourage people to begin to share a dialogue about the ideas that were really driving their lives. In fact, what was happening was the opposite. As far as I was concerned, from what I could tell, the art was contributing to a shutting down of exchange. I said to myself, "I don't really want to go on doing this work if the kind of environment that it's creating is an even more hostile one than the environment I perceived this institution to be about initially." I myself felt like a pariah in that environment. I was really seen as an instrument of senior management—I was viewed as the enemy.

I come from a very leftist position, so this was all very alarming to me because the last thing I ever imagined myself being was aligned with the "suits," over here on the right side of the equation. At that point, around 1986, we had thousands of objects on the walls, the collection had begun to be talked about nationally and internationally and was considered really to be the most radical corporate program in existence. But it was a really grim moment for me personally.

So Nathan and I started to talk about what we might do in response to this alien situation. We began to ask a number of sociologists and psychologists and people completely outside the art world what their feelings were about what we were doing and what they imagined was happening as a result of our work. From them we learned that there was a huge chasm between us and them and that the only way to bridge it was to begin to give them access to a voice and to a process of interaction around this body of material that we were dragging into the organization.

We did a massive institutional survey and asked people very blunt questions about what they felt about the art program. They could return the survey anonymously or they could sign it. We had an astonishing rate of return, which was unheard of in that particular corporation's culture—over

30 percent. People typed six and seven typewritten pages and attached them to the survey. It was very interesting because it really spoke to art's power to provoke people. More than art's power to provoke people, it spoke to what happens when people don't feel any connection to the culture of their own time. In retrospect, what it said to me was how absolutely important it was, in the minds of this population of people, since they felt alienated from this culture that was supposed to be about them, for them to speak to that sense of alienation.

We published the results, untampered with, unfrosted over, and returned them to the population of people who had given them to us. Then we instituted a series of exchanges between ourselves and the population who worked there. These discussions were held during work hours, so people didn't have to take time from their lunch hour. Management supported that.

MC: How many people came?

LS: Ultimately, many hundreds. They came in groups of 50 or 60 at a time, and it was extraordinarily hostile. The whole Legal Department, for instance, showed up together.

MC: What did these groups say?

LS: They were very alarmed about the art program. They challenged whether or not the kinds of things that we were bringing into the environment really were art, based on their expectations of what art was supposed to be like. They challenged the viability of an organization spending money on art as opposed to on things that, in their opinion, would have a more positive impact on them or on their potential to build client relationships in the community. They questioned the nature of the relationship that I had with senior management, in particular with the chairman, that would have allowed this kind of process to have developed in the institution. Frankly, some thought I must be sleeping with him. Finally, some felt that the art program was a distraction from the work at hand because it tended to divert their focus from what they were there to do, which was to pay attention to banking issues. They felt that the art became a subject for debate and exchange that had nothing to do with institutional practice.

MC: Debate among the employees?

LS: Yes, the employees found themselves at a loss when a client would come in and say, "What in the world is going on in this institution? I just passed the most dreadful thing I've ever seen in my life. What does that mean? What are you guys doing here?" And they would have no way of describing it or explaining it. They found themselves very compromised. We had a big artwork by Anish Kapoor, for instance. I discovered over time that the employees had named it "The Vagina." I guess that's what it reminded people of. It was a very, very large blue sculpture, and it hung out from the wall. One of the senior management's customers came wandering through the bank one day. She had on a white mink coat, and, as she approached the Kapoor, she brushed up against it and some of the blue pigment came off on her coat, destroying it! She went off the deep end. It was all over the bank that this had happened. After that, people were seeing penises in everything on our walls (which there were lots of, I'm sure).

What happened was that the art really, in a sense, catalyzed a debate about sexuality, about sexual politics in the institution, about religion, about death—all the things that you're not supposed to talk about at a polite dinner party, much less at work. So these issues—these undiscussables—were constantly being driven up out of the unconscious and subconscious and guts of people into a level of consciousness that couldn't be avoided.

MC: Two bank tellers working next to each other are talking about the sacrilegious piece that's over there on the wall, and then . . .

LS: Then the customer would say, "What is this shit?" It was a very intense environment for people to be working in. So we created a number of mechanisms over the course of several years to try to deal with this. First we did the survey. Then we conducted the series of exchanges with employees. After that, we created a system called "Talkback." Everywhere you went in the bank, hanging next to the works of art you'd find Plexiglas boxes labeled "Talkback—You Decide." In these boxes were forms with questions about the art—not technical questions, but questions about feelings and political kinds of questions. You could answer those or write whatever you wanted. On a monthly basis, we'd publish "Talkback" reports that reproduced people's remarks verbatim, even the most X-rated kinds of comments. We engaged people in a process of dialogue and empowered them to speak to the art, to us, to management in whatever way they wanted. We recycled it so it was a feedback, feed-forward system, over and over again.

MC: People would respond to the feedback, then?

LS: Right. Ultimately, because of the success and energy embodied in this process, we created a project called "Controversy Corridor," in which employees were allowed to banish art works to a special corridor in the building where they were on continual exhibition. It took six employees to banish any work of art. The only quid pro quo was you had to say why you were banishing it. We would post the comments. Then, by the same token, the same number of employees, from any other place in the bank, could retrieve it. Banished in November, retrieved in May! Let me read you a classic example, this one regarding a Paul Benny painting—a very large, skeletal horse image on canvas: "We, the undersigned, work in the Energy Leasing Division located on the second floor of the East Building. We put up with artwork containing broken bodies, mangled bodies, bloody bodies, and unhappy bodies. We would rather not start the same pattern now with horses. We request that *What Dark Is This* by Paul Benny be removed and that it be replaced with something colorful which does not depict violence or pain. We've had our fill of that."

MC: That one was never brought back, was it?

LS: No! We were very excited because of the intense dialogue taking place among people—it was really extraordinary.

We also created a videotape called *Talkback*. We went out into the hallways of the institution with a camcorder, without any kind of warning, and got people to talk about what they thought about the collection, the program, and "Controversy Corridor," and it's really an astonishing tape. By the time we made it, these dialogue programs we had put into place had really begun to work to the extent that there was an active discussion that people recognized as valuable for its own sake, and it was taking place institutionally across the board, from senior management right on down to the people who worked in the cafeteria. Everyone was participating.

MC: Were there other types of participation besides the discussions?

LS: Absolutely. We created all kinds of programs that people could join. For instance, we started a club for people who wanted to attend exhibition openings and lectures outside the bank. Attendance just mushroomed. As we began dismantling our own curatorial practice, we replaced it with a new kind of practice that had to do with consensus-building and the creation of collaborative efforts between different groups of people. As we did that, we began to look at the organization and its structure. We were really looking for ways to break through the hierarchical nature of the organization itself. For instance, we created committees of people on a floor-by-floor basis who would select all the art for their own floor. What you have to understand is that corporate curators take pride in the time and energy invested in installing stuff on a floor-by-floor basis so that it makes curatorial sense. They can proudly drag all the museum directors who visit the city through their collection and say, "This is the Arte Povera floor," and blah, blah, blah. But we wanted to let people make their own decisions about what would be on their floors. So for the most part, things no longer made "curatorial sense." Our reason for doing this was to facilitate communication among different groups within the institution. Every floor had both senior management and entry-level employees, and, by creating committees, we began to build a democracy based on a one-person, one-vote process that didn't exist anyplace else in the bank.

MC: Senior management had one vote . . .

LS: They had no more votes than the secretaries. The art program was the only context within the entire institution in which any person had a voice that was equal to anybody else's. We hired professional facilitators to manage these meetings, and we took people through a process. We gave them the art budget, which was very radical. We recognized that we could not control people's choices, but that we could ensure that their process was thoughtful, that it examined many things, and that people were engaged in something serious to which they had to be committed. In other words, we made them responsible participants in a democracy. What they were buying was pretty interesting. We wanted to build an exchange between people through a facilitated process that was very specifically designed to examine their relationships with each other, what they believed art's role in their lives should be, what they believed the appropriate role for art should be within the institutional culture, the issue of censorship, and so on. What does it mean if you are on a committee of 13 other people selecting art for your floor, and there are four people who want the Andres Serrano artwork *Piss Christ* and there are six of you who don't? How are you going to manage that? Are you going to, in fact, become censors for that group of people on the floor who would like to be able to look at this work? Do you find a context on this whole floor, which is 20,000 square feet of space, to manage that one controversial object, or 10 controversial objects, at the same time that you bring in this other material that you want to bring in? How will you build that for yourselves?

Ultimately, people wrote their own descriptive wall labels for the art, which was extraordinary, and they even commissioned artists to do their own kinds of interactive, ongoing projects. Dorit Cypis was invited by one floor to do a project about the relationship of the body to architecture. That was a project that came about as a result of employees feeling very disturbed about some of Cypis's photographs that we had bought for the collection and installed early on on their floor. They invited Dorit in to explain her work to them, so there she was in a bank conference room with 40 employees, talking about pulsating clitorises and all this other stuff that does not get discussed in mixed company, probably period, much less in the banking world during working hours in the conference room. That's just kind of a silly example, but it had a profound impact on people, the idea that you could begin to discuss this sort of stuff during worktime. People began to recognize that they didn't leave their sexual or emotional selves at home—that the fantasy that you brought only your professional self to work was just that, a fantasy, and that you really came to work with all of your self. To try to deny the existence of your right brain and only operate with your left, or vice versa, wasn't very useful. The more complete the self you brought to the work experience, the more fully you would benefit from it, and the institution would benefit as a consequence.

MC: What was your role in that discussion? Was it as a moderator? As a provocateur? As an educator? How did this unfold?

LS: Usually, we were just the worker bees who carried objects from floor to floor, depending on what the employees wanted done. We did work with the facilitators to design the processes that people would be asked to engage in. Sometimes we went to the meetings and sat in the back, but generally we were not even present. We found that serving as facilitators was very counterproductive because we were identified as authority figures, and as such, we interfered with the ability of people to be honest about what they really wanted and felt. We needed to exempt ourselves from that, and we did. Then it was just a facilitated process between them and a professional facilitator, who didn't know any more about art than the folks in the room did, and there were no art experts at all. In fact, one of the criteria was that they know nothing about art. We considered anybody who had art information to be sort of the enemy, not a useful person in the context of what we were trying to do because they immediately set up the "us" and "them" phenomenon—art once again had a capital "A" as opposed to a small "a," and it became unapproachable. Our goal was to demystify all that. We found that bringing artists into the facility to talk about their work was very positive. They demystified their own role, they talked about themselves as workers in the same sense that the bank's employees felt themselves to be workers. It helped to build a conceptual bridge between the cultural practice and legal practice and accounting practice and banking practice.

MC: How did people interface with you throughout this process? Did the "cold war" end?

LS: It did. I think that I never understood, until this crisis happened that I've described to you, the way I was perceived—I just didn't get it. I grew up in an ordinary household. My mother was not a formally educated person, but she had this huge belief in the value of cultural ideas and reading and art and music, so I grew up believing that this was really an important piece of one's life and that anyone who didn't have the opportunity to access it was really missing out on one of the great gifts of life. I assumed that everybody else had the same idea, and I never understood that the absence or presence of formal education around it meant anything, because it doesn't mean anything to me, frankly. It took me a long time to realize that I was perceived as an elitist practitioner whose knowledge base separated her from the rest of the folks. It was with missionary zeal, really, that I undertook to dismantle that piece of the way I was perceived. For me, that process represented a wish to get connected to people that was deeply personal as well. My work ended up being a metaphor for my own personal difficulties—my sense of alienation, isolation, and separateness was only enhanced by what I had chosen to do when, in fact, what I really wanted to do was to end my isolation and become part of a community.

MC: Do you think it's lack of education about the arts, or lack of growing up in an environment that's supportive of culture, that causes people to be antagonistic?

LS: I think it's neither of those things. I believe that it's the way culture is delivered to people that alienates them from the culture of their own time, that elitist delivery methodologies automatically set up a very unfortunate paradigm. My mother was never bothered by the little red ropes in front of paintings at the museum, but that was just because of who she was. I came to understand how everybody else felt about that. The language that we use to talk about culture and the institutions in which we experience cultural practice, the individuals who are the so-called experts—it creates two worlds: the world of those who are "in the know," and the world of those who are *not*.

MC: Do you think also that the art market itself has contributed to that phenomenon?

LS: Without doubt. It's caché, it's one more way in which the art insiders can say, "I'm different than you are because I have all this." It's sort of like carrying a Gucci handbag.

MC: People's perceptions of what defines art and culture seem to vary enormously.

LS: I think that people feel a gap between themselves and the culture of their own time for two reasons: one is because the delivery methodologies are very alienating, and the other is because the belief system that most people have about art's role in their lives is diametrically opposed to what art's function actually is. So those two phenomena set up an almost impossible set of obstacles. Cultural practitioners have difficulty recognizing these phenomena, because to do so is to admit that you must dismantle your own practice.

When Nathan and I left First Bank, we thought the logical place for us would be among museums and nonprofit art institutions. If we thought that doing our work in the corporate arena was difficult, it doesn't even begin to compare to the kind of prejudice, the kind of hermetic thinking and the kind of fear that we encountered in the nonprofit sector. We were asking people to participate in an equal process with their audiences and their constituencies. And they weren't about to do that. It was fascinating to us to discover that the wall of resistance was at least ten times as thick in the so-called community that was open to all of this radical thinking and all these new ideas as it was over here among the "ignorant" folks working in the business world.

MC: When and why did the bank's program end?

LS: The bank's program ended in 1990. Our chairman, Dennis Evans, was fired. The new leadership demanded that we dismantle our exchange methodologies. We decided that we could not continue, in good conscience, to run the project we were running, to hang the kind of radical work we were hanging and to bring in the kinds of artists we were bringing in without these kinds of exchange methodologies.

MC: The board of directors and the new CEO didn't like it that the institutional hierarchy was breaking down? That was essentially the problem?

LS: Right. We were told we couldn't have "Controversy Corridor" anymore, we couldn't do any employee art selection projects, we couldn't do any artists-in-residence projects, we couldn't do any more labeling, we couldn't do any "Talkback" programming.

MC: You could just buy art and hang it on the wall. You could go back to 1980.

LS: Both of us resigned. Ultimately, most of the collection was sold and actually made a lot of money for the bank, and that was the end of it.

MC: Who decided what to sell?

LS: I was asked to make recommendations about what should be sold. I put together a list of everything that I knew had been identified as difficult by employees. Everything else could stay.

MC: So the easy stuff is still there, as far as you know?

LS: Yes. Although it's interesting that by the time we finished up, what was easy by First Bank's standards would still be very tough by most other institutions' standards. I imagine there's still a lot of work in that collection that couldn't hang in most other places, even today.

MC: Do you know how the employees felt about the program ending?

LS: I can't tell you for sure. I only know anecdotally because no survey was ever done. But I know that when we dismantled "Controversy Corridor," there was a ceremony for the dismantling—an artist was actually retained to do a performance piece and the community was invited in. It was a really wonderful thing. Over the next couple of months, after everything was taken down, the lights were turned off, the corridor essentially abandoned, we were gone and the art was gone, many stories about the art program appeared in art magazines across the country. The dismantling of the program was actually on the cover of the *Wall Street Journal* and in the *Washington Times,* the *Los Angeles Examiner,* and the *New York Times.* Employees surreptitiously got copies of all that stuff, which was all very negative about the bank and positive about the art program, blew it up and pinned it up at night in "Controversy Corridor." It was really great! *[laughter].*

August 20, 1994
Chicago, Illinois

8

LILY YEH

LILY YEH IS AN ARTIST WHOSE WORK IS TRULY FOCUSED on rebuilding a community. Since 1986, she has stationed herself in a section of North Philadelphia that is widely regarded as one of the worst inner city areas of the country. With the collaboration of neighborhood residents, she has formed a four-street oasis of art parks, gardens, play spaces, rehabilitated housing, health services, after-school education, theater programs, festivals, and small business enterprises through the nonprofit organization she founded and runs, The Village of Arts and Humanities.

One of The Village's most recent projects has been establishing a tree farm and meadow with a mosaic of wild animals that in Yeh's words not only "turns trash land into parkland" but also generates income for the community (for example, The Village currently holds a contract to produce trees for Philadelphia's premier Fairmount Park). Given her success in Philadelphia, the China-born Yeh has initiated related projects in poor areas of Kenya, the Ivory Coast, Italy, Ecuador, and the Republic of Georgia.

Yeh states that broad collaboration among people of different ages, cultures, and abilities is essential for turning around neglected urban neighborhoods, and that, in her experience, art has been the catalyst for doing this. Art critics have remarked on how Yeh has pursued her goals virtually outside of the mainstream art world, and she herself has written that there are specific, not necessarily career-oriented paths that artists should take in order to instigate positive change in depressed communities: "Artists who come to a community to work must be modest and humble in spirit. They come to share, to listen, to learn. Then something magical happens." Following are more of Yeh's words about the remarkable experience of bringing an artistic approach to social problem-solving in North Philadelphia.

◻ ◻ ◻ ◻ ◻

Marie Cieri: You were trained as an artist, and you came here in the sixties to Philadelphia?

Lily Yeh: Yeah, '63.

MC: You had embarked on what could be thought of as a normal art career, you were showing in galleries and museums . . .

LY: I was trained as a traditional landscape painter in the Chinese tradition. Fine brushwork on silk and fine paper. When I came here [born in China, grew up in Taiwan], it was an earthshaking experience for me. It was difficult. Not so much the painting activity, but my values coming in very direct clash with a lot of values in American society. It took me 20 years to sort those things out.

MC: What were the kinds of things that were a conflict for you?

LY: For example, Chinese painter in the scholarly, classic tradition, you never sell your work. You paint in private to express your sensitivity, your longings, or your understanding of the world. And you share it only with a few intimate friends. So to sell the work in galleries, and the success of your work is based on how well you are known, how much people value you. . . . I think for me as a person, my nature, it is difficult for me.

MC: So this conflict in values was why you started doing work in North Philadelphia? How did you actually decide to come to this part of the city and work?

LY: I think it was a personal journey, a worldwide search, and I found it in North Philadelphia. When I studied Chinese painting, it was like I was given a sword, a sharp sword; it cuts both ways. On the one hand it exposed me, it taught me, it showed me what art can be. I don't like all Chinese landscape painting; actually I am very particular what I like. And what I love are the paintings produced from tenth to fourteenth centuries, Sung and Yuan Dynasty. I look at those paintings, my heart would be beating so fast. And I realized in those paintings it showed me a place, and that place is of this world, but something is so magical. It transcend the mundane, and then it become a sacred place for me. And I held very dear, I mean, I feel at home.

So I came to this country. Of course, there is totally no meaning, making brushwork and this kind of traditional painting here. And yet the way I learned Chinese painting totally bound me. I was like a woman with the foot bound. I was all in shackles. When I came to this country, I didn't know what to do, so I just totally left my tradition. I went and tried expressionistic paintings, and as I was creating them, I denied them. I said, this is American, this is not me, to the point that I reached a dead end. I had so many paintings I didn't know what to do with them, so I cut them up. I started to hang them up. So I started to work with three-dimensional space.

But I think there is a way to go back to that place [that the paintings showed her], or to move forward in order to find that place. So I remember I had this worldwide quest to find sacred place. At the beginning, in the late sixties and seventies, I would go to Europe. Sometimes I would go there alone. I would rent a car, or sometimes public transportation. I would just go and go and go. And all day long, I wouldn't be talking to anybody, but I was looking for that place. There are places that are very, very special. I found some of them. Then in the eighties there was this urge to be in touch with roots, so I would go back to China. I got to go to Tibet, go to Chinese Turkestan, all the places that fascinated me for a long time. Then in the nineties I started to go to Africa.

In '86, I began to do project in North Philadelphia, and I didn't know why, but I knew this is the place.

MC: You were living in Philadelphia, this was your base?

LY: I live in center city. I never live in North Philadelphia. Because of my Chinese connection, I set up the Philadelphia cultural exchange with China, and I was helping the city of Philadelphia host three professors from China. Of course, the city wanted to show them the African American culture in Philadelphia. I had very, very little contact. But I liked the gospel singing, I like the rhythm. Then Arthur Hall [director of the African American Dance Ensemble and of Ile-Ife, an African American humanitarian center in North Philadelphia] saw my work. So he said, "You know, I have one lot next to my building—would you build a park for me?" I opened my big mouth: "No problem, yeah, I'll help you build a park." I figured I would never get the funds. And lo behold, they give me $2,500. I said, "Wow! They give me some money. Wow, $2,500!" Then that's when I got a little scared. I got the money, now I have the responsibility. So I started to talk to people. Of course, everybody said don't do it, don't do it. You know, African American and the Asian, they've got the problem [laughter]. Then the children, kids, they will destroy everything. It's not possible, an outsider, and so forth.

But it was really that voice in me just said if you give it up, if you retreat from this, then the light will die. Then what is left is not much. The rest of me is not worth much. So I just came in. And that's when I found Jo Jo [Joseph Williams]. Jo Jo didn't want to work with me, I had to track him down. He said, "I don't know this Chinese woman. What does she want from me?" So one day, he was sitting out there. I found him. And we just bonded. It was great at the beginning, chaotic, it was difficult, there was no resource. If you need one piece of string you had to buy it from outside to bring it in. But there was just something here with the children and with hands on.

MC: How did you first meet the children?

LY: You pick up a shovel, you start digging, children come. You get two shovels, they will fight for those shovels, and they will start digging. We have fun. Just doing something positive is such a radical thing here. Here people are excluded. So if you include them, that's change. And then, nobody does anything, because, in a way, the welfare, we expect other people . . . or disillusion, "What's the use?" I think that is the reason adults didn't come. I don't blame because they've been disillusioned before. So why should they help me? It's my project, it's not their project. I understood that, so I just did what worked with the children. It was wonderful.

In '88 I came back, that's when we made the mosaic, and it was magical. I think working with children, or people untrained, it's so fresh, that creativity, it's so close to the fountain, that magical fountain. I just want to tie it up so it won't disappear. I think about your question, why did I come here from where I was, teaching in a university, showing in mainstream. I just knew. There is a beautiful poem by Langston Hughes. The content of the poem is that I used to look for the life in much more glamorous places, and then I found it in the back alley of this broken-down Negro place. And I found life stepping over my toes. Something like that. That's how I felt. With all my work in the past, nothing is like this. This project is so tremendously challenging everyday, but so deeply gratifying. You know, I'm about to resign from my university, even though my job now is what Chinese call the "golden rice bowl." I'm a tenured professor, and The Village pays me half of what the university can pay me. The Village cannot sustain me, so I have to go out and try to get other resources for myself. But still, with all that uncertainty and risk, this is the place I need to be.

MC: It really did transform you, didn't it?

LY: Yeah, it did, because I found my place here. In a way, I'm selfish. I'm doing what fulfills me. My life is made meaningful, I'm made more humane. I keep on building park. I cannot re-create that place in painting, but I need to do this. I need to live in life.

MC: One of the ways that people have stereotyped the artist is as a lone creator who is in a garret somewhere and makes beautiful things. Maybe the artist has a patron or a gallery that sells the work, or the artist is represented in museum shows. In many ways, the artist is set apart from the rest of society. There is a community of artists, but often that community seems apart from other communities. And what you are saying is that, for you, the artmaking process is now very much tied in with collaborating with people.

LY: Yes. I think we all are in search of meaning in our lives. I know that religion is coming back strong. Personally, I'm not of a certain religion, but I am a spiritual being. So to find that place of sacredness is very, very important. That fountain, the philosophy stone, fountain of creation, whatever you call it. Go back to origin. For me it is always that journey, a quest for that spiritual fulfillment. So art become a path, it become my vehicle. Through art, I get reconnected with that, what I've become severed from. So what I'm looking for, actually, is not a particular product. It's really the process. For example, when you look at Meditation Park [the first of The Village's parks containing mosaics], it's very beautiful, but the process of making it, my God, you think the world can be changed when the process was going.

I just give you some stories. For example, all my crew were on drugs. But when we came together, there was such sweetness, and it was so inclusive. Anybody who wanted to be a part could be a part. Weasel, he was a young man, early twenties, very handsome, broad built, played basketball and so forth. By the way, he was shot, last year, he's dead now. One day, he was working, and suddenly I heard this loud scream—"Eeyaaah!"—something like that. I said, "Weasel, what's wrong, what's problem?" And he said, from so deep a place, he screamed out of joy: "We are awesome!"

And then my foreman Vic Jackson, probably not in his lifetime anybody trusted him something. When he came, I sensed a wonderful quality in him. So I said, "Vic, you are going to be my foreman." I literally see him rise, expand like that—"What did you say? I'm going to be your foreman, I'm going to deliver it!"

That summer, he learned how to drive Bobcat. We all learned. Because we said we are going to pay too much money to a professional company. I said no way are we are going to do that and remain empowered. So I called up the Bobcat rental place, and they didn't ask me for license, so I ordered for so-and-so date, and they delivered it. The driver who delivered

Bobcat was very moved by what we did, so he spent time and showed us how to operate it. Vic became so professional, he was so good.

He was alienated from his father for years because of the drug. And then his father came every afternoon in summertime just there to watch his son. They got reconnected. And Vic is now not with us. I think if that project could have continued, we would have something to hold them all in. So again, he hung out around the people and the drug, so he's broken again. Like I said, even when the form is beautiful, it cannot compare to the beauty, to that light and love and warmth and affection when we got connected. Then we become whole. I think that's what my work is about.

MC: Even when some artists decide to work within communities, they often find it difficult to let go. An artist has a vision about a project and what he or she wants it to be like. Then sometimes that artist goes into a community and starts working with other people, and the artist acts very much like a director to everyone.

LY: On every level, I'm constant juggling. To begin with, when you work with other people you have to let go, a lot. But there are certain things I never let go. Because if I compromise that, I just as well give up the whole thing. There are principal issues, and there are surface issues. Principal issues you never let go. That's what I'm busting my guts for.

MC: For you, what are the principal issues?

LY: For example, the way we build houses, the way we build park, the way we do things at The Village, I never let that go. At the Meditation Park, the easy thing would be you do a feasibility study, you have it planned out, you contract out to people who are experienced, and you supervise what they do. On housing, maybe it will work, but the way we build park, it's always that I have a dream, I know where I'm taking the community, and that vision I never let go, that sensitivity I never let go. If I let that go then I can wash myself away. Because the most valuable thing about me as an artist is not my product, it's that unique sensitivity.

So what I do is I build a structure, and then I invite people in. Within that structure they have a lot of freedom. There is something ritualistic in our way of making art, in the way we do it together. We are not doing my art, we are collaborating. So through doing all those things, they come in contact with their own sensitivity. For example, with Big Man [James Maxton], I designed the mosaic of angels. I felt that life was so full of dangers, so you put a guardian angel there to protect, you create a sacred place. I painted there, and then I worked with Big Man a little bit on color theory, what makes it work, and I gave him a lot of tiles. And then, voom! It's completely his. I would discuss with him and give him encouragement, but that's all his. So I provide the structure and guidance, and that's where the vision is. That's where magic happens.

Okay, there's a romantic idea, people say, "Oh, you must listen to the community and community decide." Well, community has been for generations, you know, and community hasn't decided. The other thing is that people with not the kind of training, with not the calling or the vision, usually take the popular way. People in inner city want what everybody wants in American dream. We want the house, we want the cars. We want all the middle class things. So if you say let people decide, maybe there won't be a park—maybe a tennis court, maybe a basketball court, maybe a parking lot. So I said, yes, you can do it, but I'm not going to be a part of that. So I feel it's a calling. I really see when I deliver this vision, then I would have earned my freedom. I'm hoping in the next 15 years the vision can be really done. In my delivering, I am training staff and other people. And then I'm passing on my artistic sensitivity, too.

I think my project is profoundly American in value. It's about democracy. At one time, somebody called me from San Francisco and asked what does my project have to do with democracy—it's about not voting. I said, my God, it's about building people's self-esteem. When each one is empowered, that's how democracy work, and you have to work to believe that your action make a difference. That's how you take action and take things into your own hand.

MC: What would you say is your dream for The Village of the Arts and Humanities?

LY: For myself and The Village is different. For The Village, we have a long-range plan, and long-range plan spell out next five year, what we should do. But to really deliver The Village is 15 years or more. And our dream, it is very small, and the energy, it is about light. I came responding, my own light. So I come here to build this structure, and through this structure other people join in. And through doing things together they each get connected with their own inner light. Not other people follow your light, but people follow their own light. And yet we work together, so we have a bonfire.

What makes it work, in the day-to-day term, is we have this one-block area with more than half-abandoned houses. So our dream is that with The Village folks, and working with professionals from the outside or from inside, we will have the buildings and create beautiful parks. We nurture the young, provide education activities really connected to their own worth, their own resources, the resources in this neighborhood, and their family, their family heritage. There's a lot of resource in each individual. And then people are nurtured by attention and care from each other. Young people are strengthened by meaningful education, and the teenagers and adults are sustained by meaningful work. That is the dream for The Village. And when I talk about meaningful work, it's not just job training so that you go and get a job. I never want to work at the McDonald. With meaningful work, each person gets in touch with their creativity. I think then you have inner fulfillment, then contentment.

For example, for us to make money, we don't drop everything to do it. We don't do that. When we make money, it has to root in our resource, in our creativity, in our imagination, and then it has to be our people making the money. At the same time, the product we make is built on our strengths rather than our weaknesses, or other people's weaknesses. For example, seduction—that's a lot of our commerce. It's about how you make a buck, how you titillate people's weaknesses. You show them what they don't have, so they're craving what they don't have. Now, we don't want to do those things. So how do we make money, because even the big economy is failing? So this is really big challenge, but I feel maybe slowly, slowly for us, for this society, for our group to survive, we have to think about those things. And if we think hard, maybe there's a way. It's like it's against all odds that The Village can survive.

MC: Can you talk a little bit about what you're up against here? As this organization gets more and more established, maybe some of the obstacles change or they become more or less important. But can you talk about that within a time frame?

LY: At the beginning, for me personally, just how to deliver this project, when there is not structure here or anything. I'm from outside the community, I have no expertise, and I have little money, $2,500 to build on an abandoned lot the size of ten houses. Half an acre or two-thirds of an acre or something with unskilled people, a bunch of kids, a total unstable structure—you don't know who's coming tomorrow. But once I made the decision, the strength came. Then, it was just logistics: how do I do this? And by God, when I look at it from three or four years down the road, all our failings were the reason that we survived.

I'll give you an example. If I were male and white, and I came here, and I had all the knowledge that I needed, expertise and so forth, I probably wouldn't even begin dealing with this program. Nothing against the male or white. I think also I would call too much attention, it represents establishment in people's minds, for better, for worse. Maybe I would get more people to help more readily, or maybe people don't want to help because it represents the broken things. But anyway, I came as an anonymous person. I think that's how the project succeeded. Always anonymous. Nobody signs our paintings. It's just everybody's, it's a collective.

And because I'm a woman, because I'm Asian, and because I'm also so small. It makes me invisible. It's wonderful. And then, I worked with a bunch of kids, we had a lot of fun. We did the digging and all that, and then it's totally chaotic—some come today, and then I never see them again. Yet Jo Jo was the stable element. Despite all the difficulties, I think we bonded on a very, very deep level. Yet, with all that unstableness, this is our tenth year. If your heart is at the right place, you are right there. And so that was the beginning, lack of resource. And I think always, it's always more than I can handle. It's always about to bust me. Yet, at the end of the day, the fulfillment was so deeply gratifying. So in the exhausting process, it's like the purifying process, it's like fire. So I go to sleep; each sleep I get up rejuvenated. And next morning *[snaps fingers],* new dream. And then you come back and battle the same thing. And the other thing: I think that we are all shedding a little bit more. We are all stripped, maybe two or three layers, a little bit more naked. When we come, we try to shield ourselves, the feeling of insufficiency. The feeling of separateness, the feeling of pain that we are not together. There again, it is by default. We don't want to be in this position, yet it is in this that one is more vulnerable, more open. Then the connection is a little easier. And when the two people connect in sincerity, in openness, nothing is like this. That's a spark, that's love. When you experience that, you always come back to that.

One of our crew, his name is Ice. He came in the first summer. He's real thin, he never speak much, very quiet. He calls himself a laborer. He's always at the bottom, mixing cement, doesn't work much. He has drug problems. I know that, but that didn't change my view of him. He is in my heart, and he is part of The Village. He's a Village person, and I am still waiting for him to come back. So the third summer he came, and I knew he would disappear for some time with the drug habit. And when he came back, we welcomed him right back, so he was very happy that he can come back and work.

And I remember one day he was trying to tell me something. He said, "Miss Lily, you know, if I'm somewhere in other part of the city, and people tell me that you are hurt, I will do whatever I can to come here, and I will protect you. I will watch over, and if something happen to you, it would be hurting me so much." In a very awkward, kind of archaic way, and I realized it's not a specific thing he was saying. Through the saying, he gave me his heart. I don't know where Ice is, or where he's hiding, in rehab, or he's hiding from somebody. The heart made the connection, and nothing can replace that.

And so the product is not important. The art is only a vehicle, that is the side thing of what really happen when people working together. So I think what I do may be very radical now, but it is so ancient. It's like the people come together, build the medieval church. It's anonymous, you give what you can. Then it's an offering, and everybody do a part.

MC: You do this in a whole atmosphere of . . . I'm not from Philadelphia, but I know from talking to people here and reading things that this is a high-drug area.

LY: Right down the street. Huntingdon.

MC: Huntingdon is a big dealing area, and obviously there is a lot of vandalism that goes on. Usually drugs are associated with a lot of violent crime, and you are here with The Village of Arts and Humanities, and you're . . .

LY: Yeah, sometimes I would have images of stray bullet come through me, and I would have no fear in me. For me, my personal life, I feel that I have given everything I got. I go home, I have given everything I have. If I die, I have no regret. So that's the way I pursue my life. I retreat to that place in silence, and then I focus on my work, and I stay in the light. Everything else takes care of itself. And so I live my life so that I have no regret. So that's the only really personal issue. In the work here, I have no fear, I think because I've been here for a long time, and people have been very, very friendly. A couple of times I got cursed out, because we had squatters. But I don't have any fear, and I don't think our staff has any fear. I don't think it's dangerous here—dangerous everywhere. I work with drug users, and I love my crew. If there's anything, my crew is dearest to me. And that's the one thing I regret: because the organization has grown, I am not able to be there to do my part, and that is such a loss for me. And this is the reason why I need to go to Kenya [she has been working on a church garden with people living in a Nairobi slum]. I need to go places away from The Village so I don't deal with infrastructure, I don't deal with administration. I am the best when I do art, when I work with people hands on. It is a gift. I must spend it, otherwise it's wasted.

MC: Certainly, the infrastructure here at this point is one of the things that you struggle against. When I was talking about drugs and crime in the neighborhood, I was thinking that those are things that you, with your vision for The Village, are really in combat with, or at least competing against.

LY: Combat is the right word.

MC: Okay, you are in combat with them. But also at this point, I would think that you're in combat with what seems to have become necessary in order for this organization to grow and to have a greater impact in this community. Not just through art programs, but I know you are now rehabilitating some housing for people, you are trying to set up a health center. Narcotics Anonymous meets here. There are a lot of things beyond that initial idea that are going on now.

LY: To use the word combat: I feel that every day it's a sheer concentration, the effort, and it's like a battle. From the beginning, I have heard that what I wanted to do was not possible. You can't do education and do housing and do park building and do economic development and all that. You cannot possibly, and produce theater and publish a newsletter. I didn't think all that out from my brain, and it's not a top-down thing. It's a bottom-up thing. And this is why it's all possible. It is so organic. It's naturally grown. For example, in housing, how it started was that we have the Hermit [Richard Withers, a skilled carpenter who lives in The Village], he gave us a lot of help. And we have all this crew here who need the work. And we need space. So The Village bought some materials, nobody paid much, just skeleton. Then people all come together and wanting to give a little bit and take a little bit. So we all survive, and then we build something together.

So that's how this building [The Village headquarters] came here. That's how our housing came. And if you take community building seriously . . . I just took our children to heart. They come here for two hours every day, they have this wonderful thing [after-school workshops]. When they go home it's totally different. I took our crew to heart. They have drug problem, or they need places to stay, you figure out: wow, gee, if we build a park, maybe we have building. And then if we get somebody to volunteer to help us, maybe we can build a house. I *so* believe that these two hands can build our own dwelling. These two hands can make things change.

Sometimes I feel our society is really against the community. We all talk about grassroots building; our regulation is all *against* grassroots building. For good reason, for bad reason. It used to be we earned $5, it's for real, we spend it any way we want. Now the $5 is actually $2.75. The rest goes to pay different taxes, workers' comp. We need all that, but at the same time that suck up all the initiative. And so we raise a lot more money, but everything has gone up tenfold for us. So if you talk about what we're fighting, we're fighting against the regulation, and we are trying to work within the regulation. The city government has been wonderful, they all want to help us. Everybody. It's just that certain things are really against that.

It's about stabilization. I told you, I've been here ten years. I do all the things that I said we deliver. I deliver really, in a way, a miracle. On very, very low budget. Yet, at the same time, there is no stability, and the current government says you've got to be on your own. I took that to heart. I took everything to heart. I saw we had to build on our strength, otherwise if there is no foundation, it's all going to cave in. I'm at this age. I ain't going to spend my time, effort, and build something that's going to collapse. So most of this goes into building people, goes into infrastructure.

What resource have we got here? People. People, broken. You have to build that. So that's where crafts come into it. [The Village recently began a crafts-making and sales program.] When you talk about craft, you talk about people working. People have little work ethic, and for a long time people are against government, how to take advantage of all the loopholes. So you have to reprogram people. You say it's not about we and them, it's about all us. The bottom line is that we are all in it together. I have a good job, and I have security. I live in center city. None of that really directly affect me. But when you feel that it's all of us together, then maybe doing this makes me whole.

MC: What do you consider the community here, geographically? And also, what's the population?

LY: Physically, The Village is only a four-street area, from Germantown Avenue (or Tenth Street) to Eleventh Street, to Huntingdon, the drug street, to Cumberland. And within this boundary there are two tiny streets. That's The Village physical. Yet The Village has no boundary. People come in through our programs—the narcotic, children, adults. The squatters on Warnock Street, they have nothing to do with us, though they're right in The Village area. At the same time, other squatters have a vegetable garden. They cultivate, and sometimes in the summertime they come and get water. The Village elders, you have just seen them, they come and take part of our program, but they pretty much live an independent life. Yes, and some are very engaged with us. Our staff, definitely. Then we have a lot of people, like interns, they come in and go. They experience something. They take it with them, and when they can, they come back.

The whole thing is based on village. We have a motto here: "Together we build." And the people I work with in Kenya adopted our motto. We're thinking of eventually having exchange program for our children, for our kids. In a way, we are a part of each other. So is that a part of our community or not part of our community?

MC: Obviously, you've made a long-term commitment to this particular community in Philadelphia. It's different when you go to Kenya. I know you've been invited to Brazil and Mali, too, and that various cities in this country have asked you to come and talk or to be a consultant. There is, fundamentally, a difference in your relationship to those communities as compared to this one. I wonder if you feel there's as much potential for making a difference in those communities as there is in North Philadelphia.

LY: It's making a difference, definitely, whether it's here or there. I think it's all in different degrees. For example, if I stayed in Kenya, I would run into similar problem [as here]. They look for people to solve their problem. If I do that, immediately I get trapped in individual problem. Here I made the choice not to solve people's problems. Instead, we come together and build something new. I choose to find the one crack and plant the seed there. And it deepens through what we do. . . . So you have a new structure coming up, and then the roots spread.

The other thing is that magic is not possible if I did not have the understanding of what I've done here. To do this continuously is very, very difficult. Because I am an artist, I feel I am not doing myself justice if I don't do art at all. So I need to go other places to do art project.

MC: Has it become impossible for you to be an artist here?

LY: I am becoming a conceptual artist. The whole thing in the development of The Village is art. How it relates to education, entrepreneurship, crafts industry—I figured it out because I've been here so long. I know the ins and outs. So I work out the structure, and I get the right person with the right sensitivity [for these programs], and the person can head it. So I'm much more remote.

But with the crew, it's impossible for me now to stay there day after day and do artwork with them. And so I have to figure out the way that it becomes possible again, because that is something so important for me personally and for the crew. I tried to get a person to come in and do the same thing. The person totally had the wrong sensitivity. Could not do it. Did not appreciate the potential. In the brokenness, there is new possibility. I just know that if I start to build, I will get my crew. I cannot hire another person to take my place. My palette is not color, but my palette is working with people. I have a vision, sensitivity, so I have to be there to deliver it. But it's getting more and more impossible here. The Village has it's own goal. More structure, then I can get somebody to handle it [the structure]. Then I would earn my freedom.

MC: You started out as an artist, but you've now become an artist/fundraiser/educator/entrepreneur/health activist. . . . You're laughing, but do you feel comfortable with all the different roles? Is that your identity now?

LY: My identity is artist. I am artist. I do all that based on artist sensitivity and the vision. Sometimes I say to myself it is an artist taking things to heart and taking people seriously and wanting her work to be meaningful. And taking herself seriously. So all the other name doesn't mean a thing to me. Community is multidimensional. You can't just do one thing, but I know I do it as an artist. Sometimes thinking when I die, I'll have a tombstone that just say from year when to when, and only word I want there is "artist." Nothing else.

MC: Do you consider yourself an activist?

LY: No, I don't. If you take action, you are an activist. I just see myself an artist, take herself seriously, take what she does seriously, take people she come in contact with seriously. An artist will love life, that's how I see it. And the result is an activist—when you take action and don't wait for other people to make a change. My action, my sensitivity, is all in the arts. And the first time when I heard people call me "artist and activist," I was quite surprised. Because usually an activist is very radical. And the way I work is always with cooperation. I don't have an enemy that I rebel against, or I cast away, or I take action against.

MC: But you do say you are in combat.

LY: If you take life seriously, I think you are in combat. It's the degree of concentration, degree of determination. I always feel what we do is like walking on thin ice—you have to be so attentive and so alert and aware of the danger. Anytime, you can take a wrong step, make a wrong decision, and everything just sink. So in combat, it's that you are always alert. And especially because we do so many things, and everybody say you cannot do it. Including our funders. A lot of our funders are very, very wonderful people, and I think a lot of people bend their rules because of what we have delivered, and they saw us busting our guts. And yet, at the same time, you are against so many odds. This is a danger area. I don't sense physical danger myself, but our building, constantly people try to take away, vandalize and stuff. And so you are constantly alert, and that's like in combat. And the other one is the deadline, constant deadline. That's combat. Every time I deliver a deadline, I shed a layer of skin. You are always racing that clock, 12 midnight. That's combat. You combat deadline, you combat odds, you combat people's concept that you cannot do this.

MC: You were just saying that you are not here to solve people's problems. I'd like to know if you believe in the phrase, or in the concept of "art and social change."

LY: Perfect, perfect question. No, I cannot. It's out of humbleness knowing my own limitation and how vast the problems are. Some of the problems, physically, mentally, emotionally, I cannot solve. Some of the problems I don't want to solve. People solve their own problems. It's God's to solve people's problems. It's just knowing my own limitation. I don't go for social change, because no matter what system you install, it is always full of loopholes. Unless people have good will, people are always going to misuse the system. Our system is so abused. But for me, always humanity, always the real person, that light in each one of us. And when you help that person to get in touch with that light, you empower that person. They have their own guidance. They have to make their own decision and take responsibility. And what we do is come together and work together. And when that happens, other things change.

With Village, it was never my intention to change. Even right now, about necessity, getting teenage entrepreneur and all that—it's just out of concern, affection, and love. We see the teenagers on the street, and it's most vulnerable time, and we say let's have some program that's really meaningful for them and meaningful in our development also. In the long run, it helps this community. I just feel whatever I do here is a gift given to me. I have to give that gift out, so that it's not wasted.

The immediate neighborhood and the people we affect, it's not many. All year, it used to be 1,000. I think now maybe it's raised to 5,000 people come through our programs, festival and the performances and so forth. Still, it's only 5,000 people. You have tens of millions and billions people, what do you do? But I feel Village is at the cutting edge, just because of all the unconventional things that we do. And the most important thing is relay the mindset. You don't take no, and you really see everything as your resource. And it's all inclusive—you see people using drug as your resource. My God, it's not the other, it's us together. People in prison, we write to. Very powerful. They are the ones who can say a lot to our kids. It's all those resources.

So social change is never our target. But just be sincere, just be there, and just make a commitment. No alternative motives. We are here to work together, and eventually people respond. And also we are trying to have impact not just in Village. If this model succeeds and can be duplicated in other places, that's where it will make an impact. It's not this one light shining, but it's many, many small lights shining. Not one big light, but many, many lights shine in different places. They draw on their own resources. But it's all that inner light shared by all humanity. That's where I see the hope. If I look at human nature, I am very pessimistic, very pessimistic. I saw that we are more prone to fall, to temptation, and the Lord's Prayer does not protect us. Taking action gives me hope, takes me away from despair and pessimism. When I deliver that, when I'm free, then I paint. Then I feel that out of fullness, I can retreat in my studio. And that's like my temple, my monastery. I can be totally anonymous. Painting like prayer. And you don't ask for recognition. If you properly do the best painting, it doesn't matter. It's just a prayer through the act of painting.

MC: Do you see yourself doing what you're doing now for the rest of your life?

LY: I am seeing that I am delivering it to gain my freedom. To paint a few years in total solitude, to read a book, to not worry about next deadline. I hope not. I really hope not.

MC: You almost put it in terms of having a debt to pay.

LY: It's a gift. It's a gift given to me.

January 18, 1996
Philadelphia, Pennsylvania

9

MEL CHIN

FOR MORE THAN 25 YEARS, MEL CHIN *has produced works of art that in diverse and complex ways have grappled with major social, political, and environmental issues of the era. Sometimes these artworks are shown in museums and galleries, but more often he sets them up in everyday spaces and situations where, as he says, he tries to "create forums of discourse where there's very little." These have included a subway station, a video arcade game, abandoned inner city housing, a public high school, toxic waste sites and primetime commercial television. His chief aim is to entice people to move beyond conventional ways of thinking to explore root causes of and possible remedies for society's ills.*

In the interview that follows, Chin focuses on two ongoing, collaborative projects that typify his approach. He first talks about In the Name of the Place, *in which he organized a team of artists and art students to collaborate with the creators of the primetime television soap opera* Melrose Place *to develop props and set pieces that inserted visual messages about gender, infectious diseases, violence, environmental devastation, and global conflict into the popular weekly series. These messages were meant to be subliminal and not disruptive to the episodes—the group instead wanted to tap into* Melrose's *enormous international audience base to suggest meanings beyond standard soap-opera plots and dialogue. As Chin says, "Television has been predicated on precision, keeping it as spare as possible, or as silly as possible, to sell product. If you add texture and layers to it, then you create a more humane space possibly . . . [art] can show options that didn't exist before." Though* Melrose Place *was canceled in 1999, reruns are being shown in many countries around the world, and one of the group's major set pieces soon will be reused in a spin-off German television series.*

The other project Chin describes is Revival Field, *an environmental artwork composed of "hyperaccumulator" plants that can pull toxic heavy metals in large quantities from contaminated soils. Chin first developed* Revival Field *in 1989 with Dr. Rufus Chaney, a soil microbiologist who had abandoned research on these plants for lack of support to test them properly. Deciding to collaborate on a plant and earth sculpture that would function as a field test, they were initially thwarted in getting National Endowment for the Arts funding—then-NEA chairman John Frohnmeyer first decided that* Revival Field *wasn't art, then reversed himself. Once funds were secured,* Revival Field *was set up in St. Paul, Minnesota, and proved in a three-year test that the plants are highly effective in extracting toxic metals from the soil. The project is now entering its fourth phase in Stuttgart, Germany, for a ten-year period, which is the amount of time needed to remediate one of these contaminated sites completely. As Chin says, "The outward manifestation is the sculptural shape of the field, but the main point is that* Revival Field *calls for the sculpting of ecology, to bring it back to health. The goal is still to push the science further."*

❑   ❑   ❑   ❑   ❑

Marie Cieri: Do you consider yourself an artist, an artist/activist, or something that's not even so clearly defined?

Mel Chin: I'm doing several projects that have many pieces. There are projects where I'm collaborating with landscape architects to create sculptural works, so in that case I'm just your normal artist. I'm doing other projects from more of an activist stance, and there I'm a submerging figure, applying creative energy not just to making objects, but to creating forums of discourse where there's very little. I see it as a survival relationship as an artist. If you are fueled by ideas and all these poetic capacities, and you live in a culture where you feel they are being endangered, it seems *appropriate* to create conditions of survival for those ideas, whatever they might be. It's not just for art. If there is a future for human beings, we'd better do *something.* If we look at Africa or Bosnia or what we're doing in Central America, there is massive destruction of human potential. I think when half a million people die in Africa, that's half a million possibilities that are just wasted. I know that with myself there is a profound possibility that I could destroy, no question about it. Maybe it is about getting rid of your delusions about yourself, understanding where you stand as a human being, and then focusing on "Well, what can I do?" And then saying, "Well, what can *we* do?" because you can only do so much as an individual.

So trying to create conditions where discourse can occur seems to be a job description. Then saying, as an artist, that there definitely can be a very nontraditional approach to this. Through my experiments, I've seen the failings of public art and public activism, and the failings are not because there isn't enough commitment. It is not because people aren't saying the right things. There are *other factors,* and those are what we should be look-ing at. Having knowledgeable belief is definitely necessary. I always ask, can I have responsibility and deep ignorance? We can work on *that,* but there are other factors.

For example, I printed up these O. J. [Simpson] T-shirts that said, "Truth Hertz," like the rental car company he was a spokesman for for 20 years. I sold them in front of the county courthouse in Los Angeles on the day of his arraignment to raise money for a battered woman's center. At the same time, there was an organized protest led by a lot of artists, women activists, protesting against domestic violence—really making a solid sixties, seven-ties, kind of protest. That day, the cameras looked at them for a second and said, "No, we're going to check out the vendors, it's more interesting." I was with the vendors—I submerged myself, I was not an art project—un-derstanding that what everybody was interested in that day and where the cameras were turned was toward all these vendors making money off the case. I was standing right there with them, *not critical of them.* I was think-ing that this shirt that says "Truth Hertz" was like "Justice for Rent," or "Truth for Rent." Adding this little pun was a way of making the grounds of discourse more complex in this small world of T-shirts that were either pro-O. J. or against-O. J.—this idea of inserting additional meaning where things are so black and white.

MCi: How do you see that people respond to the gray area as opposed to the black and white?

MCh: I think that people could respond better if they had more tools to access the gray areas. But we live in a culture of forgetting, a culture that would like us to remain somewhat ignorant. My T-shirt project was small, but I took it very seriously because the world of mass communications, namely television, is a force to be reckoned with. Or if anything, here I'm saying that I am an artist, and I have ideas, and maybe a group of us has ideas, but what does that mean? I do these tests to say that we have to find meaning. We have to go deeper. The art world is a very narrow bandwidth, and what it affects is tiny. I want to go beyond that, to take an expedition beyond the existing borders.

MCi: This book project came about during discussions about the prob-lems going on with freedom of speech and NEA funding. It was not so much about the government's role in art as it was a perception that out-side the art world people really didn't care very much. A question that many art people were asking was why aren't more people coming to our defense? Isn't art important to them? Obviously there's a gap between the art world and other worlds, and it's bigger than most arts people realized or wanted to admit.

MCh: Well, it's interesting you say that. I think it was demonstrated that most of the public really doesn't have that many opinions about art other than it's fine and the NEA is fine. It's how political entities utilized it. [*Time* art critic] Robert Hughes really came down on that. Whether you like his criticism or not, he pointed out how art and the NEA have been a convenient bone to throw by conservative political structures that saw how useful and effective it could be to sway public sentiment toward conservative agendas. We're dupes, basically. I also look critically at the art world, where we preserve this mythology of rugged individualism. That makes us their easiest target. We will never be organized enough to create a political force, so what do we expect? Obviously it's political and media entities combined that create sensationalized situations and use the NEA and art as political weapons. And here we are thinking about how we can do good, and our voice is being lost on a daily basis. It's funny, I picked *Melrose Place* as a site of collaboration simply because I know that the Senate and Congress hold it out as one of the things that erodes public morals. [The series had been attacked on these grounds by some members of Congress.]

MCi: It seems that you're not that affected by these controversies, or that you've just decided that, though they exist, "I'm still going to do what I do."

MCh: We all are affected by them. What I am suggesting is if you talk about activism, you'd better go in and do something, because the capacity for human destruction is there, the capacity for destruction of ideas is there, and it happens very rapidly.

MCi: Can you talk a little bit about the *Melrose Place* project?

MCh: We call it *In the Name of the Place,* and I am only a representative of a larger team called the GALA Committee, which stands for Georgia and Los Angeles, the two sites where the original artists and students involved were working. I was here in Georgia teaching and simultaneously teaching at Cal Arts when this project was invented. The GALA Committee has been able to create sets, artworks, props on this popular primetime soap opera [broadcast from 1995 to 1997].

MCi: How did you initially get to do this?

MCh: I was invited to be part of a show called *Uncommon Sense* at the Museum of Contemporary Art [MOCA] in Los Angeles. The idea behind it is public interaction, intervention, in Los Angeles. It's a group show involving artists from Karen Finley to Mierle Laderman Ukeles to Rick Lowe. Flying back from there, I started thinking that the whole world knows Los Angeles from television, from Hollywood. My intention was to somehow get in and understand what that was about, because it is the most massive side, especially primetime network television. I hadn't even decided what to do until I heard about the *Melrose* controversy. I had never seen the program, so I turned it on and said, "Look at all those walls and all these sets and all the action—it is a modern-day *Los Caprichos* without the artistic back-up! I can't be Goya, but maybe collective invention could be Goya [the great Spanish artist whose paintings criticized human vice and political corruption in the late eighteenth and early nineteenth centuries]. If I develop this large forum, we could work together and develop a lot of ideas." Single-mindedly, I started thinking about the Goya relationship that is almost 200 years old, and who was the king then? King Carlos IV. And who is the king now? Aaron Spelling. For 30 years, he's created primetime shows that are part of a psyche, how we dress and act and relate to each other. Whether or not you know about Aaron Spelling or his productions, from *Love Boat* to *Dynasty,* the influence is there.

In its 50 years of existence, television has not met its promise to transform the world by making everybody educated. It has transformed the world, but on other terms. Then that's where you must be. My point as an artist, or as part of a group construction, is to get in as a virus or parasite, not just to tear apart but to build what has not been built before. It's too easy to critique television because it's obvious. You must respect its power and come in with a different kind of heart/mind saying, "What can we really do to this and make it truly better?" To get on a site like *Melrose* and create work, that it be not just my voice but different people working in teams, we could create collective activism, collective works that had meaning on a site where there is less meaning. There's an enormous opportunity to say some things—*Melrose Place* is seen by 100 million people internationally every week.

MCi: How did you negotiate your presence on *Melrose Place?*

MCh: I was teaching at Cal Arts and formulated the project with the students there. Through various phone methods, I was able to get to the set decorator, mentioned something about the arts and the show I was doing at the museum. I asked about the artwork on *Melrose Place.* She was apologetic about the quality of it and talked about the difficulty of procuring art work because of reproduction rights. So I offered that we would make it for her for free.

The big issue here is money. Don't ever ask for money. Do it for free. We wanted to create work independently, not be paid by Spelling, and have it add to the context of the script or beyond. So then the infection, as we call it, begins. (Recently we've been calling it "an opportunistic conception," because we are working with them.) The intent is that this is beyond *Melrose*, it's more about whether television can have multiple layers. Can it become a sculptural site, where not only the characters are important, but the image behind as well? I feel that's where freedom of thought occurs. If you have movement of the mind, you have possibilities that didn't exist before. That's probably what we're more interested in.

The work we created for *Melrose Place* then will be seen at the museum show opening in March [1997] to verify it as art. After that, our team plans a big auction of the work that will support education. We're going to try to get top dollar for it because we feel that's how you can do something. So the two most demonized factors are going to support what people say is the answer to some of our public ills. [The artworks were not only shown at the MOCA in Los Angeles, but also in Kansas City, Houston, and Kwangju, Korea. An auction of the work was held in Beverly Hills in 1998, with all proceeds going to two women's educational funds.]

MCi: Can you describe one or two of the objects that have been on the program and how they function within the show?

MCh: Many just occur in the background: a set-up of words on a poster, or bed sheets printed quite prominently with condoms, like "safe sheets." They're approved, and they go on. One of the most critical ones was thrown off the set by a producer, but somehow it was shot earlier or put back on by accident. It was an advertising poster (they have an advertising agency in the show) saying "Total Proof." The image was of the Oklahoma City bombing with the building blown out in the shape of an Absolut Vodka bottle. The Oklahoma bombing happened to occur when they had scheduled a bombing routine on *Melrose Place,* and they pulled it. Well, we got on anyway, and it was amazing because the scene was of two advertising characters, one of whom is an alcoholic, talking about the glass ceiling, talking about advertising and its limits. And the poster was flanking them. So here is where the script, by chance, was contextual to the image.

Now, of course, this image is a little more complex. It brings this complicated string of associations. Do more people die from drunken driving than all the people who died in that bombing? Archer Daniels Midland [a large soybean agribusiness] buys up large parts of the Midwest—does that create more drinking perhaps [because family farms go out of business]? Or is it just about advertising—does advertising manipulate our minds more than anything else? So you see a complicated network. "Total Proof" of what is the question.

Another advertising image says "Surreal Definitions" and has a piece of cheese floating in a sandwich. But in that cheese is the incised image of a body floating in the Kagera River in Rwanda. We did this because an army officer in the *New Yorker* described genocide in that part of the world as a cheese sandwich as far as he was concerned—just tossed away. This *is* the horror. We're going to create images for that. It happens so rapidly on the screen, we want to have a covert internet campaign that is not part of the art world but part of the *Melrose* fan club. It will be the reinforcement, just for the fans. [This site was, in fact, created and regularly accessed by *Melrose* fans.] So we're working on different levels. The art world knows about it, you know about it. The art world again is a narrow bandwidth—and people will be critical of me or the project any way they want, but there is a larger world that will carry the information. [One of the most frequently used set pieces produced by the GALA Committee is *Shooter's Bar,* which details the history of alcohol production and consumption in the U.S. from 1700 to the present. It is now a working bar in a museum in Stuttgart and will soon appear once again as a set piece in a German TV spin-off of *Melrose Place.*]

MCi: Have you had input on any of the scripts?

MCh: Oh, yes. We have to work within the bounds of television, but that's okay if we can push ideas further and further.

MCi: Well, the remarkable thing is that, as you were saying, you have this potential forum of about 100 million people internationally.

MCh: That's public art. The activism part of it is if we can show that commercial television can have a multilayered approach to information and knowledge while not trying to be dogmatic about it. Our intention is not to undermine or be so subversive as to cause *Melrose Place* not to exist or be secondary. We are dependent on the host. At the same time, we're not there just to make props. So far they have been entirely generous with us. We want a different relation to television than has occurred in the past. Usually it's art television or PBS—you separate art from television. This compartmentalization is largely what's wrong. Maybe let's not identify this as an art project. Let's just say we are working toward a goal of cooperation. We are moving into this territory, trying to collectively come up with something meaningful.

You were pointing out earlier how the social content of my work in sculpture takes time to reveal itself to viewers. I had been looking at what other artists like Barbara Kruger were already doing. [Kruger is a well-known visual artist whose work comments on a variety of social issues.] By using the direct format of advertising, she was saying it like it is and showing the grisly image. But to me, that is so similar to what you already see in the media. My idea has been to aestheticize these tragedies so they can be taken in as art, reserved poetically within the mind so they can be digested and have maybe an even greater impact. I always say you can try to read Rilke at age ten and maybe understand it, but when you're twenty you'll understand it better. At ten you don't have the life experience yet. If things happen too rapidly, you really don't have a chance of obtaining options or choices. If it's too distinctly colored one way, it only leads to polarization or perception of an impossible situation. I think if we allow more time it's more democratic, because everybody metabolizes at a different level and scale.

Some of the hope for this *Melrose* project is that we create a fan following of it, and they will understand it in their own way. We should not be so dogmatic about all these things. Maybe there will be just the basic understanding that there is something *more there.* So we are probably opening this dimensional aspect of information transfer, especially on television. Television has been predicated on concision, keeping it as spare as possible, or as silly as possible, to sell product. If you add texture and layers to it, then you create a more humane space possibly, or more defined space. Rather than so dead, like power is in one direction, in one word. There are several words now. I think art is defined between those arcs of things. *My* definition of art has changed a lot over the years. Maybe it is only important because it clears a space for language to be formed. It can show options that didn't exist before.

MCi: That brings us to talk about the *Revival Field,* because that is a project that has created opportunity.

MCh: Well, it made sense because at the time there was no solution to heavy metal pollution in the soil. I had just finished making and showing some sculptures that were stuck in the wall, about the planets and about Greek and Chinese alchemy ideas. I was really re-evaluating all that. I felt that I could be very happy doing this for the rest of my life. Okay, then, quit, stop.

MCi: Because you were happy doing it.

MCh: Yeah, because you love that, and you should be testing that. Art is something you test. So you say if that is what you love, stop. Do something else. I started researching other things. I found out this thing about plants being able to pull heavy metals or bleach toxins out of the soil. I said, "Well, I've found another sculpture." It's different, but it's the same. It's the most traditional thing I could ever do. If you can create these plants or help engineer these plants or help somebody make these plants and carve away the toxins, that's a sculpture. It was marble before, now it's toxic earth, what difference is there? Except no one's doing it, and why?

It leads you to the critical factor in this kind of activism—you must be responsible if you are going to work in the public domain. It's beside you, it's beyond you, and you start developing this collective attitude. We need to find the scientists who know how to do this. We need to find what they need. And we need to get the politicians involved and the polluters involved. It seemed quite simple but was not. You're talking about legal and political factors. To the very end it was almost stopped every minute. Dr. Chaney, the scientist I worked with, had shelved all his research on these plants for many years because there was no support.

MCi: Can you talk a little bit about what problems he came across?

MCh: There are indicator plants that grow only in sites where there are metals. This was known thousands of years ago. African smiths would look for indicator plants to dig to find their copper. So maybe it's all been there in the head, but it was never used. I think Dr. Chaney was the first to talk about it in the eighties as a process of remediation, but it was taken from Robert Richard Brooks, who in the seventies was looking at all this in Russian scientific studies. I searched for Dr. Chaney and found him. He was back working in soil microbiology—plant transfers and sewage sludge—and had shelved all of his work on these plants because there was no support for it. He was skeptical, of course—after 20 or 30 years of research, here is an artist calling him. You know what that means—like it's frivolous, not important. I didn't try to demand respect. I had to understand I had to learn *his* way of talking, learn what his world was about, too.

I was unwilling to proceed unless we could create our own grounds of cooperation. If we think about an art project, we have to talk about ego and how to diffuse that a little bit. I have to create a workable solution and a practical relationship with my collaborator. Ask him, what do *you* need? What do you need, Dr. Chaney? He said he needed a replicated field test. I said let's just change the artwork to a replicated field test because that's what's important. If we do that, it might verify the science (science can't progress into a technology unless it's proven in the field). Then here's an artwork helping to verify a scientific principle that was shown in the lab. The agony, then, is to find a site where you will be allowed to do it.

MCi: Why is that so difficult?

MCh: Because of law. There are lots of hazardous waste sites, but they are locked up for eternity by legal procedures—they're trying to find out whom to blame, they're trying to prosecute those responsible and make them clean the sites up. You have whole communities trapped by these legal problems, and the intent is never to touch the sites and never mention them. I had to bypass all that and conjoin these people to sit at one table—the scientists, prosecutors, polluters, congressmen, the mayor, the artists, and the art center [Walker Art Center in Minneapolis] to make this thing happen. And it did eventually. The original NEA grant was the only support we had and was not enough, really. Dr. Chaney expected a field test like this would take $70,000. We had only $10,000. We did it physically, my team.

The field had high cadmium concentrations. It took three years to get results: you need three years in a replicated field test, to make sure that these plants have the capacity to pull heavy metals in large quantities from contaminated soil. It wasn't until the second year that we had any results to verify because all the plants in the first year had been destroyed. There was vandalism, there was animal damage. But that verification was groundbreaking, literally, because this *Revival Field* had proven it for the scientific world. Also, the publicity related to the NEA . . .

MCi: I remember—John Frohnmeyer rejected a grant for your project after the panel had voted to give you one. He had doubts that this was really art. It was all over the papers. Then he met with you and decided to reinstate the grant.

MCh: Exactly. Oh, it was weird. The art world controversy created awareness within a whole network of scientists that this was happening. *Now,* Dr. Chaney has support, and it's all been turned around. We're proceeding with *Revival Field Three,* which is the first test of mining with plants, a major breakthrough. That's within five years of association. He says this was the pivotal project. So you don't go into this thing saying I'm here to actively transform, but that I'm here to be really passionate and empathetic to the needs of others from the start. [Chin and Chaney are now preparing to install a Revival Field of 10 years duration in Stuttgart.]

MCi: You just mentioned a problem that a few others have talked about: the ego function of art, and how you deal with that when you work with people collaboratively on a project.

MCh: I think the only thing I've ever requested from Dr. Chaney was that he call it the *Revival Field* project, and he did. But right now maybe 250 scientists claim this process, and I say great. I don't claim this idea as mine. Now it's public domain. If I were to come to these scientists and say, "No, I did it as an artwork and you're not" . . . why do that? It's about understanding the appropriate time to express so-called histories. What does that mean anyway: where did *I* take it from? So, I've developed a healthy skepticism about my own place in things.

MCi: You sound like you have found a way to be a player in a process that's historical and environmental and global in its implications.

MCh: Yeah. You can choose several things. I use Elaine Scarry's book, *The Body in Pain,* a lot. She'd probably hit me on the head because I simplify it so much. But she talks about the making and unmaking of the world. There's pain and there's imagination. Pain in its last form is war and torture, and you can guarantee it unmakes the world because it unmakes language. War of course kills people, and there's no language there. Torture removes the human capacity to express oneself. Conversely, she talks about the remaking of the world—if you close your eyes and just imagine something else, it will appear. It is the *construction* of language. That's what I'm trying to say. I want to be a part of that.

In my lifetime, the art that I've experienced, what I consider art, has stimulated my imagination and pushed me forward in a constructive way. If this can be brought to and used in the world of science, fine. And if they want to call it science, fine. If we can bring it into television, fine. While I may have engineered certain aspects of it, I don't feel my name has to be out there with it all the time. I haven't done it alone. If my voice alone was being produced in all these products for *Melrose Place* or in the *Revival Field,* I would be no better than just exercising my opinion. I want to create conditions where individual process isn't negated but actually is enhanced by collective invention. And if for some reason you can't create the art, then it's equally important to set the condition for art later to be done by others.

MCi: What you're saying is very unusual. I'm curious how you've to come take this view of yourself as an artist within the world.

MCh: Gosh, I don't know. I look at it as an evolutionary process. I remember I was listening to Cornel West talk about Nietzsche (and I think it comes from the Greek), that "the unexamined life is not worth living." But West carried it further, quoting Malcolm X saying that as a black American, you examine your life and there's pain—that's what you have. I go further to say that we live in a world that is constantly removing the tools to examine one's life. I opened up the *New York Times,* and at the top it had images of women of color weeping for Jackie O. And below the fold was that picture of a body floating on the Kagara River, the one we used later in the *Melrose* project. I was dumbstruck. Again, the world throws you back into a helpless state of saying I can't respond to this, because where are the tears for *this thing* happening in Rwanda?

I was just struck by how poetic and powerful and logical that statement is, "the unexamined life is not worth living." Now go back and look critically at the role of the artist, where you have not been creating the tools you think you've been creating. Sometimes you're just falling into set patterns, so-called creativity, because you are doing it without some kind of knowledge or some kind of poetry driving it. This ongoing critical assessment leads to this view of myself in the world. Stephen Jay Gould (he'll probably hit me on the head, too) talks about Charles Darwin citing the fossil record to verify the gradual transition of evolution. Well, the fossil record also shows a contradiction. It shows 100 million years of the same boring fossils. This interminable replication of the same thing, layer after layer. But then, all of a sudden, there's this "punctuated equilibrium," where this boredom is totally shattered by fantastic life-forms that set the course of evolution for the next millions of years. I try to think of ideas that way, and that I'd rather be in *that* period than following along the path that is being laid.

I feel that being part of this very punctuated moment sets the course, and I feel that we *are* in a jeopardized state, always. There are systems of power that would prefer that people didn't examine, didn't have ideas. I'm not talking about the state apparatus, I'm talking about just the way things go, boring, regular business. So I've led my life to believe in keeping it moving. Let's keep forcing a mutative strategy of thought. To perforate and punctuate and mutate your own self very rapidly away from what you perceive as stasis. Even single-cell E. coli knows how to band together into a colony when it's attacked by our chemicals in the water. We don't even know how to do that yet. I feel that there are so many lessons. Whether human beings exist or not later is not even my concern here. The way we're torturing the world, I don't know. But if there *is* something to be left, then we would hope it could be the grounds for other invention that would make things a little more balanced. There will always be war and torture and pain, but I'm not always quite sure if the other side will be there, the creation of the language. We should be looking at that, or I should be. So this way of being a "submerging artist," as I call it, is exciting to me.

MCi: You obviously take a long view of things.

MCh: Yeah, I think that has occurred. When I thought of *Revival Field*, I was so excited. I said finally I've come up with something that may be finished after I'm dead, and that's okay. I mean, I don't perceive myself as being incredibly original. Whatever psychological profile you could dig out of that is up to you. But it is important to do what you can. These tragedies in the world compel me. If they make you stop, then they are winning. But what you do and how come you do it also has to be understood. I don't always understand it, but I keep trying to think it over.

MCi: A lot of the activists I've spoken to have had one issue that propels them, and often it comes out of a very personal experience. Your issue is really a global one. Is there something specific that it comes out of for you?

MCh: There's one incident I've pointed to many times. I was working on this art piece about Central America, and I was collecting blood in a slaughterhouse. The piece was to be covered with blood and coffee and mud, all this stuff, the products of Central America. Equipped with all the political fever and all the rhetoric and all the history and all the artmaking practices in me, I was stuck in this slaughterhouse because I wanted it to be real. And I remember the guy who was doing the slaughtering was enjoying it way too much; it was very psychologically disturbing. It was not a business to him—he just really got into it. When he threw a goat across the room into this basket where I was working off to the side, and it died in there, I switched and became more like him. I started spraying the life of these animals all over this so-called art piece, and I remember being so psychically disturbed afterwards. Spent. Very troubled. I reassessed my whole position as artist in that moment. I realized what it was. All my life I had perceived myself to be a pacifist and an artist and that I was the alienated one. That is a way of making yourself special. That incident showed me how I'm truly linked, not how special I am, but how common I am. Under the right circumstances, whether it's art or war, I could be just like him, a killer. I could be the worst things that I've seen in a room of people. That probably started my thinking process.

When I was trying to make art, I learned about myself in a way I didn't expect, and that is probably what has led to this direction. It's not so much how special I am: when you think ecologically, you can have no pact with nature if you don't have a pact with our society. *We* are the ones doing it. If people in Harlem say "What are you talking ecology for?" or people in South Central [Los Angeles] say "It's the rain of 9 millimeter bullets, not the rain of acid that's killing us," then something's wrong. So I don't think there *can* be a specific issue. I don't consider myself an activist artist, or an ecological artist, or any of those things. I do a lot of things. I just want to have some contributing relationship in the short time that I have with others, as opposed to with myself. I'm bound to be wrong and bound to be plagued by all the things that I critically look at, and I know that. But at least it's proceeding with some consciousness. When people talk about personal responsibility, I just can't have personal responsibility in ignorance. I don't think I'm even that responsible yet, but I'm trying.

MCi: The trying, it seems to me, has to do with constantly reading and talking to people and learning about what's going wrong. But isn't it also about what's going right?

MCh: Yeah, I think this is where the invention, the art comes in. Not just to be contradictory, but to try to find the way. You're working from a critical assessment of what's happening as opposed to just doing it. I'm making less and less physical work, thinking about these forums, and some are less successful and some are more. I do believe in that. I think I'm more excited by that, because I appreciate that it could be shared. And it's not the way it's always been done. I deeply appreciate the activist work of others, of artists. I think that they are kindred. I think people truly care, but I always fear for myself how muddled I get. You can be blinded as well as enlightened, always, at every turn.

MCi: Who are the people within the art world or outside of it who have inspired you? Are there touchstones out there for you?

MCh: There are weird ones. In the architectural profession, Hassan Fathy wrote *Architecture for the Poor*. He was someone who was reviled in his time, in the sixties, when all young architects were building modernist structures, building a dam, building a skyscraper, building the tallest thing. He reverted back to mud-brick architecture to give people who are poor a decent place to live. His goals were basically that *that's* the highest thing you could build, to work in your community. That's inspirational, that has something to say. It's not always what everybody is doing, and it's not what the spirit of the time is. It's not history that is driving you, it's more just looking at really what is needed.

When I look at what fellow artists are doing, it can be those who are powerfully motivated by a community, like some of the participants in the MOCA show, from Mierle Ukeles to Rick Lowe to Karen Finley. I admire them. But there are also people making singular efforts to express themselves, whether it's a singer, or naive painter, even somebody who is in the art world today who cares nothing about social progress but who exercises the imagination to the degree that something is revealed.

But it's also like my parents. I'm always surprised by them. Somehow, in all your selfishness in becoming an artist (and it can be a very selfish enterprise), they have sacrificed so much out of just sheer love. And what can you say? How can you compare? You learn from all these sources. It can be from the most personal to the larger world, but it will always be the people who are constantly re-igniting and re-enlightening what limited imagination I have. At first I can be kind of cynical, but right now, at this stage, I'm trying to say that this executive producer, this TV film can have it as well. I have to believe that. If anything, the artist can create those paths.

MCi: Sounds like you have a lot of optimism about what's hidden in society.

MCh: *[With a smile]* But I always say that I'm compelled because I'm a pessimist. I believe that human nature has shown its head and can be very, very destructive. While it can be construed as optimism, I keep trying to correct that because I'm not encouraged by world events. It is serious tragedy out there on a daily basis. I'm just trying to say that if we can be an active fulcrum, so it can be tipped the other way occasionally, it would be a lot better. Then the question is still "Why not?" But the world has not been engineered that way. We live basically in a multinational, capital enterprise, but there's really not that much responsibility. There's no one person. It's not about individuals, and here we are as individuals, as artists, talking about responsibility. So it's time to wake up and say what we can be part of and not. Where do we really need to work? It's not where you think usually. It's not that easy, and that's what I'm learning.

Revival Field is still going on. It may happen in my life, maybe not. If a site's remediated, "That'll be the day," as Buddy Holly would say. [The ten-year duration of the Stuttgart installation should be sufficient for remediation.] With the television project, if we walk away saying that some space was created that was never there before, that would be a tremendous success.

MCi: I imagine whether that happens or not, you will keep trying to open that up.

MCh: Yeah, but it's almost like you're just trying to open up yourself. Within a world that would prefer you to be static so it can position you— art history seems to want to do that, too. We are no better. *Stochastic* is the word—it's always multidimensional, fractalized. That's what's real. We may be doing it the wrong way by trying to make it more stable.

MCi: Do you feel that what we call the art world, at this point, is irrelevant to your concerns?

MCh: It is the site that has led me to where I am now, so it's hard to criticize, but, yeah, it may be. I still absolutely have to tap into it in order to have sustenance, but it may not be as relevant to my concerns as it used to be. I always want to believe that the art world being described is not the whole art world. It's the other stubborn branches of it that are probably more important, the ones that are not in the mainstream, not in the art press, not in New York. If we can be an offshoot, then fine. (I always say "we," because I'm working now with larger groups.) I actually don't think about it too much, other than I can pontificate about its ills.

MCi: You told me earlier that at times you had required your dealer to contribute 30 percent of the sales of your work to related social causes. Do you see that there are still concrete ways that you could have an impact on the art world?

MCh: Yeah, but I'm not trying so hard to make an impact on the art world—there's so much more than the art world. Like I've said, if you can educate a child growing up in one of the worst areas in America, you are actually helping yourself. Destructive habitats and destructive nurturing processes are not serving any of our interests. So making an impact on the art world, my world, or whatever world, is the most constructive thing we could do.

September 8, 1996
Athens, Georgia

10

CARL ANTHONY

*FOR MORE THAN TWO DECADES, CARL ANTHONY has been a leader in the
urban land reclamation movement, an effort to revitalize the habitat of our most neglected inner-city neighborhoods. He came to the field in the 1960s, at the peak of
the civil rights movement, as a graduate of Columbia University with a degree in
architecture. A young African American man, he struggled to find a professional path
between the interests of corporate developers and the inner city—between midtown
Manhattan and Harlem. He turned to the inner city but only by carving out his
own path, one that links urban development with environmental and social justice.*

*Anthony founded the San Francisco-based Urban Habitat in 1989. The organi-
zation has helped to expand the agenda of the environmental movement to include
issues of public transportation, housing, health, economic stabilization, and access to
parks and open space. On Earth Day in 1990, Anthony published the first issue of
the* Race/Poverty/Environment *newsletter, a publication that explores the relationship between socioeconomic and environmental concerns, such as the siting of toxic
waste dumps in poor communities of color. From 1992 to 1995, Anthony organized
and chaired EDGE, an alliance of environmental and social justice organizations,
institutions that historically have not been aligned and have even been seen to have
an oppositional relationship. "It's great to say, 'Recycle aluminum,'" says Anthony,
"but what about the people we're throwing away?" Though EDGE no longer oper-
ates as a formal alliance, Urban Habitat continues to play a leadership role in fostering dialogue between the sectors and identifying common ground for collaboration.*

❏ ❏ ❏ ❏ ❏

Claire Peeps: Your work brings together issues of racism, poverty and the
environment. How did you come to make these connections?

Carl Anthony: An interdisciplinary approach has been of interest to me
as far back as I can remember. Sometime around 1959, I decided that I was

really interested in being an architect. Part of my rationale was that some-how I was sent here to be able to use what skills and talents and creativity I might have in the service of the black community. I grew up in Philadel-phia. I went to school in New York during the sixties at Columbia Uni-versity, where I studied architecture, and I was always struck by the dichotomy between the kind of orientation that I was getting as a student at Columbia and the reality of the world of Harlem. So I spent a lot of time trying to knit those two things together.

At one point in my life I actually had a real strong interest in being a painter. I was struck by the creativity of a group of New York artists who were challenging traditional boundaries. It seemed to me intrinsically valu-able, because boundaries are weird. I felt that it was inappropriate for peo-ple to say that this is fine art and that's applied art and that's for the museum and then this is the way you dress and that's supposed to be how you set the table. I always felt these boundaries were missing what to me seemed to be central: how do we live in the world in a way in which we can integrate our desire for beauty with our central mission and purpose? All these disciplines seemed to be going at random in relationship to that goal. It's a Humpty Dumpty problem. One of the things that the West has been very successful in doing over the last 500 years is taking things apart. We know how to take anything apart; the problem is we never know how to put it back together again. One of the strengths of art is its insistence on a point of departure, which is the human being—the anchor and spirit of whatever it is to be human. The artistic perspective offers the con-sciousness of a person looking out over the world and also looking inward. Our disciplines don't usually deal with that very well. As an architect, I was having my own problems with that. This field is not very malleable.

When I graduated from Columbia I was extremely challenged, let's put it that way. And I actually burned my diploma. It took me nine years to get my professional degree in architecture, and I found that the day after graduation, I couldn't even sleep one night with it in the room. So I got rid of it.

CP: Why? What was it that disturbed you about it?

CA: Well, what I discovered was that we were mostly being trained to make our skills available to people or organizations who were quite well-off, corporations, or what I call the nouveaux riches. Because my impulse was to help the black people in the neighborhoods and communities I came from, this thing was totally useless, it wasn't about that. We'd spent a lot of time focusing on creativity and how cute you could be. You could come up with something that was, *wow,* you get all this appreciation for it, but in the service of what? You wouldn't have any control over that. So, there we were, putting a huge amount of emphasis on our individual creativity, and we were for sale.

When I graduated, I was among the top people in my class. I had offers to go work for all these fancy architects. I spent a lot of time trying to figure out how to make this work relate to the reality of New York, but I was further apart at the end than when I started. I also felt a very strange mixture of pride and disgust. I couldn't place it at the time. I was proud of myself for having done this, but I was really disgusted at myself for being proud.

Anyway, I got this fellowship. I took my money and went to Africa. I just said, "Okay, I'm going to forget everything I learned, start all over again." I bought a Volkswagen bus in Europe, put it on a freighter, and went to Dakar, traveled around West Africa. I drove across the base of the desert to Senegal, Mali, Nigeria. I spent time in villages that had a minimal amount of Western influence. I was trying to understand how people related to their environment and I learned a huge amount. I came back and I took a teaching job at Cal Berkeley and then I got interested in what happened to all that creativity in Africa. Art permeates everything there. Everything. The houses, the women paint things on the walls. It's beautiful, they have all these carvings and there are dances and rituals that have to do with the seasons. I mean, it's just everywhere. So now I have another problem. First I had this problem with coming from a university in Harlem, now I've got the Africa/Harlem problem. You go to Harlem and you see all these tenement buildings and broken glass on the street and asphalt. So what happened to all the creativity that people had? I got really obsessed with this. To make a long story short, I decided I was going to go spend some time wandering around in the South to see what happened. I made some really interesting and important discoveries for myself, and I published a few of them; I found, in places like Williamsburg, Virginia, survival of a lot of these African traditions.

By this time, most of the people whom I considered my peers were going out and setting up their offices and doing all these things and I'm still trying to figure out who the hell I am, right?

I decided to open up an office in Oakland. I had it for about eight or ten years. I had a lot of interesting projects. But then I found some very interesting *new* problems. One was that I had hoped that I would be able to maintain a multicultural staff. I found that, with the pressures of just being in business, I couldn't afford to keep them. My staff were mostly white people, who were good, but there were certain parts of me that couldn't develop because they didn't know what I was talking about. I had a partner who was a very talented architect and we ended up parting ways.

He was primarily oriented toward the visual aspect of things, which interests me a great deal, but I wanted to attach that to something else.

I found myself running into a lot of other issues as well. I remember one particularly interesting one was the Santa Fe Realty Company. They owned the Otis land that had been under water in Berkeley; it had been a garbage dump. Over 50 or 75 years, people would dump their garbage there. It ended up being 170 acres that wasn't there before.

The Santa Fe Realty Company wanted to build a whole new downtown on this piece of land. The people in Berkeley got very upset about it and there was a huge political fight. I got hired by the city of Berkeley, along with a couple of other firms, to come up with a new plan for the waterfront—not the Santa Fe plan. This was one of a series of projects that I got involved with in which there was a clash between environmental and development issues. There were a lot of people in Berkeley, by this time, who had been members of the Sierra Club and various groups like this.

The black people in South Berkeley came to the City Council and said, "We want this development because it will give us jobs" (the Santa Fe Realty Company had promised 12,000 jobs but they weren't really real). The environmental people would boo them, "Go back to where you came from!" I felt like I was in Mississippi in the sixties. It was like—whoa!—a lack of *any* compassion. The black people were saying, "Our kids need to find jobs. The only thing they can do is sell dope and hang out on the corner and go to prison. We need something." But on the other hand, it turned out that the environmental people were right, too. Berkeley had a downtown that was dying, sitting right on top of a BART station. Why would you want to build a whole new downtown that would be totally dependent on automobile traffic, that would even be in competition to the one that wasn't working?

I thought about this a lot and got more and more involved with a group called Urban Ecology in Berkeley that was pointing out that we really need to rebuild our cities in balance with nature. A lot of the environmental problems that we have come from the way we live in cities. Look at Los Angeles. I found out from the South Coast Air Quality Management District that one percent of global warming comes from the South Coast development. It has to do with craziness in the way it's built—70 percent paving for cars. It doesn't make any sense. As we began to challenge the more established environmental groups, it began to become apparent that most of the people who were really suffering from the consequences of this lack of environmental consciousness were poor people. That's where all the pollution was. It's also true in reverse on the resource side, which nobody's really talking about much. If you live in Danville, which is a fairly wealthy place, you may use 500 gallons of water a day to water your lawn and your swimming pool and the number of showers you take. If you live in Oakland, it's 40 gallons. If you're homeless, it's 5 gallons. Energy is the same way. If you live in the suburbs, you travel six, seven, eight times the number of vehicle miles per year than if you lived in the city. There's a very high correlation between income and poverty, exposure to environmental hazards and the lack of consumption. So working in collaboration with other groups around the country in the environmental justice movement, we began to see a pattern. But for these struggles around environmental issues to be truly liberating, there has to be a core of human spirit that is a point of departure and the point of return for everything we do. I've been involved in social justice movements that didn't do that over the years, and I saw in this instance that people were getting lost.

CP: Which movements are you referring to?

CA: Well, the civil rights movement and a lot of the related social justice movements. In the beginning, the civil rights movement was kind of simpleminded in the sense that the goals were fairly obvious and innocuous: to have separate drinking fountains, to have to be sitting in the back of the bus, or not to be able to have a hamburger in Woolworth's. It was really very basic.

As the sixties wore on, the movement started to get closer to the core of the issues, but it also started to get really complicated. We got into separatism and cultural identity issues, and we also moved down the path toward militancy. There was a huge amount of emphasis on trying to prove that you were more militant than the next guy. We started out, again, in a fairly simpleminded way: can we have a boycott or can we do direct action, protest or picket somebody? And then it kind of went into more aggressive forms. Toward the end of the decade, there was a huge amount of anger and the bombing of buildings.

Looking back over that time, there were some people who, in spite of all, maintained some sense of humanity. But it wasn't very easy to do because there was a lot of peer pressure and a lot of reasons to be very angry. We were angry and we couldn't see, for example, the white working class and their pain. We just couldn't identify with them. Then, of course, the anger kind of spent itself and most of America decided that they weren't going to go that way anyway, which is one of the points where the environmental movement came in and kind of saved people. It became a cause that was safer and, at the same time, you could still be indignant about it.

It was striking to me how a wave of sentiment could cause us to lose our sense of bearings. After that, we got 12 years of Reagan. And it's partly because I think we didn't manage very well (I won't say totally because I don't want to blame the victim). We didn't really understand.

Now that I've gotten involved with the environmental justice movement I'm in a different place because I really, really feel the anger but I also feel the importance of people taking the high road. I remember a lot of us used to laugh at Martin Luther King's nonviolence and say, "Well, what is this fool going down there and getting beat up for? Why doesn't he fight back?" Now I can see that his whole point was to actually meet his adversaries on a higher level, that you actually embody the principles of the kind of world you want to create, that you don't sink to the level of the people whom you're opposed to. I sort of understood it then but I didn't really understand how important it is.

I had a moment of personal revelation after I closed my architecture office about seven or eight years ago. A friend of mine came to town. He was putting together a conference on something he called Places for Peace; it was a very creative thing. I worked with him, did a lot of reading about the environment and ecology. I read a book by the poet Wendell Barry called *Standing By Words*. It's about the importance of decorum, about how modern art seems to have lost any sense of this. He had a description of Alexander Pope's *Essay on Man*. Pope had created this hierarchy called the Great Chain of Being: angels were at the top, weeds were at the bottom, and man was in the middle. As I was reading this, I was trying to figure out where I fit in the scheme. It was an important moment for me because I realized that I had placed myself just below the white people. I said to myself, "Wait a minute, hold it! *I'm* doing this; there's nobody else in the room here. I'm reading this book of poems and I'm putting myself just below the white people?" Then I read another book called *The Dream of the Earth,* by Thomas Barry in which he talked about the evolution of life on the planet from the very beginning. I had a moment of revelation that as a human being, I stood in a long chain of life and racism was just a horrendous mistake that some people had made over the last couple hundred years. While I could see the mistake they had made, and while I could identify with the need to correct that mistake, I didn't have to actually internalize it. I didn't have to be just below the white people. I didn't need it anymore.

To make a long story short, a friend of mine talked me into coming to Earth Island. I was reluctant, but I ended up coming over here and starting a program for them. I ended up being chair of the board. We work a lot with community-based organizations in the Bay Area. Our mission is to help multicultural urban environmental leadership work toward socially just and sustainable communities in the San Francisco Bay area. We're interested in a holistic approach to things. We don't force people to make false choices. We can be against toxic waste dumps in the inner city and still like to walk along the beach and care about birds. Why do we have to create these false dichotomies? We can build a vision based on the strength of all the different cultures in the San Francisco Bay Area that embraces what we have learned through the more established environmental movement.

If the spotted owl is an indicator of the ecological damage that's been done in the ancient forest, the crack baby is an indicator of the lack of ecological health in our cities. We need to somehow be able to see the connection between those things. The pattern of civilization—the things that we make, the things that we create, the work we're doing—is going in the wrong direction. It's not pro-life, it's against life. We try to embrace whatever is beautiful, whatever's strong, whatever's powerful and use some of those insights to help people who don't seem to have a future or vision in life, so when they look out over the horizon they see a future for themselves as people who may have some responsibility for helping us move the whole damn thing in a more positive and constructive direction. We've worked with a number of groups in the Bay Area. There's a fair amount that has to do with direct action and protest but there's also just a lot of dialogue.

CP: You created the EDGE program, which is an alliance of ethnic and environmental organizations. How did you get that started? How do you actually push the movement forward?

CA: We started the program in response to the *Race/Poverty/Environment* newsletter. There had been a lot of criticism of the more established environmental groups because they didn't have any people of color. We felt that it was very important to try to create a forum for dialogue between the more established groups and the civil rights groups, so we created a statewide organization in which the members of the board were actually representatives of their groups—the Japanese American Citizen's League, the Urban League, the Sierra Club and so on. Ten organizations were represented: half environmental and half from communities of color.

CP: Has it been hard to articulate common ground between the groups?

CA: I think the resistance occurs because our brains, our thinking are so compartmentalized. It goes back to the Humpty Dumpty problem; we think of these issues as independent of one another. For example, the EDGE people are working a lot now on immigration and population issues. We thought it just wasn't appropriate to have a bunch of white people walking around saying that the population's growing too fast. They couldn't look people of color in the eye. On the other side, we felt that people of color were not paying sufficient attention to what some people think is probably the most urgent problem on the planet. So we insisted, "Hey, guys! You have to talk to each other. If the population problem is as important as you say it is, racism has gotta go. If it isn't important, we've got to stop talking about it and get to something that really is."

CP: What is the role of constituency-building in what you do?

CA: At the beginning, it really had a lot to do with people of color. When we first started, there weren't very many people of color who were consciously identified with environmental issues. If I saw a black guy in the elevator, I'd say, "Hey, brother, let me show you something." I'd just talk to people in the weirdest places. I had a really remarkable experience on Earth Day 1990, when the first issue of the *Race/Poverty/Environment* newsletter came out. I was sitting on the bus, on San Pablo Avenue, and I had a pile of newsletters on my lap. There was a lot of hype in the media about Earth Day. There was a black guy who was sitting behind me. He looked over my shoulder and said, "Hey, brother, what's that you got there?" And I said, "Oh, it's just something we're working on." He said, "Do you mind if I have one?" I said, "Sure, you can have one." So I gave him a copy of this newsletter, right? There was also a guy sitting next to me. He opened it up because there was something about the Cypress Freeway and the earthquake. They started arguing about this and he said, "See, it says that the Cypress Freeway collapsed and the community was divided in half. Other people on the bus joined in, "Can I have one of your newsletters?" So there were about five people on the bus reading this newsletter. I mean, I wasn't doing anything. So I thought, I'll try this tomorrow and see what happens. I got on the same bus and it started again. I got off the bus to catch the 51, going up University Avenue, and a guy actually got off the bus and asked the bus driver to wait for him. He ran across the street to me and said, "Can I have one of these?" I gave it to him, he ran back, he got on the bus. The next day I had them in the back of a taxicab. The box was open and the taxicab driver said, "Can I have a couple of those?" What it showed to me was really clear: what the newsletter spoke to was an unanswered need to help people understand how environmental issues were relevant to them.

CP: If you simply talk about the "environmental" issue, for example, it may conjure up an image of affluent people who don't want oil wells off the coast of Santa Barbara. If you attach the words "race" and "poverty," people can make the leap.

CA: Yes. We started telling people, "Okay, it's fine to talk about recycling your newspapers, your bottles and cans. But in Washington D.C., in Philadelphia, in Boston, in Detroit, in Los Angeles, they're throwing away streets, they're throwing away houses, they're throwing away schools, they're throwing away firehouses, they're throwing away whole communities of people." To some extent, it's great to say, "Recycle aluminum," but what about the people we're throwing away? We don't have to say that's wrong, but we have to say, "Hey, our system has reached the point where the extraction of profit for a certain group of people has become so dominant that anything that doesn't accomplish that is out." There are connections that have become extremely obvious to me, but five years ago they were not obvious.

CP: What are some of those connections?

CA: Consumption. For the last 50 years under the Defense Highway Act, every time you bought a gallon of gas, you spent five cents to build a freeway—a freeway for a lot of the white people to leave the inner city, take their money and their resources with them, to build the suburbs. In building the suburbs, they destroyed the farmland. Farming became integrated into the global market, and at the same time, we saw the abandonment of the city by this mass of people.

Today, 86 percent of the European Americans in this country live in neighborhoods where less than one percent of the residents are people of color. The only information they have about people of color is what they see on TV. The reality of a Rodney King, or me for that matter, is an abstraction. They don't really know it. They have no direct experience. So when it comes to practical matters, like voting or immigration, people are reaching conclusions that are just totally ridiculous. "There are too many people in California," they say. Well, the immigrants are not the ones who are chopping down the trees, they're not the ones who are destroying the salmon runs. If you have a situation in which 35 percent of the world's resources are being consumed by people in the United States, by that logic, 35 percent of the world ought to be living here. To be blaming undocumented workers, who are necessary so that we can buy a head of lettuce at a price that we can afford, is a misallocation of the real problem. The real problem is that our economy depends on putting Pepsi-Cola ads all over the damn world and having naked women sit on top of automobiles telling everybody that this is a good life, so everybody gets hooked and they want to live like that. We all have these terribly wasteful lifestyles because our advertising and our economy depend on making people want things they

don't need. We may not be able to face that, we may not be able to do anything about that. But let's not blame somebody running across the border
to try to find a way to connect with family or have a better life. That's not
what's causing the environmental degradation. It's that we haven't found a
way to live, within a set of limits, a good life.

We need to come to terms with getting our necessities without having
to have this class of exploited people, whom we have to somehow keep at
a distance. Almost all the nurturing functions of our culture that are really
important have been delegated to, "out of sight, out of mind." We have dis-
placed so much of the public consciousness by this imbalanced emphasis
on materialism. We have very little experience of what it means to be
born, about raising children, how to deal with old people, dying. None of
this has been put very much in the center of our attention. Yet we are
spending millions of dollars on equipment that keeps somebody alive for
ten minutes, after they're 85 years old, in order to have an organ transplant.
When my mother died, I actually had the good fortune of being in the
room and holding her when she breathed her last breath. That was one of
the most beautiful moments in my life. AIDS is a terrible, terrible thing,
but at least it tells people, "Hey! Pay attention to how you die." Pay attention. You know, you love somebody and you're going to lose them.

I think one way that artists can help us is to have clarity about who we
are, what we're for and what we're against. We deal a lot, in our multicultural lives, with pieces of our communities that we know nothing about.
People have come here from the Philippines who may be physicians who
can't get jobs in our medical establishments. So they're taxicab drivers. We
don't know who the hell they are. In our midst we have all of this strength
of experience, but we have no idea. If somebody could just tell us the story
of who our neighbors are, that might help us find a way out of some of
our problems. It's not just the people of color, it's even the white people—
we don't know who they are! People who came from a dairy farm in Wis-
consin to Los Angeles—what has that transition been? What does their
story mean? Artists can help us to see that, I think.

August 17, 1994
San Francisco, California

11

MARY ELLEN BEAVER

As Mary Ellen Beaver puts it, "One of the greatest sins in this country is to be poor." For more than 30 years, this white-haired grandmother of five has devoted herself to countering this notion as an advocate for the thousands of migrants who work for little pay and under substandard conditions on farmlands of the eastern and southern United States. She has done this as a paralegal for a variety of legal service agencies, working long and unconventional hours in far-flung, isolated places, often under dangerous conditions, to collect information that can be used both in and out of court to leverage better working and living conditions for migrants. One of her former bosses, lawyer Greg Schell of Florida Legal Services, has called her "the best farm worker outreach paralegal in the country," and she has not only been cited for her work by several legal organizations but also has received a medal of honor from Pope John Paul II.

Beaver spends much of her time at the camps where migrants are housed so she can speak to them directly and intervene quickly if their rights are being violated. She says that the most common offenses are wage violations, though she has been known to help workers flee the camps when they are being beaten or otherwise abused. She is famous for keeping copious records on everyone she meets, her philosophy being that "Just because they are poor and have nothing doesn't mean they're not important."

When Beaver was interviewed, she was working out of Belle Glade, Florida, a small town in south central Florida that is one of the poorest in the U.S. and also home base for one of the largest concentrations of migrant farm workers in the country. She left there in 1996 but continues her work as a paralegal for the Pennsylvania Farm Worker Project of Philadelphia Legal Assistance. Though she says she would still be working for Schell in Belle Glade "if I were independently wealthy, because there's so much to do down there" (she sometimes had to work without pay for lack of funding), the move has enabled her to return to the farm in rural Pennsylvania where she raised her seven children and where she first decided to take up the cause of migrant workers.

☐　☐　☐　☐　☐

Marie Cieri: How long have you been working with migrant workers?

Mary Ellen Beaver: Since 1969.

MC: I understand that when you started out, you lived in a rural community and observed that migrant farm workers there were not being treated well.

MEB: I lived on a farm. I started out very naively. I used to see all these black people going by in buses. The local migrant ministry committee of the Pennsylvania Council of Churches would put little notices in the paper: "We need health kits, we need shoes, we need people to take people in the camps to the doctor." At that point I had seven children, and the youngest was three years old. I was a member of the Council of Catholic Women in the Diocese of Harrisburg, and I thought why couldn't the Catholic people work with the [Protestant] Pennsylvania Council of Churches? And then I started visiting camps with the priest and sisters and the Presbyterians and Methodists.

The workers eventually knew that I lived in the country and would come to my house and tell me they weren't getting paid and were being threatened with beating if they wanted to leave. I literally had not a clue. What could you do? At the same time, I was active in the local parish and in the schools. That's all I had time to do with raising my family.

Then the Council of Catholic Women was having its annual convention in Bloomsburg, Pennsylvania, which is the largest town to where I live. They asked me to organize a workshop about migrant farm workers, and I knew nothing. But a priest in charge of the Hispanic ministry helped me because he knew people who had labor camps, and he had some experience dealing with migrant farm workers. He took me to meetings in Harrisburg of the Governor's Interdepartmental Council for Migrant Farm Workers.

The council had programs in migrant education, health, and day care. When you went to the meetings in Harrisburg, it sounded wonderful. Pennsylvania was a garden spot for migrant workers! But once I started finding out that things were not what they were saying, it was outrageous. They had a migrant education program, but I found out a lot of these people were related to growers or had growers as friends.

MC: You mean the state officials?

MEB: Yes, the state officials. So all this was like window dressing. They were not really advocates. In fact, it was the crew leaders' children who would go to these special education programs and summer recreation programs. As time went on, there were fewer black farm workers' families that would come.

MC: You must have made a decision at some point that you wanted to devote more of your time to helping the farm workers and their families.

MEB: I just knew things weren't right. By that time, in 1969, we had given up the farming and sold most of the machinery, but we kept the land, thank God. It was a struggle. My husband had taken on a part-time truck driving job. He belonged to the Teamsters Union. He had good pay. We had health insurance. He had a pension. Even so, it was a struggle to raise your family and make ends meet. The fact that people who were working in the fields couldn't even get paid . . . there had to be some way to deal with that. I didn't know how.

In 1974, Legal Services started up in the area where I live. In 1975, the Pennsylvania Department of Community Affairs designated $100,000 to provide legal services to migrant farm workers for one year. So they started the program in Bloomsburg and Gettysburg. The lawyer was a very bright young woman, Justina Wasicek, and they hired a young man as a paralegal who was real gung ho, Mike Folloni, who had just graduated from Harvard, had spent time in Guatemala, and could speak Spanish. But they didn't know what to do. They didn't have any guidance from anyone. There was just, "We hired you, here's the money, good luck."

So what they did was go after all the labor contractors who were selling alcohol on the camps. It took a month to convince the Pennsylvania Liquor Control Board to prosecute. It was hard to convince them. Nobody wants any part of that. Who wants to deal with all these dirty people, you know? They think migrant workers are dirty. They put them in a camp with no showers and no toilets and no way to keep clean and then blame them for being dirty.

Simultaneously that year, the American Friends Service Committee had a contract with the State of Pennsylvania to investigate the food processors, the farmers, the labor contractors and the workers, and they hired ten really great young people. A bunch of them came into our area, and in fact, some of them stayed at our house. I can't imagine anybody wanting to stay at our house. We had one bathroom, seven children, Fresh Air children from the city, cousins, you know, wall to wall. It was a big farmhouse, but still.

MC: Sounds like fun.

MEB: We had a lot of fun *[laughter]*.

MC: This was all shortly after Cesar Chavez's work was in the news, wasn't it?

MEB: Yes. My oldest son was either a junior or a senior then. Chavez was promoting the lettuce boycott. One of his people wanted to come and talk to students. The only high school in the area that would even hear of it was the Catholic high school where my son went. So I remember taking that man over there, and he showed a movie and talked to the kids. See, California has a state law that gives farm workers the right to organize. Arizona also has a law, but the rest of the country, good luck.

MC: There still isn't a law?

MEB: No. Farm workers are not covered by the National Labor Relations Act. They can organize all they want to, but off with their heads. They hire new people the next day.

MC: So there can't be a union?

MEB: No.

MC: Does that also mean they can't band together in groups and protest?

MEB: Well they certainly can do it. But there's no protection under the law.

MC: Do they give a reason for excluding farm workers?

MEB: Well, the law was passed in 1935, and the farm interests have always been powerful. They're in charge. There's nobody more organized than farmers. They have all kinds of associations. In Pennsylvania, there's the Pennsylvania Farmers Association, Pennsylvania Mushroom Growers, Pennsylvania Apple Growers, Pennsylvania Vegetable Growers, etc. And they all know each other. On a national level, the American Farm Bureau Federation is strong and powerful.

MC: I imagine when you visit the farms and migrant labor camps you find there are a number of growers who don't pay minimum wage. Then there probably are some that do and who treat workers better than others.

MEB: There are.

MC: In the states where you've worked, what's your sense of the percentages of farmers and farm corporations who treat their workers according to the law?

MEB: Oh dear. I would say, for the most part, workers are not paid correctly. But it varies from place to place. What has given the farmers impetus is getting sued. If it costs them enough, they'll do it right.

MC: Having the legal weapon . . .

MEB: . . . is the only way to help the workers. That's my conclusion. You're not protected to organize. The farmers don't have to honor any kind of agreement the workers have amongst themselves to stick together. But the law is very clear on how they are to be recruited and paid.

In 1983 the law was changed to say that the farmer and crew leader are joint employers. They're both responsible. And the test is an economic test: where does the money come from to pay the workers? It comes from the farmer. The crew leader on his own can't do anything. We just lost big time on an appeal to the Eleventh Circuit on this. The three-judge panel said that a certain crew leader was the employer because he directed the people in the fields, which is totally wrong under the law. We're getting ready to appeal it to the Supreme Court.

When we bring suit, what we try to do, ideally, is say, "Mr. Farmer, you pay that person directly." Because of deductions for beer, wine, food, transportation, whatever, the farmer has taken the person's wages below the minimum wage. Write a check to that person so he can get his own money.

MC: Right, so he can make the choice about where he's going to spend it.

MEB: Yes. But again, they have ways to deal with that. "Oh, here, sign this on Friday." On Saturday this labor contractor goes off to the bank somewhere and gets all the workers' money and gives them their change. They still do it in South Carolina. It's a lot less prevalent around here. We've had strong legal services in Belle Glade for many years. The workers' unemployment is paid in. Their Social Security is paid in. But when you give this former migrant worker, who is now a labor contractor, a couple thousand dollars and say, "Here, pay these people," where does it go? Into his pocket.

MC: I'd like to know how you do what you do and how it fits into the legal system of helping the farm workers.

MEB: Well, what we do is visit labor camps and talk to workers and give out booklets on their rights. We say, "We're from Legal Services." "What kind of service is that?" Some of them think we're going to hold religious services. We explain that we can help people get paid correctly. If you're a farm worker and you're picking with the piece rate, if you don't equal the minimum wage at the end of the week, they have to pay you build-up. If you're working in a packing house and getting paid by the hour, you still get paid if you have waiting time. A light goes on—they never heard of it before. Then we say, "Here's a book to tell you about the laws that protect farm workers. There's a place in the back of the book where you can write down how many hours you work a day and so on. Keep your own record—it's a very good way to see if you're getting paid correctly." Some guys will do it, and they'll call us when they leave the camp (because there are no phones there). If a crew leader doesn't like us being on the camp, and we are two people, one of us engages the crew leader while the other runs around talking to the workers.

MC: So you usually go in twos?

MEB: It's good if you can, but I started going on the camps in South Carolina by myself in 1992, even on Sundays. For the American black people who drink, the weekends are not good, especially Saturdays. They've been paid, they don't often leave the camp, they don't have their own transportation. There's a lot of economic and physical abuse. The Hispanic groups often have relatives with a car and can get around better. There are so many undocumented people among them, though, that they will put up with anything because they are afraid they will get deported if they complain. We don't investigate their immigration status. But if we file a complaint about wages to the Department of Labor, the Department of Labor has an agreement with the Immigration Service.

MC: And they'll investigate.

MEB: Yes. So in that situation it's more difficult to get people to complain. But if it's bad enough, they'll walk for days to get off the camp. They've been doing that up in South Carolina, walking over to Augusta, Georgia, where Catholic Social Services is.

MC: How far is that?

MEB: Thirty-five miles. A long way. Or they walk into Aiken. They've been promised they can make $300 a week, that there's even a swimming pool in the camp. Fairy tales. So when they get off the camps, they call us. We try to get the Department of Labor to interview people. They've been very resistant in the past, but we've gotten some cooperation since last year when the new administration came in.

MC: Has it gotten better?

MEB: We think so. It's a combination of our putting pressure on the people in the regional offices, and sometimes we're able to get the media interested in abuses that are going on. There was an instance in South Carolina last year where the woman in the Department of Labor office in Columbia wouldn't interview the workers, we put the pressure on, they heard the media was coming, and they sent a strike force of 17 people into three counties to clean house. That was the first time they ever did anything.

MC: So you've been able to use the media.

MEB: Oh, absolutely! They've been wonderful. In 1991, we interviewed workers at the Catholic Social Services office in Augusta. Catholic Social Services was crying poverty. They had spent $35,000 in the past four years on bus fare for all the people leaving the peach camps in South Carolina. They were getting 15 people a day. So we sent a letter to the South Carolina Peach Council saying, "Oh, we've spent *x* number of dollars to send people home who have been working in the peach camps; how about reimbursing us?" We also called up NBC who had been down here in Belle Glade doing an exposé on the sugarcane industry. I called the producer and said, "Margaret [Margaret Mackavoy], this is what's going on in South Carolina. Why don't you come up here?" She did, and they did an exposé of the peach business. Frank Heflin, a reporter for *The State* newspaper, the biggest newspaper in South Carolina, got himself on one of the labor crews and did a big series of articles. So we had Frank's articles, we had the letter to the Peach Council, we had the NBC exposé. We caused all this uproar. It was wonderful.

MC: Can you see concrete results from that?

MEB: Well, they hired a man named Dan Bautista to work for the state under the Commissioner of Labor. He spoke Spanish and was a real good person. But he just quit this year because they gave him no power to do anything, just listen to workers and try to talk to farmers. It didn't change anything.

MC: You're working in a lot of different states now besides Florida. Is that because of a perception by Legal Services that there are major problems in these areas, but there aren't local entities to deal with them?

MEB: That's correct, and it's because workers who come back here tell us they didn't get paid in South Carolina, they didn't get paid in Georgia. "The guy took our money." "We were in an accident, and there was no insurance on the van."

MC: Do a lot of migrant workers around the country end up at some point in the year working here?

MEB: Yes.

MC: And you talk to them about experiences they've had in different parts of the country?

MEB: We do, yes. At this point, after doing a lot of outreach and giving out a lot of cards and so on, half the farm workers on the East Coast have our phone number. We're getting a few more lawyers now, but the best we can promise the workers is to file a complaint immediately with the Department of Labor and try to get them to investigate. Whether we can really bring suit or not depends on how terrible the situation was and how many people were involved.

MC: Legal Services in Florida can bring a suit for a group in another state?

MEB: If we're not licensed there, we have to get a lawyer there to sign off on it. The problem in South Carolina has been that Marvin Feingold, the lawyer, has been the program for the whole state. He has no outreach.

MC: He doesn't have somebody like you?

MEB: No, so I get loaned out to him, and that's worked well. But we didn't dare do that under the old administration because the farmers could easily say "What's that woman from Florida doing up here?"

MC: To whom would they say that?

MEB: To the Legal Services Corporation, which doles out the money. You have to have them be in sympathy with what you're trying to accomplish.

Actually, it's Florida farm workers that we're seeing for the most part in South Carolina.

MC: How long are the workers usually in one place?

MEB: The peach crop in South Carolina starts in May with the early peaches and goes through to the end of August. But it depends on the weather. Last summer there was a terrible drought. It didn't rain for 55 days in South Carolina, so that cut the season short. The tomato harvest in northeastern Pennsylvania starts about the second week in August and goes on until about the third week in September, so it's a short time. In those states it's hard if you have to concentrate your outreach and services during the season.

Now they're all going to North Carolina to do sweet potatoes. That's where they have the most abuse. And other ones are going to start to go up to do apples in the northern states. For the majority of workers on the East Coast, Florida is the home state. This is where they come back to in the winter time.

MC: How do the workers get from one place to another?

MEB: They travel on buses or vans. The Department of Labor for years had regulations for high insurance on these vehicles so that if the people were in accidents, someone would pay the hospital bills and pay the migrant workers when they weren't able to work. But they didn't enforce that. Here in Florida we have had constant accidents in the wintertime with people who have taken the seats out of the van and put in boards on blocks or had workers just sit on the floor. When you get hit, there's no protection.

MC: These vehicles belong to the farm owners?

MEB: No. They're owned by the labor contractors who are employed by the farm owners.

MC: I see, so the labor contractors are the middlemen who take groups of workers and hire them out.

MEB: That's right. They recruit people to work.

MC: Are they also the people who go down to Jamaica to get workers?

MEB: Well, no. Jamaica's a different story because that's a foreign country. The people who come here to do the sugarcane have to be approved by the Department of Labor on the basis that there's nobody here who will do that work. The sugar companies have been bringing people in for 50 years and cheating them out of everything.

MC: Do the Jamaicans come only for sugar?

MEB: No, they come for apples too. They're H2A workers—that's the designation given them by the immigration service. They come here on a special immigration contract that says they can only work on certain jobs, and then they have to go back.

MC: Are the abuses against people from outside the country worse than they are for citizens or permanent residents?

MEB: The physical abuse hasn't been bad, but the cheating on wages and workers' compensation has been astronomical. The United States government is looking the other way while the sugar companies do it. It's regulated by the federal government, supposedly, but they cave into the sugar companies, and they have for years. They found a way to cheat the very poorest people. They know it doesn't matter what they do to them: they will still come back and work because there is nothing in Jamaica. These sugar companies know that the $3,000 or $4,000 they are able to earn in a year is big money back home.

MC: I'd like to get back to the evolution of how you do what you do. You started out as somebody who didn't know very much about the farm companies, the farm workers, and the conditions under which they worked. At some point you realized that the best recourse was through legal systems. Now you're here at Florida Rural Legal Services. How did your methods evolve over a period of 25 years and why? *[MEB laughter].* I know you've become famous for that pad of paper you carry and for taking extensive notes. [At the time of the interview, Beaver had compiled more than 200 steno pads containing information about thousands of workers.]

MEB: Well, yes, I do. Even back in Pennsylvania, people started calling me, like the Red Cross or some minister, asking if I had heard of this person because his mother died or something happened to his family or whatever. That's why I started writing down names of people. In the beginning, we couldn't do much except keep them alive and get them to the next place.

I started keeping notes, and I've become much better at it because I've had a lot of practice.

When you write names down you don't always know. It's amazing how they come back through the years. In fact, I ran into a man two winters ago, a little old raggedy white man, God bless him, his name is Lawrence Cole. He was in Pennsylvania in the late seventies. The reason I remember him is that he had broken his jaw, they had wired it shut in another state, and the wires were growing into his face. So I had to take him down to the hospital, and they were able to help him. In fact, I had to go back on a Sunday to pick up his false teeth which he had left on this terrible ragged mattress that was in the camp. The crew leader was walking around with a big club to keep order in the camp. Two years ago in Florida, lo and behold, I went into this horrible room up on this labor camp called Spuds that used to be a prisoner-of-war camp. I went in to give out cards and books and said, "What's your name, sir?" "Lawrence Cole." The same person! I could not believe that man was still alive.

And I've had workers do the same with me. About the same time, I went to Arcadia [Florida] to pick up someone who was running away from the crew leader, and I didn't want to stay long because I didn't know where the crew leader was. When someone's trying to leave, the crew leader might not be happy about it, and you don't want to make a lot of conversation. I noticed these guys I hadn't seen before and said, "I'm Mary Ellen Beaver from Legal Services, here's a card if you have a problem with your pay—" This guy looks at me and says, "Mary Ellen Beaver, Bloomsburg, Pennsylvania, Leroy Thomas." It was a worker named Johnny Cook, and Leroy Thomas was his crew leader in Bloomsburg in the late seventies. He remembered me!

MC: So a lot of what you do depends on keeping records.

MEB: Keeping track of people. I think so, because every person is important. Just because they are poor and have nothing doesn't mean they're not important.

MC: You were also, though, keeping track of crew leaders and farm companies?

MEB: Well, I was. We didn't have any Legal Services for farm workers in Pennsylvania when I worked for the Pennsylvania Council of Churches. All we could do was help people get away. We passed a law in 1978 to give us access to labor camps and to see that people got paid correctly. The same year we passed the law, Dick Thornburgh got elected governor in Pennsylvania, and the whole thing went down the drain. He positively ignored the law, wouldn't have people enforce it. He ignored letters from the church groups and the League of Women Voters, who were requesting him to reconvene his Governor's Committee.

I decided: enough of this. I went to the women's legislative conference in Harrisburg and got Mrs. Thornburgh in a corner about this. "Oh, I was just visiting labor camps the other week," she said. I asked her, "Well, where were you?" "Well, I was in the mushroom area, but those camps were the most horrible places." I said, "Well, Mrs. Thornburgh, they wouldn't show you the worst. . . ." I knew what she thought was a terrible place was the prime camp down there. I told her we had not been able to reach Governor Thornburgh. She said, "Well, send me a letter." So I did, and her husband got one of his flacks to send a letter back to us saying, "The State of Pennsylvania has a law on the books, and there's a committee created with this law to administer it"—never admitting that the committee was not in use. But it *was* something in writing from the administration saying we don't give a damn about the whole thing. The only way we ever got them to enforce the law was when we were able to raise money and sued the state in 1983.

MC: So early on you tried to talk to some people in power or near people in power. Do you do that now as part of a strategy developed with the lawyers?

MEB: It's sort of my own. I'm at the point where I'm not listening to the lawyers right now because I'm very angry about this whole situation with the sugarcane cutters. When they had the immigration reform in 1986, anyone who worked 90 days in the field from May 1 of '85 to May 1 of '86 could apply for amnesty if he didn't have the correct papers. The sugarcane workers were excluded from that. Legal Services went to bat and got them put in the law. Then the government appealed it with the help of the sugarcane companies, and they were taken out again. To this day, I get calls from sugarcane workers saying, "I long to see my family; I can't go home." Their work permits have expired, and the sugar companies opposed them getting green cards because then they could work for anybody—they wouldn't have to continue cutting cane. The sugar companies presented agricultural experts who testified that sugar is not a vegetable and it's not perishable; therefore, these guys aren't entitled to that green card. Greg Schell and the other lawyers all say there's no way anybody is going to get a green card, that it's an immigration problem. That makes me all the more determined. It's a question of justice—they've been cheated out of it. There has to be some way. I won't accept that.

MC: Do you know what you're going to do?

MEB: No. But in 1991 the Okeelanta Sugar Company kept promising us we could go on their camps, but they weren't letting us. So we arranged for Jim Green, an ACLU lawyer, to represent us. I went on the biggest camp, where there are 2,000 men, on a Saturday night and started giving out books and cards, and I got through half of one barracks and down the other side before they found me. If I had been some young whippersnapper they would have removed me physically. They didn't know what to do with me. They said, "You can't be here." And I said, "Listen, these people are tenants. They have the right to receive visitors, and I'm not going to leave." There were five people from the sugar company, and they were almost jumping up and down, they were so mad.

They sent three of them off to call somebody and left two of them to watch me. So I just stood there and waited. They came back and said they'd like me to talk to their lawyers, and I thought, why do I need to talk to their lawyers? So I said, no, I was going to call Jim Green. Jim Green told me to just keep right on going. So I did. I gave out two big boxes full of books and cards. They didn't know what to do with me.

MC: The law had passed that allowed you to go?

MEB: Not in Florida. But we decided to challenge it.

MC: I see. And you were the challenge?

MEB: Yes.

MC: Did they try to arrest you?

MEB: Well, that's what we had hoped. But they wouldn't do it. Instead, Okeelanta filed a suit to keep us off, and we countersued. The suits went on for quite a while, but the upshot is we have an access law now in Florida.

The funny thing was that when a reporter called Greg Schell to see what was going on, Greg said, "You mean to tell me that this 60-year-old grandmother who has a medal from the pope for helping migrant farm workers is going to disrupt this big international company?" And that made the business page headlines in the *Palm Beach Post*. Seeing that, another large company, U.S. Sugar, immediately said, "Oh you can go on all *our camps,* we have no problem." They didn't want any bad publicity. They hadn't been paying the correct workers' compensation, back wages, and transportation fees. They then voluntarily agreed to pay in exchange for our not suing them. They started correcting all of their abuse. But Okeelanta never agreed to any of that.

MC: The information that you collect from workers about the conditions on the camps—is it primarily handed over to the lawyers? Do you strategize with them about what might be done with it?

MEB: Yes, we do. After working this long with Greg Schell, who's a very good lawyer, we know what to ask people: how they were recruited, what kind of vehicle they're transported in, how they're paid, do they get pay receipts, do they get their money free and clear or do they just get change after the crew leader takes out all the deductions? But we haven't had enough troops to bring enough lawsuits. We interview everyone who leaves a camp and say we'll file a complaint for you with the Department of Labor. We're not sure what else we're going to do until the season's over and we see how many people we have. If we think we have a strong case, and the complaints are from people we can find, we'll bring suit. We have to see how many people are solid, meaning a person who has a good home address. We always ask: "Who's someone you contact at least once a year? Give us that person's address because then if we can't find you, they may know where you are." We've been able to keep pretty good track of people. But people also have to know they can trust you. If we tell somebody we're going to do something, we do it. Or we say we're not sure; we don't want to fool them, either.

MC: I imagine there's some amount of fear about talking to you. How do you deal with that? How do you get the workers to cooperate with you so you can help them?

MEB: It depends on who's standing around. If there's nobody that they trust around, you can tell from the look they give you. They know who the crew leader's henchmen are, so sometimes they will only talk to you after they leave the camp.

MC: Are the workers who complain afraid of going back to the camp?

MEB: I'll tell you, if they live in the same community as the crew leader, they're afraid. They've told me that. "This guy will pay somebody $25 to beat me up on Saturday night or worse." It depends on the worker. Some guys are not afraid. They've been doing farm work for a long time and just want their money. But others are rather cowed because all they've known all their lives is rejection. They're afraid because they know this guy has power and has people. All crew leaders have henchmen. They sell crack cocaine and beer and do the beatings so the crew leader keeps his hands clean and can keep his license.

MC: Many of these stories have made it into the press over time, haven't they?

MEB: Yes, but they have to be pretty bad to make it.

MC: Do you feel that the coverage has affected public opinion? To what extent has it really helped things?

MEB: I think the press helps to constantly keep the situation before people who go and buy their fresh fruits and vegetables every week. The people who are out there in the fields cutting the lettuce and picking the corn and getting the apples and peaches can seldom afford to go to the grocery store and buy anything.

MC: There are a lot of things you're working against—sometimes it's big business, in other cases it's politicians who don't feel that taking up the cause of migrant farm workers will get them the most votes.

MEB: Exactly. Farm workers don't vote.

MC: I would think also that a lot of it has to do with racism and prejudice in this country.

MEB: There's a lot of that too. The thing is, so what, it's a challenge. You have to find a way to deal with it, whatever it is. You just don't sit down and say, "Well, what's the use?" You don't belong in this job if you do.

MC: I was wondering if you could talk a little more about life on the camps beyond the work that's done.

MEB: Well, workers oftentimes have their own radios, and usually the recreation room or the dining room in the camp will have a television set. A lot of the Jamaican sugarcane cutters will drive you mad. Every one has his own boom box playing, and there's so much noise. I think music helps them. And they like to hear the news. But you know that song, "Lucky Old Sun?" "Up on the morning, out on the job, work like the devil for my pay." Well, the workers get up at the crack of dawn and work all day.

MC: Generally how many hours?

MEB: It depends: sometimes 12, 14, 16 hours, until dark. In South Carolina, the growers like to have too many workers. Whenever they get an order for peaches or whatever, they can throw the workers into the gap immediately. Maybe they'll work all day for a couple of days, and then they'll sit down for two or three days until the next job.

MC: And the farmer doesn't pay them when they're sitting down?

MEB: No, they only have to pay them for the work they do.

MC: Do farm workers complain that this is all about work and there's no concern about the quality of their lives?

MEB: They don't even think about it. The main complaint is they don't get paid, or they don't get paid right, or they're taking out too much money for taxes or whatever. It's a survival thing—it really is.

MC: Are there other people around the country who do what you do? Are you in contact with each other?

MEB: We're in contact with other Legal Services programs all the time. I had a call from a farm worker in Virginia because he had our card. I told him to stay by that telephone and I'd get the lawyer to call him. I called a lawyer on the eastern shore of Virginia who's in charge of the farm worker unit for Legal Services. She called the guy back within ten minutes. So yes, we work together, especially on the East Coast, because that's mainly where our people go from here. It's real important, the networking. If they can keep you isolated in your own little state, you're not as effective.

MC: Do you have any other observations about organizing people and working for change that you'd like to talk about?

MEB: Well, what is organizing, really? It's mostly an education process to teach workers so they can help themselves. So that they know when something isn't right and that they should have courage to do something about it. Oftentimes, it depends on the people. Haitian people are very good at organizing. They're not afraid of anything. They stage their own strikes if they don't think they're getting paid right. If the guy fires them, they'll go home and call "*Avoka* Gregory" [*avoka* is Creole for "lawyer"].

I guess what we do is some organizing, but I see more results in helping to get the law enforced. We've had some effect. Greg has brought more lawsuits under the federal law than almost any other lawyer in this country.

MC: Do you have much hope about bettering the condition of farm workers?

MEB: Well, I think you just have to continue. If we all gave up and went home, God knows what would happen. As long as I'm healthy, I'm going to work. Greg is relatively young. I think he's going to be 41 this year. (Don't tell him I told you!) He's a person who's not intimidated by anybody.

MC: Well, you don't sound like you are, either.

MEB: Well, no, I'm not, but we have different approaches. He charges in faster than I do. I take it a little more easily. But when push comes to shove . . . I've gained courage, I think, from working with him. He says you learn from your experience as you go along, and he's right. I used to have horrible experiences in Pennsylvania. One woman wouldn't let anyone visit her camp. If the workers needed a doctor, they had to walk out to the end of the road, and we picked them up there. I went on the camp anyway, and she accused me of soliciting for prostitution. In other cases, they said I was giving people $50 to leave the camp, or I was handing out wine to the workers. You name it. They think of ways of damning you somehow.

MC: Has it gotten any better? Are you in less fearful situations now?

MEB: Yes. Back in Pennsylvania, I used to get sick in my stomach. Many times it was so unpleasant, and there was just so much turmoil. I began going through a lot of problems in my personal life, too. So I had a lot of years when there was a lot of trauma. But that's part of what you have to do if you want to do anything.

It's really changed now since we got the access law in Florida. I feel much more confident because we do have the right. We don't have the access law in every state, but our position is that the workers have the right to receive visitors.

The things that we have done, and Greg Schell's reputation, have given us strength. The farmers know not to argue with Greg. If he says he's going to get your money, he's going to get it. Now when I go on a camp and see a labor contractor or someone who looks important, I'm much more confident in confronting them. I just say, "I'm Mary Ellen Beaver from Legal

Services. Are you the crew leader?" I get it out in the open right off. If they don't like it, they'll tell you, but they usually haven't challenged us. They just let us go.

So I don't know for the future. I hope I'm able to work a long time. I have too many things I want to do; I'm not going to be able to live that long. I want to do work on the family genealogy. I want to open a little shop. I have a big farmhouse back in Pennsylvania to live in. Greg says that after we end poverty and injustice, I can retire.

MC: It seems to me, though, that you've really become part of the migrant labor community here through your work.

MEB: I didn't think about it until just now, but I feel very much at home with them, more than I do with people in higher places. I live in Palm Beach County, but I feel much more at home here in Belle Glade than if I lived in [the city of] Palm Beach. People there have a whole different attitude toward poor people. I grew up on the farm, and I lived on a farm all my life. I guess that's why I feel more comfortable with the farm workers.

August 16, 1994
Belle Glade, Florida

12

JOAN ROBINETT

A NATIVE OF TENNESSEE, JOAN ROBINETT WAS propelled into activism by the grim discovery that the mobile home park she and her family had moved to in Dayhoit, Kentucky, was located on a federal Superfund site. Unknown to residents, the well water had been massively contaminated with carcinogens by the mining machine repair company next door, and many of them, including Robinett's young son, had developed severe but inexplicable health problems. Though they didn't at the time suspect that something was wrong with the place where they were living, Robinett and her family moved about a mile upstream, and her son's health began to improve. A year later, the government tested the water and began to warn people to stop using it, without revealing the severity of the problem. It was this lack of full disclosure, as well as the contamination, that spurred Robinett into becoming a community activist.

In the following interview, Robinett tells the story of how she and her Appalachian neighbors taught themselves to counter business and government misinformation and indifference to their plight. This involved not only versing herself in the chemistry of complex contaminants and their impact on human health but also learning how to organize herself and others to function effectively within the legal and political arena. On a personal level, she talks about how difficult it was to stand up to the intimidation tactics leveled at her by corporate mining interests and how she struggled to reverse the ingrained perception in many poor Appalachian communities that they are powerless against the forces that have ravaged the regional landscape.

Robinett and her neighbors eventually filed suit in federal court against the owner of the contaminated site in Dayhoit and received a settlement, but this struggle just marked the beginning of Robinett's commitment to grassroots community activism. Since then, she has continued to work on environmental issues but has broadened her involvement to include battles against political corruption and initiatives to lessen local economic dependence on the mining industry. Along these lines, she has been working with her second husband, Andy Jones, on the marketing of

*local arts and crafts outside the region through the Appalachian Heritage Arts
Guild. Finally, she is optimistic that conditions in the area are improving, mainly
because she feels that people of different political persuasions are beginning to work
together on what they perceive as shared problems.*

☐   ☐   ☐   ☐   ☐

Marie Cieri: Can you tell me a little bit about yourself: where you're
from and how you got involved in activism here?

Joan Robinett: I was born and raised in a little town called Erwin, which
is in the mountains of Tennessee. I was raised on a farm. After we moved
here, I learned the difference between farm and mountain culture, and
there is a big difference.

My parents still have a farm, and we were very self-sufficient, mainly
dependent upon the land. We were much more independent in our area
than folks are here because we didn't have to deal with answering to the
coal company. We didn't have the coal camps and the control. My husband
at the time worked for the Kroger Company grocery chain, and in '81 we
were transferred here to Harlan, Kentucky, from Tennessee. The first time
I came here I was pregnant with my son, who is 13 now, and I cried all
the way home because I had never been in these parts.

MC: You hadn't been in the mountains of Kentucky.

JR: I had not been in the mountains and the coal fields of Kentucky. I was
devastated for a long time. It was very sad. It was terrible. The mountains
in our area, they hadn't been mined. I mean, there's environmental problems, but it's nothing like what we see in this area. I guess the biggest thing
that touched me was the quality of life that people *don't* have here, basic
things that they should have, but they just don't. So we moved here, and I
worked in the Head Start program. I worked in the school system as a
teacher's aide and a substitute. I was active in community things, like
Scouts. Just normal stuff. I jumped in and thought I was doing my part as
a community person. In '84, we moved into the mobile-home park in
Dayhoit. The National Electric Coil plant's property line—their fence—is
adjacent to the Holiday Mobile Home Park. During the time that I lived
there, my son was very sick. He had to go to the doctor and to the hospital a lot—several hospitals. We had to fly experts in, and he was diagnosed
with failure to thrive and severe gastroenteritis and diarrhea. Nobody
could find out what was wrong with him. So we went through about three

years of a lot of hospital stays, and I did not know at the time that our drinking water was polluted. I knew the plant was there.

MC: What kind of a plant was it?

JR: It was a mining machine repair shop, and they rebuilt motors and transformers, and then they brought equipment in from paper mills, steel mills, chemical plants. But the whole time that my son was sick, I just assumed that that facility was permitted and was operating legally. Environmental pollution never entered my mind, ever. His doctors even questioned me: "Do you live near a chemical plant, do you live near an industrial complex?" I said, "I'm in the mountains of southeastern Kentucky," you know.

MC: So he was in hospitals far away from here?

JR: Tennessee, University of Cincinnati.

MC: Teaching hospitals where there were experts.

JR: Yeah. At one point, they did question the drinking water, not for chemical contaminants per se, but bacteria. So we would have the water sampled. At the mobile home park, at the time, there were probably over 100 residents, and we had a drinking water well that was our public water system. So we had the water screened for bacteria, but nobody ever thought about chemicals.

MC: Were other kids sick?

JR: Yeah. But not as severe as mine was. They were lifelong residents, most of them third, fourth generation. I shouldn't say not as sick as Danny. Some of them had other problems, but it wasn't as apparent as it was in Daniel. Anyway, we sold our mobile home, and we moved into a house in Rio Vista, which is about a mile upstream from the National Electric Coil Plant. When we moved into the Rio Vista community, we were on a public water system, which is the Harlan municipal water system and is totally different from the well there. Within six months' time, Dan began to show an improvement in his health. We had not been moved out of Dayhoit a year, and the Division of Water came through the area doing sampling, which is required under the Clean Water Act, to test public water systems for volatile organic compounds. They tested the well where we had lived, and the water supply was shut off almost immediately because the levels of vinyl chloride, trichloroethylene [TCE], and sys–1, 2-dichloroethylene were just so high in the drinking water. So in turn, they began to sample wells within the Dayhoit community, and some of them had to be shut down. They began to look for a source. The National Electric Coil was determined to be it.

Even though I had moved out of the community and moved upstream, I still had a lot of friends there, and they began to talk to me. I went to some of the public meetings the EPA [Environmental Protection Agency] held, and I called Dan's doctors and said, "You're not going to believe this. We don't know how long this stuff has been in the water, but this is what they found." Besides the VOCs [volatile organic compounds], they found lead and PCBs [polychlorinated biphenyls] and mercury and cadmium and you name it. Dioxins have been found in the soil afterwards. There were a lot of contaminants.

His doctors began to supply me with fact sheets. The first one I got was, I think, from the New Jersey Department of Health on exposure to vinyl chloride and TCE, and the doctors said, "This could be it. This could be why what happened to him happened, and why it hasn't happened anymore. The fact that you moved is probably why he's alive."

So we began to do living room meetings in my house. I began to get information that you couldn't get locally. The Federal EPA would not give it out, the state EPA would not give it out. They came in here and said, "Don't drink your water, don't wash your clothes in it, don't wash your car, don't water your lawn, don't water your garden—but you're going to be okay." I swear. "You're going to be fine, just don't do anything with this water anymore."

MC: What were you supposed to use?

JR: They were supplying residents with some two gallons of bottled water a day.

MC: How were you supposed to wash your clothes?

JR: It was awful. People would come to my house and get water because two gallons a day was nothing. It was in the summertime. They couldn't flush their toilets. It was terrible. The only way we were able to help was that people would just come and turn our faucets on.

MC: You had good water.

JR: Right, I was upstream on a different system. These chemicals had to be really bad if one day you could use the water, and then the next day, "No, you can't ever use it, ever, ever, we've capped the wells off." I didn't know the extent of the danger, but I knew I was going to find out, and I knew that I wouldn't get it from the regulatory agencies. That was very clear.

MC: They were keeping everything secret.

JR: Yeah. Then, finally, one of the health experts came out and said, "Well, yeah, there are cancer-causing chemicals in this water, but your chances of developing cancer are very slim." And I said, "Well, how do you know that? You only know what you found on this day. This plant's been here since 1951." But that's the way they were handling it.

MC: To your knowledge, over that period of time, were a lot of people dying from cancer?

JR: Yeah. We went back and did surveys. We have plant workers in our citizens' group as well as community folks. Plant workers averaged at least two a year dying of cancer. Just this past summer, we had four residents die of cancer. This is a population of somewhere between 350 and 500.

MC: What kind of cancer do they get?

JR: There's different types. There's a multiple melanoma, Hodgkin's disease, non-Hodgkin's lymphoma, some leukemias.

MC: So it's all through their systems.

JR: Yeah. And that's not counting the folks who've been diagnosed; those are just those that have passed away. So we began to look at all that. But in the living room meetings, it was mainly moms who pulled together and said, "You know, our kids had this, they had the rashes and the stomach flus all the time." We weren't officially organized yet. We didn't even know we could organize a citizens' group, okay? *[laughter]*.

The plant workers began to come to my house to talk about their health problems, and it was so overwhelming. A lot of these guys didn't live in Dayhoit, they lived somewhere else in the county, yet they had the same medical problems, only more severe than the children and the lifelong residents in the community. We began to try to sort through all of that.

This friend of mine, a coal miner, called me up one day and said, "There's a lady in Harlan County who you need to talk to who can help you. You need to call Hazel King who lives at Clover Fork. She's fought the mining industry for years and years and years. When you talk to her, you can't tell anyone that I referred you to her. I work in one of the mines above Hazel's property, and if my boss finds out that I've put you on to Hazel King, I'll be fired. So call her and tell her that an anonymous coal miner. . . ." And I did [laughter]. I told Hazel what we were doing, and she said, "Well, I read about the pollution in the paper." Then she said, "Where'd you get my name and number?" I said, "I can't tell you. He said to just tell Hazel 'an anonymous coal miner.'" And she said, "Okay." I've never asked her, I probably should, but I often thought that was a code or something [laughter]. She said, "You need to call Tom Fitzgerald with the Kentucky Resources Council, and you need to call Larry Wilson on Yellow Creek in Bell County, he's fighting the pollution problem down there. You need to call Kenny Rosenbaum [a local musician and activist], and you need to make contact with Kentuckians for the Commonwealth [KFTC, a major statewide citizens' group that had been fighting the coal companies]." So she gave me a list of folks to make contact with.

So I made contact with Tom Fitzgerald, and he began to help right off the bat. Larry and his wife Sheila came up, and they have a citizens' group there in Bell County that has been organized for about 15 years, I guess. They've been fighting the tannery down there. They were real knowledgeable about the importance of organizing, which we had not gotten to the point of yet. Kenny came in and practically lived with us, helping us to organize a citizens' group. Then we began to attend the monthly KFTC chapter meetings at the library in Harlan. There were about 70 of us who met. I was nominated as the chair, and I've been chairing that group since '89. The pollution was discovered in March of '89, and by June of '89 we'd formed a citizens' group and had set up our by-laws.

MC: That was pretty quick.

JR: Yeah. By July, we held our first public meeting with the state EPA.

MC: You moved here in 1981, so between '81 and '89 was when all this was happening?

JR: Yes.

MC: What's the name of the citizens' group?

JR: It's Concerned Citizens Against Toxic Waste.

MC: Is it just people in Harlan and Dayhoit?

JR: Mainly it is Dayhoit community folks and former NEC plant workers (some of them were current at the time, but they're not now). Probably about 60 percent of our group are plant workers.

MC: How did the plant workers get involved? Were they afraid of losing their jobs?

JR: Yeah. There's still a lot of fear. You see, their drinking water well was polluted, too. I must say that for some of these fellas—and there's a few women who were in the plant too—it was really devastating to them, not only because of what they had been exposed to, but what they had carried home to their families. A lot of them went through a lot of guilt because they had no idea the stuff that they were working in caused cancer. They had no idea when they were told to dump this stuff in a drain that runs into the river or pour it out on the ground that it would seep into the ground water. But they made contact with us when their drinking water well got shut off at the plant. One of the contractors that was doing the sampling let it slip that it contained cancer-causing chemicals.

    The fact that my husband works at Kroger, in the public, we knew a lot of these folks. They had become like family to us. Workers could tell us what they used, what time frames they used it in, where they dumped it, when they dumped it, why, what the different processes were. By doing that, we were able to push the company and the EPA and say, "No, you're not just going to address ground water pollution because there are dumps here and the stuff's here. You're going to test for other chemicals because this other stuff was used." It was in this exchange between community folk and workers that we found out what all their health problems were, what all these chemicals caused, what levels OSHA [Occupational Safety and Health Administration] says you can and cannot be exposed to in the workplace, and that they were supposed to have MSDS sheets (Material Safety Data Sheets) for workers.

MC: So this company was in violation on many fronts.

JR: Many, many. This company *never* had a permit, *ever*. They were never, ever permitted to use or dispose of the chemicals the way they did. Never. There was a questionnaire that asked, "Are you in violation of any environmental permits?" And they said, "No, we don't have any permits." Technically, you can't be in violation of a permit if you don't have one. But we began to learn about the process and the system, and the fox-watching-the-henhouse approach. When these companies set up, it's up to them to tell the regulatory agency, "I'm going to use this chemical, I'm going to dispose of it this way, this is how much, etc." I call it a license to kill, because it is.

MC: In your opinion, were they just ignorant, or did they know that by moving into a remote place it was really hard for the regulatory agencies to know what was going on or that it would be ignored?

JR: The company knew. McGraw-Edison was the original owner of this particular facility, and McGraw-Edison is worldwide. In 1985, McGraw-Edison became a wholly owned subsidiary of Cooper Industries, which is a multinational corporation. They knew. McGraw-Edison had the same type of plant in Bluefield, West Virginia. They had plants in remote areas of Ohio, New Jersey, down in Tennessee. They knew.

MC: Were they doing the same kinds of things in those places?

JR: Yes, very similar. Bluefield was exactly the same, just a smaller operation. They knew. I work with community groups all across the U.S., and I believe that certain areas are singled out, either because it's low-income or it's in a remote area where regulatory agencies are not going to be on the site every day, or in communities with people of color. I think that in our situation it was because we're looked upon lots of times as poor, dumb hillbillies.

It was a really neat thing to be an employee at the National Electric Coil plant here because it was an alternative to going into the coal mines. The pay was good, very close to mining wages, and they had a little union. They had good benefits and retirement, so from a social status, everybody wanted to work there because that meant that you could make a good living and not go back into the mines. We talked about that a lot with the workers, because they looked at the coal mines, as everybody does, as very, very dangerous work, which it is. You never know, when you go in a mine, if you're going to come out from your shift. So with the NEC plant, because they didn't know the extent of the chemicals and the dangers, it was like, "Wow, if you can work there, you're doing really good."

MC: Did any people lose their jobs because they were fighting against the pollution?

JR: Yeah, some did. Some who were not actually employed with NEC also lost their jobs. They were employed in the coal mines, but because NEC's customers are coal operators . . .

MC: . . . It was all connected.

JR: Yeah.

MC: What was your approach as you got more and more information? You went to the company and to the regulatory agencies to keep exposing what you were finding out?

JR: We just kept digging, yeah. In fact, at one point it got so bad that we kept making regulatory agencies hold public meetings with the community. We kept going to the table. We went to Frankfort [the state capitol] in August of '89. And you've got to keep in mind that none of us had ever done this before.

MC: You said to me earlier that mountain people feel like they're not going to be listened to, they're not going to have an effect, they don't have the right skills to communicate with anonymous people in high places. How did you overcome that?

JR: It became a matter of survival. I think that most of the people felt like I did—this is the straw that broke the camel's back, and you are not going to do this and get away with it. This is it, these are our kids we're talking about here. I think that was probably the key. The mixed emotions between fear and anger. None of us had ever been in a situation where we had to stand up and speak before 200 people or relate to a corporate vice-president with Cooper Industries or a ground water hydrogeologist. For months I would call on the phone, and I would spell trichloroethylene because I could not pronounce it, and vinyl chloride and all these chemicals and say, "What is this? What is a site assessment? What does that mean?" The mix of emotions brought about a determination, and we said, "We're not going to take this. We don't believe what you're saying because we know—here's the paper—you're not telling the truth. You're not being honest with these people." If the regulatory agency had done what it was supposed to do, it wouldn't have taken until 1989 to find it, number one. So we began to weigh all that out.

MC: They wouldn't have looked, probably.

JR: They never did. Publicly, they said, "We didn't even know this plant was here." And we said, "Wait a minute, there are employees here. OSHA was in this plant twice—two times in 37 years an OSHA inspector came through the plant, cited it both times, but never came back. Somebody paid taxes here, you know." Of course, our immediate goals were to determine the extent of pollution within the community and the extent of health problems as much as we could. But at the same time, there was—and there still is—a constant learning process of the domino effect, of how the system does not work in relationship to *everything*. Everybody knows that it doesn't work, but they don't really think about it until they actually have to deal with it or are confronted with it. In our situation, within the community, we were reacting to a disaster. What we try to tell people now in other communities is, "Don't wait until you have to react—act now, be aware, look out around you at what's going on and take preventive measures." I think it's just human nature that we just all go along; I know I did it. I wonder sometimes, if I had not experienced what I had experienced with my son, would I have reacted the same way to the pollution problem?

MC: You might not have been the spearheading force.

JR: No. I would have been involved, I'm sure, but I probably would not have taken on the role that was handed down to me *[laughter]*.

MC: I understand you've been talking to other communities around here about how to organize against other existing or potential problems.

JR: After we were organized about a year or so, these folks began to call us. "You know, there's raw sewage running in the creek up here," or "There's black water running from this pond, who do I call?" This friend of mine had lived in Dayhoit, and she was reluctant to get involved at first because she worked in the courthouse and was afraid she would get fired.

I felt like everybody should have the same convictions that I did, and I'd get real angry because people didn't jump on the bandwagon. I asked her, "Why did you not get involved? Your parents live there and da-de-dah." And she said, "Well, we wanted to see what you all were doing, if you continued to do it, and if you lived to tell about it." I didn't realize it at the time, but a lot of folks were watching to see what really happened, because it was not common for a citizens' group to spring up in this area and be as active as we are. We had to learn right off the bat how to deal with the press and how to do all of these things.

MC: What was that like, learning how to deal with the press?

JR: It's terrible *[laughter]* because it's really hard. I had never done interviews. What we found was that we had to educate ourselves and help educate the news media as well. When we would come across documents or new test results that showed much higher levels than the company was saying, we had to be able to relay that to the news media: "The Federal EPA maximum contaminant level for vinyl chloride is two parts per billion, but we've got 898 parts per billion in this well." It was really tough, it still is tough, for me. So you have to learn to do all that. It goes back to reacting to something—you don't realize you're doing it, you just do it. None of the work is planned. I mean, you do plot and plan for particular meetings and rallies and things, but most of the stuff is thrown at a community group so fast, you just have to react and trust your instincts and hope that you do the right thing.

MC: Have you ever felt that you've gotten burned by being instinctual, especially with the news media?

JR: Yeah, yeah.

MC: You have? Because they quoted you out of context or got it wrong?

JR: There have been times that I would pick up the paper the next day and I'd say, "This is not the meeting we were at last night, I wasn't in this meeting." It hasn't happened a lot, but it has happened. One thing about dealing with a company as large as Cooper Industries is that they have lots of money—they bought full-page ads in our local newspaper and ran them for weeks at $600 an ad and said, "The levels found are not of concern, they're not going to cause any health problems." They hired a toxicologist and did press conferences. So we had to fight a lot of money.

MC: How much time do you spend on this work?

JR: Lots *[laughter]*.

MC: *[Laughter]* Is this a job for you now?

JR: It's a job. I'm the coordinator of the Local Governance Project, which is a countywide group that was a spin-off from the Dayhoit citizens' group. But if I had a paying job, a real job . . .

MC: This is not a paying job?

JR: Citizens' group, no. Local Governance Project, there's like a $400 expense stipend that I get every month.
 The fight is still going on. You can work day and night, and I've learned that the hardest part for grassroots groups and activists and community folks is that it can be so time consuming. I've been fortunate enough to

have a husband who's very understanding and with extra income coming in the house. But most of the time, when these things happen, folks are not as fortunate. They either have to work or have very little income. Money is one of the big barriers, getting access to available resources is another. But there's no way that I could do what I do if I had to leave my house at eight in the morning and come home at five. Most of the regulatory people and the people that you need to get in touch with and bend their ear go home when you go home. So we've been fortunate in that.

There's been times that we've worked day and night for two or three days straight, when reports come in, when different things are going on at the site, a lot of testing being done, plans being developed. You have to be able to sort through all this stuff to get your comments in, knowing good and well that they're probably not even going to be acknowledged, but if you don't respond they're going to say, "You didn't care, you didn't comment anyway." So then you comment, and they say, "Well, no, we can't do that." That's the process. We know that if we keep going and going and going . . . It's happened, we've had a few victories along the way, and they do eventually listen. The point is, we don't always get what we ask for, but we just have to keep doing that. It's very time consuming; it's very stressful on families and children.

This has probably been the most difficult thing I've ever done because of some people's way of thinking. The coal operators just went haywire. Even though we were not focusing on their operations, they felt we had public meetings in "their" courthouse. It's theirs, you know. I had a judge tell me one time, "This is my courtroom," and I said, "Excuse me, but . . ."

MC: It's the people's courtroom.

JR: It got really scary; it still does sometimes.

MC: In what way? Physically?

JR: Physically, yes.

MC: You've been afraid? That one woman said to you that she wanted to see if you'd still be alive, and she meant because somebody would harm you?

JR: Would kill me, yeah.

MC: What kinds of threats have you gotten?

JR: People would call me. "You better watch your back door," was one real common one and, "You're going to get yourself killed, you don't know what you're messing with." In the beginning, they would call my husband a lot at work and say, "You better stop your wife." So I knew it was someone local doing that.

MC: *[Laughter]* Oh, because that's an attitude here?

JR: Yeah, that's a cultural thing here *[laughter]*.

MC: They wouldn't have said that in Tennessee?

JR: I don't think so. One day, he came home, and he was real frustrated, and he said, "I really support what you're doing, but we really didn't think this thing through." And I said, "We didn't have time." And we didn't. I mean, we discussed it, but you never know what the outcome is going to be. I've learned that. He said, "I got one of those calls today, and this man said, "You better shut your wife up, you better do something about your wife, Joan Robinett, you gotta do something." And my husband said, "Hell, I can't do anything with her. Don't call me anymore. I can't shut her up" *[laughter]*. I've been followed before, for a long time.

MC: In your car?

JR: Yeah.

MC: Did anybody ever try to run you off the road?

JR: Yeah, up here on the curve, at one point, someone tried to run me over. It was about 8:30 at night, I was going to a meeting at Holy Trinity School. I still don't get out a lot at night by myself. If it's going to be late, I don't travel very far alone at all. Because you never know.

MC: Do you feel that there is some kind of protection in numbers, because you're part of a citizens' group, or do you feel that you're singled out because you've been a spokesperson?

JR: I think that when you're dealing with companies and regulatory agencies, if they feel like they can single out one person, the one who will be screaming the loudest, it could be an example to the other folks: this could happen to you. But we've been organized so long—so many different folks across the county are involved—that it's not going to make any difference. I probably used to be in more danger than I am now.

MC: I understand you're really branching out from environmental issues into other things now.

JR: Yeah, very much so—learning about election laws and state laws and city government. I served on City Council within the city of Loyall; for two years I was appointed to an unexpired term, and then I had to run on a ballot. So I've been in an elected official position. Last year, there was only one candidate for county judge executive on the Democratic ticket, the incumbent, and she was going to run unopposed. So I let some of these hellions, rebels *[laughter]* talk me into filing for county judge executive. Not necessarily to win, but to say, "You're not running unopposed this time." So I did. I filed an hour before the deadline shut off. Fifteen minutes before the deadline, they brought this fellow in under me, so there were three candidates. It was a hoot. It was really a learning experience. I did the old-fashioned door-to-door, but what happened was that I couldn't campaign because people knew me as "that woman that helped them people in Dayhoit get clean water" or "that woman that fights with the EPA all time," or "fights with the courthouse all the time," or "she can get information for you." So as I was going around, I learned more and more about the severity of the problems throughout the county. I couldn't campaign for taking complaints and helping people. It was very hard. Whether they were dealing with the school board, or their kids had to walk six miles and cross a swinging bridge to get on a school bus, or "This bridge out here's been broken for four years and I can't get it fixed." But I learned so much about Harlan County and about the people, I wouldn't take anything for what I learned.

MC: You definitely are what someone would call a grassroots organizer and activist. Are you at all afraid that if you actually got into an institutional position, maybe you couldn't get anything done?

JR: Right. I thought by being an elected official I would be able to help people more. In some ways you can, but I learned that the bottom line is that sometimes, even within the system, it's tougher because you feel like your hands are tied. It was like wearing two hats. When you go into a council meeting, you don't always know where your fellow council members are coming from with things that they want to do, or don't want to do. In a grassroots citizens' group setting, you know where folks are coming from, okay? You know because you work with them, and you can tell.

Most of the time they don't have anything to personally gain or financially gain, it's because they do it from the heart. In the elected official setting, you never know what their motives *really* are. Sometimes I would assume that they were the same as mine and found out three months later it was totally for other reasons. That was the most difficult thing for me because you want to do what's best for the people, *all* the people who elected you, not four or five, or not just the business people. I wanted to make sure that *everybody* in the city of Loyall was fairly represented. In that setting, because of the political factions and control and money and power structures, everybody else doesn't feel the same as you.

I don't regret running for public office because it taught me a lot, but I probably would not do it again. But one thing did come out of running: I said, "I want to see a more open government in Harlan County, I want everybody to be able to participate in their government, and we want the garbage cleaned up," and these things are slowly happening. Even though the incumbent beat me out, she's having to follow through with things that came out of my campaign. We didn't plan it that way, it just happened.

MC: When people tell you what they want and need, there must be conflicting interests sometimes. How have you been able to deal with that, to get people to agree on what actually to do, even if it might go against one person's interests or another's?

JR: It's really hard. Probably the first time I was confronted with it was with the Harlan Area Ministerial Association, the group of ministers throughout the county. They called me as the coordinator of Local Governance and said, "We need some help. We're tired of looking at the garbage strewn all over the county. We were the first county in the state to implement mandatory garbage pick-up, yet we've got all these problems." I said that first we need to document where all the illegal dumps are. That's something I've learned: you've got to have something you can show people. Even though the elected officials know, they're saying, "We don't have a solid waste problem in Harlan County." So we began that process.

Some of the areas where we found illegal dumps were owned by coal operators, which makes them responsible for cleaning these dumps up. I said to the ministers, "Some of the folks who are putting money in your collection plate every Sunday are going to wind up being responsible for some of these dumps. They're going to own the land, they're going to have to clean it up." They had not thought of that. I've found that if you're honest enough with folks on the front end and let them weigh it out, they'll usually make the right decision. It's very hard to do, though. In that situation, this particular minister had to decide if the money coming into the church would be cut out, but his attitude was, "That'll work out. This is something we feel strong about doing and we're going to do it. We'll take that chance."

The most important thing is people being responsible enough to take the time. The reason I think most people don't do that is because they don't think they can make a difference, when indeed they can, even if it's just writing a letter or sometimes making a phone call. It's a problem all over the U.S., but it becomes more prominent in the mountains. Because of low education levels and different social factors, people don't feel like they're knowledgeable enough to say what they think in opposition, or even when they're supporting something. They feel that because they're in the mountains of southeastern Kentucky, they don't have the right or they have to be of a certain social status to be able to speak out and accomplish things—which is not true at all.

MC: Where are things with Cooper Industries? Have they come under compliance about what they're supposed to do about contaminants? Are you still agitating?

JR: Yes, we're still agitating *[laughter]*. According to the federal EPA, Cooper is in compliance, and they're under federal consent orders because they're primarily the responsible party. But they're still not doing what they should be doing to protect the public's health and the environment. It's a very slow process, and we've learned that in some ways, it's good to have a company come forward and spend their own money, because when that happens, you don't have to wait on federal Superfund money. But they also tell the regulatory agency, "We're going to do what *we* think is best in cleaning it up, and we'll do it in our time frame because it's our money," which again takes the control away from the community that's most affected.

MC: You said earlier that when you moved here, you were really depressed because people just didn't even have the basics. Could you describe this community and the ones around it a little more—what life and culture are like here, what people do?

JR: We have folks around here who are very talented with their hands. For instance, my dulcimer was made by Mr. Cornett in Cumberland. That's one thing about mountain people—most of them can do all sorts of things. This little piece of furniture, for instance, was made by a coal miner. The talent is overwhelming sometimes in a lot of the folks. A lot of the homemade things are handed down through generations—the quilting, ribbon-working, making the instruments and so forth. There's that part of the culture. Then there is another part of mountain culture—what's been handed down in their family is having to survive on the system, which means welfare and food stamps and no education. I'm trying to be real careful how I explain this, but I saw this a lot during the campaign trail. Independence was not passed down through the generations. So when the dependence on the coal industry is gone because the coal's not there or the coal mine just shut down, folks seek dependency on something else, which is public aid. It's not that they want to. In some cases they don't know any other way of life; in other cases there's nothing else available to them. I have friends who are single mothers who would love to be able to work and support their children, but they can't survive, financially cannot keep a roof over their heads, food on the table, and provide proper medical care on minimum wage. So the only other alternative is to depend on public aid.

I have learned that when people are dependent upon the system, they are least likely to resist anything. It's the same thing in the coal industry. I work with coal miners who do raise hell, but it's like, "Don't bite the hand that feeds you." We had lots of folks who were so afraid that their disability benefits and Social Security would be cut out because they were participating in a citizens' group.

MC: Do you think there's the potential for people who make art or music to help a cause you're involved in, either through a direct reference to the issues or just as a way to bring people together?

JR: Survival is the key; we have to keep focused on that, but at the same time I think we have to stop and look at these children and think about how important it would be for our kids to be able to experience some type of exchange.

MC: They're not at this point?

JR: Some of our kids are involved in different things that we, as adults, do. My son just recently went with me to Appalshop [a community arts and media center in Whitesburg, across the mountains] to do the radio talk show over there with me. Some kids are involved, but I think that during all this survival stuff we mustn't leave the children behind. If we're doing it so they have a better future, we have to include them in whatever way we can. Daniel was involved in the Appalachian Youth Leadership Conference in '91, where children were involved in different cultural exchanges—music and readings and stuff like that. There's a photography exhibit currently at

Southeast Community College called "The Women of Coal." So there are things that happen from time to time.

MC: A lot of ways that people participate in culture, especially if they're in smaller, more isolated areas, is through television or the radio. That's a very different experience than the one you get seeing things in person or making things with other people, especially if it has to do with your own life and your own experience.

JR: Which I think is very important. It would be good if we could do some things like that locally. Even from the environmental fights, we've learned that all of us are from different communities, fighting different companies, fighting different chemicals, but the bottom line is that it's the same rotten system, the same rotten regulatory agencies. As I'm going along doing that, I know about folks and their struggles, but I don't really know about their culture.

MC: What they think about and what they like doing.

JR: Yeah. There are workshops about networking and trainings, which we all need, but I'm not aware of anything where you can just come together and say, "I was born and raised in the mountains of Tennessee, and what I like to do is make quilts, and my grandmother taught me how to do it." I think that would be really good if at some point, in some type of setting, you could pull folks together.

August 25, 1994
Loyall, Kentucky

13

AMALIA MESA-BAINS

AMALIA MESA-BAINS IS AN ARTIST AND CULTURAL ACTIVIST whose work emerged from the Chicano movement of the 1960s and 1970s. Her evolution as an artist paralleled her work in education. With a degree in clinical psychology and her background in elementary and bilingual education, and as a scholar of the Chicano movement, Mesa-Bains perceives strong ties between art and social practice. Art is "a series of ethical reflections," she says, "a relationship of private narratives and public dialogues."

Mesa-Bains's own artwork takes the form of altars, or ofrendas, which are contemporary interpretations of the Mexican/Chicano tradition of the home altar and the celebrations of the Day of the Dead. Her ephemeral installations of flowers, candles, family photographs, memorabilia, and Catholic imagery are about redeeming and maintaining the continuity of Chicano culture in the face of American cultural hegemony.

During the past two decades, Mesa-Bains has turned her attention increasingly to discriminatory practices within the academic and art worlds. As director of the Institute for Visual and Public Art at California State University at Monterey Bay, she teaches her students how to be organizers as well as artists, encouraging them to make artwork that is responsive to community needs as well as expressive of the individual voice. In the following pages, she reflects on the integral role of art in the Chicano movement and the more recent politics of culture in America, which she believes have been focused on "a deeper agenda about controlling a shifting demographic."

Claire Peeps: I'd like to hear about your personal background. How did you begin your work as an artist? And how you have identified opportunities to cross borders between the arts and other sectors?

Amalia Mesa-Bains: Well, I would describe myself as a product of the Chicano movement, although I was already out of school by the time it was really hitting campuses hard. My work has always been within the art movement of the larger Chicano movement. Luis Valdez and I were in school at the same time. He was starting Teatro Campesino and doing the first premieres of *The Shrunken Head of Pancho Villa.* But it wasn't really until I moved to San Francisco that my politicization occurred. In a lot of ways, I think it came largely from my husband Richard's work with the Congress on Racial Equality. He was working for CORE when I first met him. He did a lot of the housing law work—you know, where you'd be around the corner for a rental property and you would call up the landlord and speak without an accent. You'd say, "I'd like to rent," and they'd say, "Come right over, sir." You'd go around the corner and they'd say, "Oops! It's already been rented." And we'd say, "Well, it's been three minutes and 47 seconds, how did you manage that?" So Richard used to do that. I think that probably more than anything had an influence on me, because I was not raised with a clear picture of that kind of discrimination.

CP: Where were you raised?

AMB: When I was born we were still living around the Mountain View/Sunnyvale area south of San Francisco, but this was before Lockheed headquartered there. My father came into this country as a child during the Mexican revolution, around 1916, so it's sort of debatable as to whether they even registered him at the point of entry. My mother came across with her mother on a day pass when she was about five, to clean houses on the American side. Both of them entered the country in very unstable times and in very unstable ways. I remember as a child knowing that my parents weren't citizens but also sensing that they were not here under legal circumstances. They got their papers and green cards along the way, but we grew up in a time when they were still very connected to a Mexican community. Going to school and going into the "other world" was a shift.

Racism in California then was much more subtle than in someplace like Texas. People didn't wait on you in certain stores; it wasn't comfortable to go to certain movie theaters. There were unspoken things going on. I grew up in white 1950s America, and it really wasn't until I got out of college and moved to San Francisco that I became conscious of these issues. Around 1969, I got connected to political work in the Mission district through a national project called Teacher Corps. The first Chicano exhibitions were being mounted in Delano around the same time, and my artwork became connected to that group of Chicano activists and artists who were really beginning to move into a community base. The Galeria de la Raza was formed around 1970, and I affiliated with it around '73 and began exhibiting there around '75. So my work really came through a slow awakening of consciousness. Teacher Corps was of course a radicalization process for me. I was there in the era when the FBI was really doing in the Panthers, and a number of people in our program were associated with the Panthers.

So it was a whole coming of age. I think by virtue of marrying Richard I already had a kind of crossing over concept about cultural work. Richard was and is a musician, and I was trained as a visual artist. But we didn't really think of ourselves as artists at the beginning. We called ourselves cultural workers. And that's really been my base all these years. As time has passed, I've crossed over into lots of areas. I went into public education and taught in the school district for 20 years, so I did my time in the trenches. I was able to finish my dissertation during that period. I did research on Chicano culture and identity formation by looking at artists. That opened doors for me to go out into the art and museum world, not simply as an artist, but from the point of view of talking about the relationship of cultural identity to visual representation. Having been groomed through the years by the Galeria and other groups that I worked with, I really had a sense of the issue of access. I think I'm really of the first generation of the Chicano movement that was very much driven to open doors. I wasn't in the group that opened doors at colleges and universities, but I was within the group that was working in public education at the grade-school level, and then later within the museum world and gallery world, demanding equity of representation.

CP: Can we talk a little bit more about how Teacher Corps was organized and what it did?

AMB: I was part of the third national cycle for Teacher Corps, between 1969 and 1971. They recruited adults who had not been in education to come in to be trained as teachers to work in inner city schools. I worked at a school that was actually up the block from my house. We formed teams and had to spend a third of our time in a community-based organization, a third as student teachers at the school sites, and a third on campus. It was in the middle of the Third World Student Strike, so we refused to cross the picket line and they had to house us in an old Victorian flat outside of the campus. So it was a rather alternative education in the beginning, to say the least! *[laughter]* The people they brought in were all totally radical.

CP: Why did you have to spend time in community-based organizations?

AMB: The concept was that if you were going to provide a relevant education to young people, as teachers you had to know the conditions of their experience and existence. I worked with a variety of programs, like summer schools for what they then called disadvantaged youth. We all worked in advocacy in some form or another, and so a lot of the skills I gained as an organizer, as an advocate, really came from that period of time. I think that's very common in our community. If you look at artists Carmen Lomas Garza, Ester Hernandez, or Judy Baca, every one of them worked in or led a youth movement, founded an organization, or developed a particular constituency. Their works have always been within the visual advocacy of a community. We began our careers that way. It isn't something we had to learn to do later in our careers because we couldn't show our work. It was from the beginning the purpose of our work.

CP: At what level did you work in education?

AMB: I was a classroom teacher. I taught from kindergarten through fifth grade. I went to work in childcare centers because that gave me the flexibility to go back and forth to school. I also worked as a therapist in a night clinic. I got a Ph.D. in clinical psychology, but I didn't continue practicing because by the time I finished I was more entranced by critical theory and more convinced that public dialogue was more important than the privatization of the therapeutic relationship, even though I was always fascinated by it. Anyway, over the years I ran programs in professional development, bilingual education, English as a second language—I mean, everything. I was a multicultural resource teacher, so my teaching work completely paralleled my advocacy and my cultural work. It's always been very easy for me to shift from one space to another because they're really all the same space, they're just in a different form. When I do curriculum development with the New Museum, the Mexican Museum, or the Museo del Barrio, it is not unlike what I did in the school district.

After I left the school district in '89, I went to work at Far-West Laboratories in educational research. I wrote a casebook on cultural diversity in the classroom. One of the biggest problems in public education is that the bulk of the teachers who are working now are in their fifties and are racially completely inconsistent with their students. The bulk of them are white. There's a growing number of minority teachers but it's still very, very small. So you have this discrepancy between teachers who culturally are not like their students and therefore have no personal experience or wisdom to fall back on. On top of that, they were trained sometimes as long as 30 years ago by school districts that had neither the money nor the interest in mandating staff development. Consequently, you have teachers who came in forming their worldview from personal experience and training models that are absolutely irrelevant to the young people they face now. Rather than live constantly with the sense that they're deficient, I think their experience more often is to perceive that the student is deficient. That's one of the real dilemmas of teaching—teachers feel overwhelmed by the students and don't exactly know how to deal with them.

CP: Throughout this period while you were working in education, you were also making art. Could you talk a little bit about what was going on in the early seventies within the Chicano movement, and how artists were manifest within it?

AMB: It's something I've been thinking a lot about because I worked on the PBS series, *Chicano.* No matter what we did, we couldn't get the people producing the series to deal with the fact that art is not a separate function. We're looking back now on almost 30 years. The political movement was tied to the cultural movement, and the cultural material was a way of solidifying the inspiration for the political action. Yet, years later, I see that it is being separated out. The only stories being told now are the Corky Gonzales, the Alurista, Reyes Tijerina, the political figures who organized around land grants or around the Chicano Youth Movement. But equally important were the people who created images. There would be no Chicano movement without people like Rupert Garcia, who produced posters for almost all the events. There would be no Chicano movement without people like Judy Baca, who worked on murals. So the artists were at the core of creating images that helped people to organize social action. The *centros,* or Chicano cultural centers, became a sort of national system, almost like a vascular system where people were connected to this web of centers, where ideas would pass from one to another. People would drive in caravans from the Rio Grande Institute in New Mexico to the Royal Chicano Air Force in Sacramento to the Galeria in San Francisco to Plaza de la Raza or SPARC in Los Angeles. They moved around. There were organizing councils where there were representatives from all the organizations.

CP: Were artists at the table with the other social organizers?

AMB: Yes. Luis Valdez and Alurista who were side by side with Corky Gonzales and Angel Rodriguez, and all the others who were doing the political organizing. The *Plan Espiritual de Aztlan* was written as much by the poets and theater people as it by the political figures. They really were integrated.

CP: What kind of training did the artists have that enabled them to speak an organizing language so easily?

AMB: I think sometimes it's in the blood! I always say that if you put more than two Chicanos together they form a caucus *[laughter]*. It seems like a natural function.

You have to remember that the Chicano movement is just another iteration of political struggle. You had people like Emma Tenaynea, Luisa Moreno, all these women and men who were labor organizers. We were raised with the concept of *huelgas*—strikes. That has been a tradition from Mexico into the United States—labor strikes, labor organizing, fasts, sit-ins. There have been forms of those forever, extending across generations of people. From 1848 to 1851, for example, when they were parceling out the annexed territories, there were groups like the *Goros Blancos* or the White Caps who were basically guerrilla fighters organizing to retrieve the land back to Mexico. They were never successful, but we inherited that tradition, that sensibility, as activists. We really followed from that. We had important Marxist training sessions. Saul Alinksy was an important model, he had great influence on Cesar Chavez. I would say Cesar and Dolores Huerta were also important figures in teaching people how to organize. But the concept and spirit of it was always there. Artists did their art training, and then came out and realized that that wasn't enough.

CP: How did your artmaking practice function within the community?

AMB: Well, one of the key functions of the Chicano movement was the idea of cultural reclamation, a sense of consolidating our identity and resisting the feeling of erasure by the dominant society that excluded you, and affirming those things that your family had taught you. But we had begun to forget those things because many of us had moved far from the original places in which people did the Day of the Dead, or traditions of the *Posada* for Christmas or the *Tamalarda* (the tamale-making). So we consciously turned around and went back where we had come from, picked up all the things our parents had given us, collectively dusted them off, and recreated in a new contemporary form from the traditions we'd been raised with. For me, it was the concept of the home altar, the permanent ongoing record of the family's life, the sacred space. My work came to be about the traditions of the offerings for the days of the dead which I had not been raised with—except that I hung out in graveyards all the time because, as a Mexican family, you're always looking after your dead; it's a very big function in the family. I worked with other Chicano artists, particularly in the late sixties to the mid-seventies, who were also retrieving the traditions of the Days of the Dead. We did big communal *ofrendas* or offerings; we sometimes called them altars. When people like Carmen Lomas Garza came from Texas in the late seventies, she began to influence the way we worked. Carmen, Rene Yañez and I made the first *ofrenda* for Frida Kahlo in 1978. We took what was traditionally a familial and personal practice and we turned it into a community, public practice. We mixed our families in with historical figures who had died. We used that as a way to historicize our past.

CP: Where did you do that?

AMB: Mostly in and around the Galeria de la Raza and the Mexican Museum in San Francisco. It was a very collective practice, and I really didn't take it on to my own until around '81 or '82.

CP: What do you mean by collective practice?

AMB: I mean we did them together. We would build the parts for the altar and we would create an overall aesthetic, but then we would leave it open to other people to put their offerings. We didn't control the aesthetic in the way a single artist would. In fact, we created a public space that people could participate in.

CP: People from the neighborhood?

AMB: Yes, people from the neighborhood and other artists. The altars were tied to the *danzante* tradition of the Aztec dancing, the processionals for the Day of the Dead. They became part of an overall cultural practice that engaged communities in different ways.

CP: At what point did you begin working in museum environments?

AMB: That started around '82 or '83.

CP: How did that affect the content of your work and your relationship to audience?

AMB: Early on, I always worked in the context of a Mexican museum or some sort of ethnic museum, so it was slow and gradual. I can't quite remember when I started crossing over. I do remember that I knew instinctively that my practices would have to change. The regular museums wouldn't let me do *limpias,* or cleansings, for instance, in which I would ask someone like a *curandera* or a healer to come in and bless my space, or I would do it myself using *copal* incense. I couldn't do that because it would set off the fire alarms and sprinkler systems. That was my first little lesson. Little by little, I recognized the concept of interpretive devices. In fact, in some ways that's how I got into criticism and writing. I discovered that people didn't know what these things meant, so I had to write about Mexican traditions like honoring the dead, because otherwise Americans would simply feel that those candy skulls were ghoulish. They didn't understand them. So that was the next step.

The notion of building anti-elitist spaces was in the tradition of the Chicano movement. So to find yourself in the elitist space meant to question within yourself, am I in the system or outside the system? Am I attacking the system, resisting the system, subverting the system? It forced many of us into ethical debates among ourselves and within ourselves. I had to make peace with the fact that part of me wanted to really change the very nature of this nation's patrimony. I wasn't willing to stand outside the system that I as a taxpayer was subsidizing. If municipal and state and federal monies that came from our tax base were going to be used to sustain institutions, we had every right to demand to be in those institutions and to have those institutions reflect our reality. That was another shift for me—from being in museums as an artist to intervening in the practice of museums. I began to take on that aspect of artmaking in the mid-eighties.

CP: Do you feel like you've been successful?

AMB: No.

CP: How do you measure your progress in that environment?

AMB: Well, I guess I've learned certain things, one of which is that museums are governed by old men, more often that not, who at the end of their lives are the last people who will ever question the rightness or logic of what they did. If you want to make change, shaking your finger at a 65-year old white man who runs the National Gallery is probably not a great idea. But what you *can* do is teach in the systems that prepare people to take on those roles. You can prepare young people from a variety of backgrounds to aim for those positions. So in a certain sense, I never gave up shaking my finger. I used to call myself the Cultural Attack Dog, but then I found myself making jokes about what happens to old attack dogs when no one really wants them or trusts them! *[laughter]*

CP: Did you think you were attacking the system or subverting it?

AMB: I thought I was attacking it. But then I realized that that was not going to work. So I began trying to subvert it for the next several years, and then felt for a period of time that I was the one being subverted, and I had to get out of the system. That was in '91, and in '92, I came back home again. I think of it that way. That's when I began to spend more time at the Galeria and the Mexican Museum again, and when I started the Regeneration Project. Now I see myself in a different stage of my life, which is working to codify the knowledge that we developed as artists and activists and bring that into the preparation of young artists and thinkers. I feel that's an important goal that has emerged from the Regeneration Project, which has been such a life-giving experience for me.

CP: What is the Regeneration Project?

AMB: It started out as a sort of ad hoc gathering of young people at the Galeria de la Raza in San Francisco. The Galeria was approaching its twenty-fifth anniversary, and there was a focus on the idea of renewal. We recognized that one of the chronic problems in community-based institutions is the exhaustion of its leadership. Where are you going to get someone who's going to continue to do this? People in our generation started because the necessity of building an alternative space was so critical. And once you got into it, it became your life, your plan, and your community. But for some young person, why would they do that? We recognized that we were aging, people were becoming exhausted and burning out, there were a lot of chronic illnesses arising among us, and we perceived that there wasn't going to be anybody to take this over. Sometimes there have been as many as three organizations within the Southwest all looking for a curator at the same time, and you couldn't find one single Chicano or Latino curator to take any of those jobs. It was clear that the schools weren't really producing them and at the same time young people were coming to us, as artists and as role models for themselves.

   It also had to do with my serious illness and regeneration, and the resources from the MacArthur Foundation grant which freed me to begin Regeneration. We decided to develop this project where established artists would reach out to young people through a series of intergenerational dialogues. People like Judy Baca, Carmen Lomas Garza, Guillermo Goméz-Peña, Ruben Trejo, Yolanda Lopez, and others started doing . . . just talks. We recruited through different college campuses and art schools, young people from their mid-twenties to early thirties. We decided to produce three exhibitions in 1995. We set up a committee system, educational programs in curating, archives, and writing, and then we eventually got enough money to hire a young person, David Contrares, as our coordinator. We just set about with these committees and it developed a life of its own. The young people in Regeneration produce their own catalogues now, their writer's manifestos, and they've gone into the Galeria and archived materials. Actually, in a lot of ways, they've helped us to make sense out of our own history.

For a number of the kids, this has been their first collective experience. They are the product of very isolated, individualistic, and competitive models in higher education. It's a strange contradiction. Our generation basically kicked open the doors and set up programs and opportunities for them, but in the backlash over the years we couldn't sustain the faculty. Now as our kids get recruited, particularly into the Ivy League schools, they get there and find there is no there for them. It's a totally isolated experience. Some of them don't even last a year. So, in a way, the Regeneration Project is filling a gap that the colleges and universities have not been able to fill. These young people have become educated in a way that makes them different from people in their families, different in their communities. For some of them, this is the only project that has enabled them to feel connected again. They don't feel that they're the only ones. They spend a lot of time either asking us questions about our lives or exchanging information with each other in sort of a support group model. It started about access and exhibitions and venues, but it has become much more about life experience and support and collectivity, which they just didn't have where they were.

CP: How has Regeneration evolved?

AMB: It's been amazing. The makeup of the Galeria's permanent staff has changed. More young people actually work there now; they're not just volunteers. The project has a capacity of about 200 or 300 participants. They have an incredible network, they have a 'zine, a website, monthly spoken word/poetry readings, they sponsor arts education in the neighborhood, in the *barrio*. They went so far beyond anything we ever foresaw. One of them now is in an internship at the Smithsonian; more and more of them are going on to do other work.

It started out with a small group of kids. They still come to us for advice, but they run it now. I think it could be used as a model for other organizations to revitalize their own energies. We're coming to the end of the founding generation of community arts. The founders are now in their sixties, facing health problems, facing retirements with little or no benefits, locked into struggles and concepts that aren't flexible anymore. You have to prepare this young generation, because if you really believe in what you're doing, you know it can go on without you. A good parent can let a child go, a good teacher says goodbye. You have to be able to do that. It's very hard.

CP: How are you preparing them for this different environment?

AMB: We try to keep them connected to people in the field, get them internships, build a network for them. We try to teach them and then step out of the way. That's the most important thing, stepping out of the way. You can't stand it when they make mistakes, but you have to. I see that as the legacy of this generation of founding arts administrators, the hand pulling up the next one. They don't look like us and they don't behave like us, but we need to accept that.

CP: And do you think a new generation of cultural leaders will emerge from this process?

AMB: Absolutely. That's my dream, that many of our organizations would regenerate themselves. I think in a social sense, the role of the mother is somehow at the heart of Regeneration—because the bulk of the people who've put the energy into doing it have been women. Some men have come and gone, but it's really been the women. The kids that we've attracted have also been largely women, young women, and gay and lesbian kids.

CP: We spent some time talking about the profile of the teacher in relation to his or her constituency. What do you think the profile of an artist should be in relation to the community?

AMB: I think one has to ask the question: what context can an artist work in that is useful? Now, artists often go into residencies in public school settings. Often the school is unprepared for dealing with the artist, and the artist is totally unprepared for dealing with the reality of school-based schedules, recesses, bureaucracies. So it's not always a good match. I think there are very few models for artists working in community-based organizations.

CP: Then how can artists learn to do this kind of work effectively?

AMB: It's important to encourage artists to see art as a part of social production, not just cultural production. They need to acquire a variety of skills because the bulk of their work will not take place in a studio. They need to be able to write well, they need to be able to articulate their ideas, and they need to know something about organizing. One of the things we had to do with the Regeneration group is that we had to teach them how to run meetings—how to set an agenda, how to solicit ideas from the people who aren't talking, how to develop task models and how to make systems that are accountable. They knew how to do things by themselves, but they didn't know how to do it in groups.

One of the nineteenth–century romantic models of artists is that they're highly impractical, that they live in this individual dream world and that contact with social reality would only tarnish their experience. I think it's really just about the opposite, that being in contact with social reality provokes you and gives passion to what you want to do. If it's just for yourself, you'll run out of things to do by the time you're 40, but if it has to do with the world around you, you'll never run out of things to do. Most of these kids will go their own individual path. Regeneration has had contact with well over 500 kids in workshops. Out of that, you'll get maybe five really good leaders who will probably spend their lives working in communities. But that's what you need. You just need five.

One of the problems is that too many artists have bought into this art-world hype—you know the Julian Schnabelization of American art where you think that you're going to be rich and famous at the age of 33. Before the fantastically high art market of the eighties, most people went into art school not really thinking that would happen to them, making art because they had to but not really imagining they were going to make a great living. Now we have all these kids with these real fantasies about—

CP: "I'm going to be a star."

AMB: Yeah, "I'm going to be a star." Art schools should be talking about the business of art, which is part of it, but also the activism of art. Because by and large these young artists can expect that certain experiences will not be available to them in their lifetime unless they organize around everything from finding venues to learning how to do public processes like making murals. At some point along the way they are going to have to learn to organize. Even if it's only for self-serving purposes, they should at least have that in mind. I look at it from the other side, too, which is that I think that the social service sector doesn't recognize the power of art. It's hard to get groups who are not art-oriented to see art as a relevant experience and a tool in consciousness. I think that the general public's view of art is that it is an elite practice and that is something that is bought and sold, and that it really belongs to a particular class and race of people.

CP: Do you think that the arts community has cultivated that view?

AMB: Yes, I do. At least in visual arts what's been cultivated is a joke at the expense of—you know, Joe Q. Public. The quality of work has to be esoteric because if the average viewer could walk in and figure it out, then you aren't being sophisticated enough. I feel like our artists in the Latino community really get caught in that. Our work is in fact an outgrowth of our general public, and so consequently we suffer from the perception that our work is simpleminded narrative, embedded in popular culture, that it isn't intellectually rigorous or relevant to critical contemporary issues. No one would say that to me, but I sense that. And worst of all, that it's politically self-serving, because people still think of us as a minority and they don't recognize that give or take about ten years, we'll be the majority. Our story is an American story. We are still perceived as marginal to the real American culture. So if we pay attention to ourselves, we're seen as a sort of one-note song, chauvinistic, narrowly focused—unlike mainstream white culture, which sees all of art and culture as itself and therefore does not see itself as self-serving, because it is universal.

But if a group of people represent nearly a majority of the population, don't they have the right to representation? And if they do, shouldn't there be a sizable amount of leadership and resources put in their service? If that's not happening, then we have to say what it is: it's educational and cultural apartheid. If you want to support that, you can, but don't sit there and tell me it's because I'm a one-note song. The art world is more sophisticated than the world of education, so they never say those kinds of things so overtly. But the system is set up in such a way that you're seen as having a specialty, whereas a person who talks about Impressionist art is never seen as having a specialty; they're in fact part of the canon. So part of the dilemma, I think, of trying to set up models of activism within the arts is that there are a lot of hidden agendas about what issues are really significant and what are not.

CP: Your own activist work in both art and education has focused around issues of race and ethnicity. Do you think class figures into this discussion as well?

AMB: It's a hard one. We always talk about this "complex identity," that there's something about the composite of race, class, culture, and sexuality that makes it impossible for us to make any sweeping statements about, say, Chicanos, or Latinos, or lesbians. But I guess if it's put to a test, I still think that, by and large, race/culture intersects with class as a formative worldview.

CP: Do you think issues of race or class have figured into the debates around public support for the arts?

AMB: At a certain point early in the censorship discussion at the National Endowment for the Arts, many of us in communities of color were approached by people from what I consider the white avant-garde to stand shoulder to shoulder in the battle. We did at the beginning, because people like Andres Serrano were involved, and even the issues around the Robert Mapplethorpe controversy were racial issues. But then things seemed to move further and further away from a common ground, and communities of color stepped back. We are made up of both traditional and nontraditional constituencies, and many of our organizations have to serve both. I think this is one of the complexities of diversity. We're very respectful of certain cultural lines, so pushing the boundaries around sexuality, for instance, isn't really an issue.

At some point, some of us asked, "Why would you send a sexually explicit tape to the National Endowment for the Arts? Is it really necessary to push people that far?" People of color learn, and I'm talking as an individual, you learn from the day that you can walk and talk and go to school that things are dangerous. You're not stupid and you're never a fool about those things unless you become so angry and self-destructive that you just become provocative. I think leadership in our communities has developed because they have been able to judge what battles are worth fighting, and what are not, what is wise politically and how to organize so that your communities are protected.

It was a battle forged in our names, without our participation and leadership. It's analogous to one of the models of identity politics that people really loathe, which is that white spokespersons fight on our behalf without asking us what we want and what we think. Yet, when the battle is won or lost, we get lumped into the decision making and the result.

If you peel back the cover of sexuality from the NEA debates, the deepest and most abiding source of fear, the real political target group, was not gays and lesbians. It was about us—Proposition 187, anti-affirmative action legislation, all that has come to pass in the national agenda around immigration. I believe sincerely that what was going on in the censorship and freedom of expression battle at the NEA is really about cultural change—cultural manifestations and cultural expressions that are not in the comfort zone of the white right. I think that fighting it out over the level of sexual politics was probably the most obvious level, and certainly one that the religious right could really hook onto and get the general public to be alarmed about. But I think implicit within that has been a much deeper agenda about controlling a shifting demographic that makes them very, very nervous. We're really the Other.

CP: More and more often now, the arts are pitted against social services as an either/or in debates over public funding. Why is that?

AMB: I think it has to do with this issue of what's life threatening. If you're operating at a level where people are blowing each other away outside the door of your institution, then the idea of working on a cultural project, an exhibition or a mural, seems like a real luxury. You have to keep these kids safe, you have to give them alternatives to conflict and violence. I'm working with a group of people on a violence-prevention initiative. We're trying to position the initiative around the idea that violence in the community is no longer a criminal justice issue. It is a preventable public health issue. Consequently, art and recreation are part of the alternatives for a healthy life, and therefore can be seen as relevant to reducing violence and giving young people tools for expressing themselves and for resolving conflictual circumstances that they're in.

CP: Who is your audience for that argument?

AMB: Social service people. And they're sort of understanding it. First you have to start with convincing them that you want to help, and then second, together you have to convince funders that that kind of art is worth investing in. It isn't about a private market, it isn't about career individuals, and it isn't about an elite esoteric. It is life saving. It has to do with giving young people an experience of being able to be competent, to be relevant, to be useful, and to be able to communicate what they see and think about the world in terms other than words. Because I think the inarticulateness that they suffer from turns back in on them and is destructive. And the one thing artists learn is that they can transform momentarily their dissatisfaction into terms of a world they want. That's what art is. And if you can give that to a young person, then they can also experience this capacity to transform the world in terms that suit you.

CP: Have you encountered a tendency for social service workers to want to measure art quantitatively?

AMB: Yeah, and that's one of the things that artists fight—being asked to provide art that can be measured by its relationship to literacy, or to a reduction of violence, or skills enhancement. I think all of those things are important. If you're an activist, you want the art to be associated with literacy, you want people to have the organizational and communicative skills to reduce conflict in their lives, you want them to be able to feel competent and to believe that there is power and purpose in making something. So personally I don't really fight it a lot, but I know a lot of artists are uncomfortable with it.

CP: I think maybe they're uncomfortable with trying to reduce art to a statistical outcome, which overlooks the fundamental, spiritual nature of art and the artmaking process.

AMB: I think that's something that we have to educate people about. I think there is a great myth about art. Just like that nineteenth-century model we were talking about, people don't really know how it happens, the mental process that artists go through—these very subtle and sometimes unarticulated or unconscious processes of judgment and interpretation. It's essentially a cognitive process of transforming raw materials into meaning. There is something about that that people need to know, how to see the relationship between the process of learning and the capacity to be a person, to know inside when to change and when to stop, when to think and when to experience and feel. That making art is a series of ethical reflections. We don't really know a lot about that in teaching. I think that that's the interesting thing about art that has not yet come out, that is beyond quantification. It would really help people to see the relationship of art and social practice, art and education, art and human development. That's key.

You see, I think it's incumbent on arts organizations to go talk to the people around them. The Galeria de la Raza is a block around the corner from St. Peter's Church where the immigrant youth go for a *Joves Y Ninos* program. Well, they have to walk by the Galeria to go to the project, so they peek in the window. Another youth organization, RAP, is a half a block down the other direction on Bryant Street. So you have an arts organization that's right between two major stakeholders in this violence prevention initiative. When you're on Twenty-fourth and Bryant, you go across the street to the paint store to get more paint, they say what are you working on, and we go "Oh, yeah, well, we have a new show over there, you have to come and see it," or people walk by and the old ladies stand in the window and discuss things. They might not always come in but they talk about it and observe it. The first question artists need to ask is how close are they to any constituency of everyday people and what can they do to get closer to them? Because if they got closer to them, they might see then what relevant issues for them as artists or as organizations could be brought to bear.

CP: Now that you are working within an academic environment, what do you teach your students about how to find their place as artists in the community?

AMB: As artists, we're teaching them how to analyze information, how to work in a community, how to organize and collaborate, how to produce work, how to revise it and change it in respect to the community's responses. More than any single thing, I feel as though we are asking them some very simple questions. Why do you make art? Who do you make it for? That's about it. The making of it, the technical skills are important, but to understand your impulses, to be committed to it as a reciprocal process is much more important. It takes years to master the technical, but that means nothing if you don't know why you do it or who you do it for.

For me, on the bigger level, it's about private and public. When I was younger, it was minority/majority. Then in my museum and critical theory years, it was center/margin. The paradigm that makes sense for me now is public/private—asking questions about who controls those spaces. We live near Pebble Beach, which is a gated community. We say to the students, here you have people who are leading their public lives in private because they have the resources. And then just go over to Watsonville or Salinas, any of the farm worker camps around here, and you will see people living their private lives in public. We don't provide the farm workers adequate housing or recreational space. So what's your responsibility? If you're going to work in public spaces, who is the public? What is public and what is private? What is your responsibility to transform that space, to create opportunities for exchange for people? There's a whole push in public art that's very corporate. It's about controlling space—benches no one can sleep on, beautiful wrought iron gates that lock people out and protect the people who are in. I feel that we are in an age when we have to really question the goals of public art or they will become as locked in as the ones about private work in museums. The goals of public art are still porous enough for us to be able to influence their development.

CP: What do you tell your students about why you make art?

AMB: I tell them that it is a relationship between what others might call private narratives and what I call public dialogues. That my family is a Mexican family, and like many Mexican families, when I extrapolate the stories of people through this work, I am telling an Everyman or Everywoman story. That I still continue to make art to transform people's sense of themselves and their relationship to each other. I don't believe anymore that I make work only for Chicanos or only for women, but I make it for people who want to reflect on the condition that they are part of, whether they are creating that condition or are victimized by it. Either way, that's what I want. I want them to stop dead in their tracks, look at the relationship of these objects, look at the little words pencilled on the wall and say to themselves, "Oh my God, I never thought about that." I realize that it's not something I can control. Once they leave my environment, they will do whatever they will do.

CP: Are you working at all in public sites now?

AMB: Yes. I've been working on a piece called *Private Landscapes and Public Territories, 1848–1998—the Reannexation Project.* It's my own version of taking back the territories, my own little joke. I've been tracing my family's geographic history. I'm using the data I gather to create interior/exterior garden landscape spaces on a very temporary basis. My first piece was done in Copenhagen, of all places. I'm also going to do it at the Galeria de la Raza and a public park near there. I'm excited about it. My parents are getting older and they'll die at some point, as all parents do. I feel like the one thing I never learned from them is the way they grow things. So this has been an opportunity for me to learn from them.

CP: What do your parents think of your work?

AMB: They love it. My mom thinks it's like spiritual work. She saves things for me, she dries her rose petals. My father is always so thrilled when I show him pictures of his mother in my work. I've made my family history quite well known. I feel like this is what I was supposed to do. My work is part of my own human process. The pieces are signposts of living for me. I don't think of art as separate from living, and I don't think of teaching or writing as separate from living. People used to ask me, "Why do you do all these different things? Don't you feel too spread out?" I said "No, it's my way of gathering things together."

CP: How do you read the signposts of living through your art?

AMB: Some pieces are signposts about how to be well when I've been sick, how to age with grace, how to love people without hurting them, how to find a space for myself for when I'll be gone, how to live and leave myself behind. How to survive without having been a mother, how to be a person without being wedded to a narrow identity. These are all things that I've struggled with along the way. I've never labeled myself as a feminist. I was never part of that movement. But I have come to realize that my stories are as much about a woman's life as they are about a Mexican or Chicano life. Maybe I can't really separate being Chicano from being a woman. Learning to be a woman really comes through lenses of ethnicity, race, and class that makes the idea of being a woman different for each one of us. Even though you and I could have in common very specific things, and have, I'm sure, there will be parts of my life and parts of yours that could never be the same.

CP: As you look back over your life's work, from pieces early in your career to the more recent ones, do you read them as a progress?

AMB: Yes, I do. I've come to realize that I have this domestic tension. At first I completely affirmed all the things I'd been given. Then I went through a period of time of contesting them. And now I have learned to live with the tension that I can never clearly live in or out of them. I can't leave them behind because they're what made me, but I can't totally accept them because they're what limits me. So I live in this tension and consequently create pieces around that tension. I've made slow progress.

CP: Has most of your work taken the form of altars?

AMB: Always. Up until about six years ago, my altars were always ephemeral installations. They weren't permanent. It was only illness that made me decide to make work that was lasting. But my great love is still installation because it's momentary. It's more fragile, and therefore more valuable to me. I think the greatest passions you have in your life are for those fugitive moments which you know will never last. They become in your memory the most powerful things that happen to you. Memory has been the vocabulary for me. If I ask, at this point in my life, what is the contribution I have made in my writing and thinking, it has been to place memory as a device, both of identity and artmaking—creating a ceremony of memory, a ceremony of spirit, and writing around these themes and tropes. I feel good that I was able to select out the function of memory and give us, as Chicanos, a more critical space in the eyes of the outside world—that we aren't just nostalgic, chauvinist nationalists trying to hold onto the past. It is within the remembering that one resists annihilation; in remembering, one claims the past and lives it forward for those that can't be there. I think of memory as a very political practice.

CP: How does memory figure in your work for future audiences if your work is ephemeral?

AMB: That's why the writing and documentation is the thing that really matters to me now.

CP: Are any of the current pieces participatory?

AMB: Somewhat, but not as much as they used to be. It's something I've been thinking about returning to because of being involved in this program at Cal State. I'm teaching these things and I want to live them again. They're based on what we did as young people. And yet, as we become older, more well known and more fiscally stable, as we take on the institutional life, we do less asking. I want to go back to it now.

CP: Do you see yourself moving into the role of an elder?

AMB: Yeah. I'll be 55 this year. Together with others in the Chicano movement, I lived a generation of time that won't come again. We created directions that were very common among ourselves. We need to record it in some way, because then other people will feel they can create new directions themselves. We're still fairly invisible in the cultural landscape of this country. I feel like if we don't do this we will have no one to blame but ourselves.

I have Louise Bourgeois as my model. I look at her—she's in her eighties or nineties, and she is kicking it! I'd like to do exactly the same thing. I want to make art until I just fall down dead. I think it's the best thing for you!

May 18, 1995
San Francisco, California

April 16, 1998
Monterey Bay, California

14

SKIPP PORTEOUS

A FORMER FUNDAMENTALIST MINISTER AND ACTIVIST for the religious right, Skipp Porteous is now one of the religious right's most knowledgeable and outspoken critics. Under his mother's influence, he became a born-again Christian as a young boy in the 1950s, but he became disillusioned with many of fundamentalism's precepts toward the end of his ten years as a minister in the 1960s and 1970s. Initially wanting to stay as far away from his old life as possible, Porteous decided to use his firsthand knowledge to counter the religious right's growing political influence in the 1980s by founding the Institute for First Amendment Studies (IFAS) with his wife, attorney Barbara Simon.

A nonprofit organization located in Great Barrington, Massachusetts, and New York City, IFAS vigilantly researches and reports on the activities of the religious right. Among its many activities, IFAS publishes Freedom Writer *newsletter and maintains a website featuring daily reports on issues pertaining to the First Amendment. In his capacity as director, Porteous has been quoted in a wide range of regional and national newspapers and magazines, has appeared as a First Amendment spokesperson on national television, and has participated in hundreds of radio talk shows, sometimes entering into live debates with such highly vocal conservative leaders as Jerry Falwell and Pat Buchanan.*

Porteous is also a licensed private investigator in New York and Massachusetts, and through IFAS has used undercover volunteers to report on various right-wing groups, including militias. The arts, as well, have figured in his activities, and in the interview that follows, he has very cogent things to say about the motives behind right-wing attacks and how people working in the arts might most effectively diffuse them.

◻ ◻ ◻ ◻ ◻

Marie Cieri: You were a born-again Christian when you were a kid . . .

Skipp Porteous: Yeah, when I was 11 I became a born-again Christian.

MC: Was that through your parents?

SP: Through my mother.

MC: And you later became a minister.

SP: Somewhere in between there I had a few happy years, in what they call a backslidin' condition.

MC: In a what condition?

SP: Backslidin'. Backslidin' is the act of leaving the faith to turn back to the world.

MC: Was that in your middle teens?

SP: Yeah . . . sex, beer, and rock 'n' roll, I guess. A brief period, then I went back into fundamentalism, studied for the ministry, and became a minister.

MC: How long were you a minister?

SP: From the time I was ordained and became a pastor, it was ten years. I started off in upstate New York where I was raised, then went to California to Bible college. I was in California for nine years and came back to upstate New York, which is only a few miles from here.

MC: From your experience, what would you say are the main attractions of adopting a fundamentalist mindset?

SP: We used to try to get people into it by saying Jesus would give them peace, love, and joy. And that's what people tend to find. The reasons they do are important to understand. It's really because they find an easier way of· life. There are many gray areas of life, and in fundamentalism everything is black and white. There is good and evil, there's wrong, there's right. There's God on one side and Satan on the other, and there's no in-between. So you just try to follow God and the Bible. That gives people peace, because they don't have that turmoil.

MC: But you don't have peace if you "sin."

SP: Personally, I don't consider it sin anymore. "Sin" is a theological term that has no basis in reality. So when Christians sin, they just ask Jesus to forgive them, and they go on. But in reality, most fundamentalist Christians have a lot of guilt because they have thoughts. If you lust after a woman in your heart, you have committed adultery. So all these fundamentalist men are going around thinking they have committed adultery because they looked at a woman in the wrong way. Or you might have the case of a gay person who is a fundamentalist who's wrestling with this thing and can never accept his sexuality. Fundamentalists are totally guilt-ridden, and they're most unhappy, I think.

MC: I guess they don't feel that it's religion that's making them feel bad or guilty, but their own bad natures.

SP: There are three things that fundamentalists fight against: the world, the flesh, and the devil. The world is this other thing out here that's not controlled by God, and everybody's crazy. Then the flesh is their own sinful nature that makes them do things they don't want to do. And then they think Satan sends demons to tempt them. They're always fighting this battle; they never relax.

MC: At the time you were a fundamentalist, did you ever consciously attack liberals, or fight against freedom of speech or pornography, any of those things?

SP: I went through phases. In an early phase, I was very anti-Catholic. I was convinced that the Catholic Church was this great harlot or whore in the "Book of Revelations" and the pope was the anti-Christ. I got over that. Then for a while I had a ministry on Sunset Strip in Hollywood to get as many hippies saved as I could. Then for a while I had an interest in getting Jews to accept Jesus as their savior. I never really went after pornography. I guess the thought never occurred to me.

MC: Were you also engaged in political action?

SP: I believed for most of my ministry that if a person accepted Jesus, that person's heart was changed, and then other things would change. I thought you had to make change on an individual basis. And that's true—the only way society's going to change is one person at a time. It wasn't until just about a year and a half before I left the ministry that I became politically active. A friend of mine convinced me that America was supposed to be a

Christian nation, and the only way we could get it back was for Christians to be politically active. So I got involved with a national movement called "If My People." (It was based on 2 Chronicles 7:14, which starts off with those words.) So in 1976, I headed a rally in Albany, New York, where 2,500 born-again Christians came out. Our purpose was to try to get them registered to vote, get involved in politics, run for office and vote for Jimmy Carter, who is a born-again Christian.

We also were always taught that as Christians, our citizenship was in heaven, not of this earth, so we shouldn't be involved in earthly politics; we're like foreigners here. Only since the seventies has this begun to change. This is now one of the main thrusts of the religious right: to get Christians to see that you've got to do it now. Some actually believe that Jesus won't come back until the church has control of the world. That's a strong motivation.

MC: Do you know how all this started in the seventies?

SP: Powerful conservative political leaders, like Paul Weyrich and Richard Viguerie, got together with Jerry Falwell. They realized if they could get conservative Christians to become political, they would have a massive movement. So they set out to do it. One of the things they did was to try to convince Christians that abortion was murder. When I was at Bible college, we used to look at the Scriptures for answers to problems. Somebody asked the teacher one day when human life begins. So we looked in the "Book of Genesis," and it said that God breathed into Adam the breath of life, and he became a living soul. So when a fetus takes the first breath, it becomes a living soul, and that happens after birth. So, I never had a big problem with abortion. Anyway, for part of the religious right in the seventies the whole purpose was to get the church to change its mind about politics. You are seeing the fruit of it now.

MC: You told me earlier you left the ministry in 1977. I know you had a period where you were an undercover cop, and then you founded the Institute for First Amendment Studies. Was that pretty much the sequence?

SP: Sort of. Barbara [his wife] and I met in '79, and in '84 we started this. That was a result of a couple of things that happened in Lenox, Massachusetts [Lenox is about eight miles north of Great Barrington]. A ministry called "The Bible Speaks" took over the town. They had a campus with over 1,000 people of voting age. One of the issues there was whether or not to fluoridate the water. Conservatives go way back with bizarre thoughts about Communist plots and fluoridating the water to dumb-down American brains, and they defeated the measure. Then they bused people into the Republican caucus in Western Massachusetts, took that over and sent the delegates to the national convention in Dallas in '84. Tim LaHaye, Bev's husband, and Jerry Falwell were trying to take over the Republican Party down there in '84.

I'd been familiar with Tim LaHaye for years, followed Pat Robertson for 25 years. When I got out of the movement, I was just so glad and relieved that I never even wanted to think about it again. I thought they were a bunch of nuts and would never get anywhere, but then they started to do some of the things they set out to do. I became alarmed. I thought we would see the end of First Amendment freedoms if they ever got their way. Free speech, press, art—there are so many things they are against that I didn't think it boded well for the country. So I said to Barbara, let's do something. We started publishing *Freedom Writer* in '84 [the Institute's monthly newsletter, which now has a circulation of 54,000]. We mailed 100 copies to friends and family, everyone we could think of.

MC: To other people who had defected?

SP: I have no association whatever with any of the old friends—they cut me off. For a while, they used to call me. They'd say, "Skipp, I'd like to share some of the Scriptures with you," and I'd say, "I can't imagine what Scriptures you could share with me; I probably know more than you do." However, we did publish a newsletter called *Walk Away* for people who had left, and we still publish it on the Internet. It's very popular.

MC: What do you think are the key reasons why "do it while you're on earth" has caught on? You yourself thought they would never get anywhere, but this is a powerful movement at this point.

SP: Sure, and if you ask them or read their literature, they would say God has started a revival. But it's been really shrewd planning and hard work. After the fall of Jimmy Swaggart and Jim Bakker, the mainstream media said the religious right was dead. We didn't say that because we knew it wasn't. What they did was just go back to the drawing board. For example, the Moral Majority had been focusing on national politics, the White House and so forth, and it was mostly a PR movement. After that failed they realized they had to do it differently. They didn't just give up. They began working on a grassroots level. And for grassroots organizing you have to train people. This is why the Christian Coalition has held thousands of training schools; so has Focus on the Family, with community impact seminars. Through training, they are establishing footholds all over the country and organizing through that.

MC: What's the training like? Do you go away for a couple of weeks?

SP: No, it's usually just two days, like a weekend. And it's intensive. It lays out the problem and gives simplistic solutions. The way they take control is by organizing, so they'll tell people they have to have precinct captains and block captains, state chairs. They organize right down to the precinct level, and they have the whole country divided into little voting blocks.

MC: It sounds like people are so obedient. Is that because this is so tied into religion?

SP: Yeah, they're obedient because they feel that Pat Robertson is God's servant, or Bev LaHaye is God's servant. They trust that these people are hearing God and passing the word down to them. They emphasize authority a lot in those circles. The wife is under the husband's authority, the husband's under the pastor, and so forth. That helps people to be obedient.

MC: It certainly helps avoid one of the pitfalls of being an activist: trying to mobilize people who often don't agree about methods for reaching goals. But it sounds like people know where they fit in because of this structure of authority, and they just do it.

SP: The activists we're talking about do. However, the religious right is by no means monolithic. There are many divisions. You asked what the institute does. One of the things we do is look for weaknesses among the religious right and try to divide them. I'm pretty sure Jerry Falwell can't stand Pat Robertson, and Pat Robertson probably can't stand Jerry Falwell. I know a lot of ministers who hate Jim Dobson because he's raking in so much money. There are intense jealousies and bickering.

MC: Among the leaders.

SP: Oh yeah, and among some of the followers, too. Baptists hate tongues-speaking Pentecostals, and a lot of the Pentecostals still don't trust Catholics, and the Christian Coalition is trying to recruit Catholics. So we play on all these things. I think that's important to do, divide and conquer. We work with Christian organizations and Christian publications. There's a Christian magazine that uses stuff from the *Freedom Writer*. They don't have to say it's from the *Freedom Writer* because their readers would reject it if they knew we provided it. So we end up giving some Christian groups ammunition to fight their Christian brothers.

MC: Is that "divide and conquer" strategy one you developed from a right-wing model, or is it just a general premise?

SP: We try to present the radical right in its own words. We don't have to *accuse* them of stuff; we say this is what they've done, here's proof. We go for the jugular; we don't mess around. We're not objective, never pretend to be. But this is the way the right wing is. Radical papers like Don Wildmon's *AFA Journal* are hysterical—it's sort of like a *National Enquirer,* it's so wild and crazy. I take on that style sometimes. The difference is that we have the evidence to back up what we're saying, which they often don't. But I'm not sure where I got the strategy of dividing and conquering. It's an old strategy, but I don't think the right wing has done it. Coming from within, I just know how their minds work.

MC: I think they have used "divide and conquer." For example, I've heard stories of the religious right trying to divide African Americans who are truly religious, true believers, over the issue of gay rights. Most African Americans are progressive in terms of civil rights, but there have been concerted efforts to dissuade them from forming bonds with religious gays and lesbians.

SP: That's probably true. African Americans tend to be more liberal; even though they might go to conservative churches, they're for civil rights. So I think the gay issue is used to try to convince them that they should be joining the religious right. Do you know who Mel White is? Yeah, they had a real problem with Mel. He used to work for Falwell, Robertson, Billy Graham, Oliver North. He knows how they can't stand each other. [Before coming out as gay, White was a ghostwriter for many evangelists and political conservatives. At the time of this interview, he was dean of the Cathedral of Hope in Dallas, the largest gay/lesbian church in the world.]

MC: I imagine that people like you and Mel White have an advantage in doing what you do because you know the Christian right from the inside.

SP: Yeah, I think so. I can talk their language. Here's an example. We went out to California and had a meeting with Bob Simonds of Citizens for Excellence in Education. He was saying that if he didn't have Jesus in his life, he'd be into gambling, prostitution, and drinking—there would just be no control. I said, "Bob, that's bullshit. You know as well as I do you would not do that. I don't have Jesus in my life, and I don't go out doing those things." A lot of Christians are taught or convince themselves that if they didn't have Jesus as an anchor, they'd go out and do all these things. As soon as he started saying that, I knew where he was coming from and where he was going with it, and I just stopped him. And he said, "Yeah, well"—he admitted it. But that's the kind of stuff they practice and believe in.

MC: I know there have been instances where you've been on radio or television with someone like Jerry Falwell, and when Scripture is quoted to you, you can either debunk it or quote it right back.

SP: Yeah. For instance, I'll do a radio talk show, and somebody'll call in and say "Well, Jesus said" and then quote the Bible. I say wait a minute now, where did Jesus say this? Did he write it? Then he says "Book of John." So I say, "Jesus didn't say that, John said that Jesus said it. We don't know for sure that Jesus said it or not because in another Gospel, Matthew reports something else that Jesus said during the same incident. So what did Jesus really say, what John said or what Matthew said? We don't know." And they get so flustered by that time that they forget the point they're trying to make in the first place.

MC: But truly for them, you're not changing what they think.

SP: No, no, you can't change what they think at all. There are few that have open minds. I get calls from people whose loved ones have fallen into a cult or fundamentalism, and they want to know how to get them out. The fact is 90 percent of these people come out of it in two years anyway. They see that it's not all it was cracked up to be. Something happens somewhere along the line: they see the preacher's on the take or whatever. Then you can reach them. But when they're first really involved and think it's their life, there's no way you can reach them. You just have to be patient.

MC: At this point, the religious right's agenda has evolved into a whole set of principles about how this country ought to be. They often hark back to "better times," to what they consider was the founding fathers' vision for this country. This seems to appeal to a lot of people right now, not just religious people.

SP: I think most Americans think there was some time in our history where everything was wonderful, the golden age. There's a 1958 article that we reprinted in the *Freedom Writer* that talks about the problems teachers faced then in the public schools: "vulgar or obscene language, indecent or improper dress, the formation of infamous clubs, smoking on school property, defacing or destruction of school property, gambling, use of illegal weapons, petting in school, pornographic literature, physical violence against teachers." And this is 1958.

MC: That was one of the times when it was supposed to be perfect, right? *[laughter]*.

SP: It's a myth. Around 1800, only 10 percent of Americans went to church. And this is supposed to be when we were truly a Christian nation.

MC: Also, how do they reconcile the fact that the founding fathers established freedom of expression for this country, and now in many cases they are attempting to squelch freedom of expression, especially from outside the mainstream?

SP: They say that the founding fathers didn't know how far this would come, that they didn't know about gay rights or pornography (although Ben Franklin was supposed to be an avid collector of erotica *[laughter]*). They say that the founding fathers wrote the Bill of Rights in a biblical perspective, and that they didn't think people would really go so far with it by saying or printing anything they wanted. There would be some inner guidelines, inner restraints.

MC: Who do you think formulated the strategy of harking back to "better times," and how do you think they've been most effective in implementing it?

SP: Who is hard to say, because we are talking about many people. You can go back to every well known fundamentalist or even evangelical preacher since the fifties, sixties, seventies—they've all been harping on this. Billy Graham added to it. Falwell certainly has. Pat Robertson has had a major effect through television. In fact, because preachers like to talk so much, they are very much into electronic media. There are about 1,300 Christian radio stations and 300 Christian television stations, and they really use the airwaves to harp on this message. The right wing has perfected direct mail more than the left has. So they've used every medium there is. Now they're on the Internet. There's probably more right-wing stuff on the Internet than anything else.

MC: Christian religious leaders were especially effective in using electronic media to raise large amounts of money, especially before Bakker and Swaggart were exposed in the 1980s. There were a lot of exposés about the Christian right's fundraising, how their followers were being manipulated into giving money through faith healings and such things on television, and about how those funds were being used. Has that kind of fundraising abated somewhat, or is that still going strong?

SP: It's still going. It may not be as strong through television as it was, but they're doing it through direct mail. It's an age-old gimmick: "Send us money, and God will bless you" is really their bottom line. They always make it sound like what they're doing is God's work. What people don't realize is that millions of fundamentalist Christians tithe—give 10 percent of their income to the Lord. Well, the Lord ain't here to pick it up. So who's here? Pat Robertson's here, Jerry Falwell's here. Jimmy Swaggart falls from grace so they feel the voice of the Lord has stopped speaking to them. They pray about it. Then they happen to turn on the TV and somebody else is on it—"Ah, *that's* God's message to me." And they send the money over to that guy. When we had those scandals, the money didn't dry up; it just went to different places. For a while, some of it went to local churches, where it's a good idea to put it anyway. Getting back to politics: these TV evangelists themselves were not very political. The most political thing Jimmy Swaggart ever did was endorse Pat Robertson for president through his magazine. That cost him $265,000 in a fine because he used a nonprofit vehicle to endorse a candidate. We filed charges with the federal government about that.

MC: Your organization did?

SP: Yeah, we felt very good about that. So when the media thought the religious right went away, it just showed its ignorance of what the religious right was. It's a lot more than just a few loudmouthed preachers. You know, we're talking about a movement.

MC: Also, a lot of people tend to think that all fundamentalists are like sheep, unthinking people, but I don't think that's true.

SP: No, a lot of them voted for Bill Clinton *[laughter]*. Normally one would expect that they voted for Bush because the religious right was behind Bush, but they don't always vote the way the religious right's leadership wants them to vote. For example, the Christian Coalition, unofficially, is backing Dole.

MC: They're not backing Buchanan?

SP: No, because they never thought Buchanan could win. But within the grass roots, Christian Coalition people are backing Buchanan. So they're not doing what Robertson says.

MC: So the grass roots is starting to show more power than most believed it had.

SP: Yeah and, as such, it's like a monster gone out of control. This is what scares me about the religious right. I don't think Pat Robertson's any Hitler. I don't even think Buchanan's a Hitler. I think he's probably anti-Semitic and racist, but he's not a Hitler. But with the *climate* they've created, how many Hitlers are there out there waiting to come into power? This monster they're creating might eventually get out of control.

MC: It sounds like there was a sort of core to the religious right, but now it's got a lot of fingers going out in different directions.

SP: Nobody owns it. That's scary too in a way. I think Christian Coalition is just about at its peak. After this next election, they're going to peak for sure. There are signs that they are already starting to break up. They've had a split in Pennsylvania, which had their strongest state chapter, and the director started a new group that seems to be competing with them. They're exaggerating their numbers. Actual circulation of *Christian American,* their magazine, has gone down. Dobson [head of Focus on the Family] has had a couple of heart attacks; I don't think his empire will survive without him there. The religious right won't die, but who's going to take over? And it could be far worse than what we have now. By no means is the movement itself falling apart; it's like an undisciplined army, and somebody'll come along to unite them.

MC: What do you think the majority of Americans are thinking about all this?

SP: Most people probably aren't thinking about this, really.

MC: Yes, I agree. But what's happening now seems like it could be a little more central and potentially threatening to people's values.

SP: Well, you could ask why Buchanan is so popular. Unemployment is high, people are losing their jobs. Major corporations are laying off lots of people. He makes it sound like our jobs are going overseas while Mexicans are coming across the border taking our jobs here. On the other hand, I don't know many middle-class American whites who are going to pick oranges. And he is typical. He presents simplistic answers to complex problems.

MC: Tell me more about your organization and how you're attempting to fight this. What do you think works?

SP: Legally, we're an educational research organization, a nonprofit. We feel that the more people know about the radical religious right, the more they will rise up against it. We feel that an educated public is an informed public. You know, take action. For 12 years we've been trying to warn people what's coming down the pike, and now it's come down the pike.

MC: Who are you trying to warn? It's a big country.

SP: I'm a Unitarian Universalist now, and I've spoken for years in Unitarian churches all over the United States. For the first ten years of our existence, people acted like they knew everything that I was saying. Oh, yeah, we've heard that before. We just released a video that went out to 1,000 Unitarian churches, and the phone's been ringing all day. They saw it this weekend and they're calling. But for so many years we couldn't get them to believe there was a problem developing.

MC: So churches have been a target area.

SP: Liberal churches. And today we're trying to reach more mainstream groups. There are Catholic priests and bishops who agree with us. We sent a mailing out a few years ago to a list of religious leaders Don Wildmon said had supported him. In the mailing we sent evidence of his anti-Semitism. John Almay, who was head of the U.S. Catholic bishops at the time, wrote back saying he didn't support Wildmon in his anti-Semitism. We got a lot of religious leaders to turn against Wildmon. We feel that we have a lot in common with religious leaders. I think religion is basically good for the country, but it's got to be free; everybody has to be really free to make their own choices.

MC: It's part of freedom of expression, I would think.

SP: Yeah. Earlier our organization was involved with a lot of atheists. To some degree we still are, and I don't have a problem with atheism, but I called some of them "fundamentalist atheists" because they are so dogmatic.

Their only message was that there is no God. You're not going to go too far with that. They were just as dogmatic as the religious fundamentalists.

MC: Are religious groups the main audience?

SP: It's a big part of our audience. One thing we try to do is reach into new areas. We don't want to preach to the choir. So many groups keep preaching the same thing to the same people and don't grow. We want to find new people and convince them there's a problem. So, again, we reach out to different religious groups. I've spoken at a lot of temples and synagogues. But then we're trying to reach just anybody. We try to get into magazines and newspapers, publications that normally don't talk about this stuff. Okay, practically everybody who reads *Mother Jones* would agree with us, but not everybody who reads the *New York Times* agrees with us. That's always a struggle. And we have testimonies from a lot of people who said they had no idea this was a problem until they read the *Freedom Writer*.

MC: Is print your main communications vehicle?

SP: Print and the Internet. We have a home page on the Internet. We're getting 25,000 hits a week now. *Playboy* is featuring our home page in its April issue. They warned us we're going to be bombarded.

We have something called the Electronic Activist on our site. You can click on your state, see who your elected representatives are from your town right up to the state and federal level. Click on a name with an e-mail address, type a letter, click again, and that message goes to your representative. We have radio stations and newspapers on there so you can send letters directly to the editor. This is a vehicle that people can use to communicate.

MC: Since the religious right has been so heavily involved in television and radio, have you considered trying to set up your own program?

SP: No, but for five years I was doing 100 radio shows a year. That's two a week. I was probably on most every talk show in the country. I was on Pat Buchanan's show twice *[laughter]*. I've been on Donohue, Morton Downey. A little television, but mostly radio. In fact, when Robertson was running for president, I scheduled radio interviews in the cities he was in at the same time he was there.

MC: That's great. One of the things I hear a lot from progressives is that it's an unfair battle because religious conservatives have all these electronic weapons, and they don't have any. That's certainly changed somewhat with the Internet, but it hasn't changed that much with broadcast media.

SP: You see that flag there? That was America's first non-burning flag. When they said you could burn the flag, I said all right, we'll give the right-wingers something they've been primed for. I fireproofed the flag with chemicals. When that hit the AP wire, I was on that phone doing interviews for 15 hours straight. To go to the bathroom, I had to take the phone off the hook *[laughter]*. It was amazing. So we work all kinds of media. We work with Frank Rich at the *New York Times, 60 Minutes.* Often the media is more conservative than I wish it would be, but at least the minds there are open to ideas. So we give a lot of information to the media to expand our outreach. We don't usually get credit for the work out there, but it doesn't really matter. We had sent somebody undercover to a conference in Branson, Missouri, and he came back with some devastating tapes of the glee that was going on there after the Oklahoma City bombing. *Time* magazine called, and I said I have this tape. They sent a limousine from New York to pick it up, and they printed something about it in the next issue.

MC: That's amazing. You have people who are connected to this organization who go undercover and are actually members of these groups?

SP: Uh-huh. We are always trying to present what the other side is saying from their own sources. And one of the best ways to get inside information is to get inside. We've penetrated virtually all the larger groups, and we have people working in different capacities there.

MC: Is that dangerous for them?

SP: Yeah, very much so. Especially in militant groups.

MC: Have you sent anyone into the militias?

SP: We have some people in a militia group now. Their lives are literally at risk. But they're volunteers, they want to do this. They think it's important and so do we. We go to great lengths to protect their identity. CNN wanted to interview one of our people in a militia. The way we arranged it was to have CNN rent a hotel room in Washington. The mole flew in, knocked on the door, and the whole crew went into the bathroom. He put a hood on his head and went in. They came out and interviewed him. Then they went into the bathroom again, and he left. We had to deal with

CNN's lawyers because they said, "How do we know you're not just making this up?" They just had to trust us.

MC: Are the people who go undercover of a certain occupation or personality? And how do you find these people?

SP: I speak at seminars and conferences a lot: the Anti-Defamation League, NOW chapters, Planned Parenthood. After these talks, I often ask for volunteers for the Institute. Many people come up afterwards, and I try to see where they're coming from. Sometimes I suggest they monitor their local papers and send clips to us. There are literally hundreds of people who send us stuff. Then a lot of times I'll say that the Christian Coalition is having meetings in their area, could they just attend and let us know what's happening. And then others have been developed into moles who actually go in there, join and become very involved.

MC: These are people in different parts of the country, not just here.

SP: Oh, none of them are here. In one state, our mole helped start a Christian Coalition newsletter, actually desktop-published it and wrote half of it. And when they were ready to mail it, he'd call and say we're ready to mail it. We have all the addresses of their membership on our computer, so we'd get him the labels.

MC: That's a good mole.

SP: It was hilarious.

MC: How long do these people usually function within an organization?

SP: Usually they can be effective for two years. We have somebody now who has been in for three years, and he's worked his way up quite a bit. But it's very difficult. For somebody who is joining the hometown chapter, it's very intense because they all know where the person lives, what his phone number is and everything. The person has to act like a fundamentalist all the time. But if we send people to Colorado Springs or San Diego it's a lot easier because they only have to act during the day.

MC: What do you feel at this point is your most effective weapon?

SP: The truth. Doing good research and getting good material out there.

MC: Given the enormity of the situation, do you ever feel frustrated or discouraged because, compared to the Christian Right, you don't have as many financial resources?

SP: I like what the late Supreme Court Justice Thurgood Marshall said: "I did what I could with what I had." And that's all we can do. We don't have millions, but we've been hanging in for 12 years now. For 10 years I wasn't on salary.

MC: How did you make a living?

SP: We had to do all kinds of stuff. Barbara and I ran a movie theater in town. I mowed lawns. I did just enough to pay our bills so we could keep doing this. One summer we mailed out the *Freedom Writer* and had ten cents left in the bank. If you asked Don Wildmon about this, he would say God hasn't called me to be successful, just to be obedient. I can't say that. I can only do what I feel in my heart I should do and do it the best I can. And keep my passport renewed in case it doesn't work *[laughter]*.

MC: I now want to get into the area of freedom of expression as it relates to the arts. Have you been involved in that struggle at all?

SP: When I was in high school my favorite class was art. Then I went to art school for a year in New York City. When I was a young teenager, I belonged to something called a Community Activities League. We had an art show, and Norman Rockwell came to speak. So they asked me if I'd go out to his car with him and carry a painting in. The paint was actually wet—he had just finished it. So I got to meet him there. Later, when I was in the ministry, I came back from California and went over to his home one night and tried to convert him. He was funny. He just was totally . . .

MC: *[Laughter]* He must have been, "Who is this guy?"

SP: And he remembered.

MC: He did remember you.

SP: Yeah. People think he's like a Pat Buchanan or something, but the guy is a secular humanist from way back, I'm sure. He indicated that he didn't know there was such a thing as hell; he wasn't worried about it. The whole thing was sort of amusing.

I've always appreciated art, and when I saw Wildmon and others start going after the NEA or after Mapplethorpe, I saw it, immediately, as a fundraising gimmick through and through. Most of these people don't know what art is, and they don't care for it. They wouldn't go to an art show if it opened in their front yard.

I remember back when one of Wildmon's members at the AFA [American Family Association] found *Piss Christ*. Wildmon checked it out because he couldn't believe it at first. Of all the maybe 60,000 exhibits or pieces of work that the NEA has funded, they got two or three that they were upset about. I guess if the cross wasn't immersed in urine, it would have been all right. It would have been funding religion. They never listened to Andres Serrano, who did *Piss Christ,* to hear his explanation. He said he was making fun of the commercialization of religion. And that's a good way to do it. Art has always been a way of expressing viewpoints. That's all he was trying to do, but they thought if they positioned this properly they could get people to think the government was funding anti-Christian art. His purpose was really pro-Christian, it wasn't anti-Christian at all. Serrano was Catholic. I debated with Wildmon on the radio about [the film] *The Last Temptation of Christ*. Again, [the campaign to ban it] was an anti-Semitic attempt at raising funds. The bottom line about all this objection to so-called obscene art is that it's for fundraising. That's all it is.

MC: Why art?

SP: Well, again, they look for tools they can use. They wouldn't go after art if it wasn't publicly funded. People think, "My hard-earned money is going into taxes, which are funding this anti-Christian, obscene art. I'm pissed and don't want anything to do with it." Wildmon can use that. But if they destroy the NEA, they're going to lose a valuable fundraising tool. I don't think they would want to.

MC: That's an interesting perspective.

SP: They need that there. It's a devil for them. They need something to keep banging at.

MC: Let's just hypothesize that one of their people, let's say it was Buchanan, became President, and Congress was still controlled by Republicans. Do you feel that they wouldn't then abolish the NEA?

SP: They could; it's possible. They've cut it back a lot. But if they do, they're gonna be kicking themselves, because it's a great fundraising tool. I get mailings from Wildmon, and he has warnings, do not let children open this envelope and so forth. You open it, and you can see reproductions of *Piss Christ* and all these things.

MC: I was thumbing through your book *[Jesus Doesn't Live Here Anymore]* and reading the transcript of your session with Jerry Falwell on the Morton Downey, Jr. radio program. You and Falwell were going back and forth, and he had said something about not using the misdeeds of a couple of people, namely Bakker and Swaggart, to condemn fundamentalism. One of the defenses the art world has made is why throw away government funding of the arts if there are only two or three things that are objectionable? What I'm proposing is that the argument is the same.

SP: It is and it isn't. First of all, taxpayer dollars don't fund religion. That's one thing we don't want. We want separation of church and state.

MC: No, you're right about that. And your premise is that the trouble comes from the arts being federally funded.

SP: Yeah. If corporations decided to fund the arts and government didn't anymore, it would change the whole picture.

MC: But the religious right also condemns pornography, commercial pornography, doesn't it? And some elected officials have started condemning Hollywood movies because of sex and violence.

SP: Well, go back to the arts for a second. I think that if this government put more into arts than they do into defense, we'd have a kinder, gentler society. We live in such a violent nation—most of our sports are violent. But, by and large, Middle America doesn't really appreciate art.

MC: I agree. As these controversies about the arts have gone on—the undermining of the NEA, various censorship threats—a lot of people in the arts have been surprised and disappointed that more people didn't spring to the defense of the arts to say they're so important, and we have to support them. My feeling has been that in general, people are apathetic about the arts because they don't feel the arts are important to their lives.

SP: I agree.

MC: When it comes to entertainment, people are really into it. But when it comes to work that's intended to make you think, upset you, or not make you feel happy . . . people may not actively try to get rid of it, but they're not going to actively try to keep it either.

SP: Right. They won't back it, that's for sure.

MC: I'm curious: do you think that the government should fund the arts?

SP: Yeah, I do. I think the government should double the NEA's budget. I think it does so much good for communities all over the United States. There might be a community affair with line dancing in some town, might be an art exhibit in another or a play. There are so many ways it benefits communities, and I don't think we pay enough attention to art in this country. It's a wonderful expression of life and beauty in our culture.

MC: So you see it as the government supporting what our culture is and can become as well as freedom of expression.

SP: The government is the people. People who hate the government forget that. These are people we elected—they're our neighbors. But our society is violently oriented. Sports-minded. The movies reflect our society. Sometimes I think the movies shape the society. I agree about violence in the movies and on television. Not the sex part. Sexual violence is violence, but there's nothing wrong with sex.

MC: You agree with the criticisms of violence.

SP: Yes, I do. But I don't think it should be curtailed through law. I think people should take responsibility. But filmmakers have to constantly outdo each other, try to find better ways to blow people up. Competition drives them to further lengths to entertain, and it's disgusting.

MC: One of the arguments used against government funding of the arts is that the arts should just participate, without assistance, in that marketplace.

SP: But I think the government has the responsibility to keep art alive. Frankly, there probably isn't enough interest to keep a lot of art alive. But it should be kept; it's a way of teaching people. I think it's almost a mandate for the government to teach people this way.

MC: Has your organization been involved at all in the arts controversies?

SP: Only when I debate Wildmon and others when I see them using art falsely. They *lie* constantly. I thought Christians aren't supposed to lie, but they do all the time. Whether it's with *The Last Temptation of Christ* (which isn't anti-Christian at all) or Mapplethorpe, they use one little thing, totally taken out of context, just to raise money.

MC: Do you think it's usually about sex?

SP: Not always—it can be what they call an anti-Christian image. That and sex are the two big things. Fundamentalists are totally hung up about sex, so they can use that easily. You couldn't throw enough sex at people to hurt society. It's only when the violence comes into it

MC: There's been a lot of frustration within the arts community because people feel that they're very vulnerable, that they don't have any power, and that they've been pretty ineffective in answering the attacks. Do you have any suggestions or ideas about how the cultural community might deal better with all this?

SP: I would say one way is to try to get involved with churches. Many go practically unused all week long. They can't use the sanctuary, probably, for an art exhibit, but many of them have a banquet hall or meeting halls. They're great places for art. Synagogues, too. I think every community should have some kind of arts council, a group that can move quickly if it has to if acts of censorship come along. It should be connected with national groups. People for the American Way, for instance, is a strong defender of art. That way a local group can learn what others have done when they've come under attack. They can't be isolated.

MC: I think they do feel isolated. I think coalition building is an important thing to do, but I'm wondering if you have suggestions about *how* coalitions can be built, especially when controversial work is involved, a real freedom-of-expression issue. I'll give you an example: if someone wanted to put up works by Andres Serrano in a church, it could be a real struggle.

SP: It would have to be a pretty liberal church. But the point is that people in the arts should try to get as much and as diverse community support as they can for their events, so when trouble comes, they've already got the majority on their side. It could be through printing a program and getting businesses to advertise in it. Let them know what it's all about. In the majority of the cases, they wouldn't have a problem, but if they were ready for it, it might make a difference. And even if the event isn't in a church, get some members of the church to back it. If trouble came then, they'd have religious people behind them.

We shouldn't have to think that way: this is a free country, supposedly. We should be able to show anything we want, but that's not the climate we're living in. We need to realize that while it might seem innocuous or very innocent to us, you don't always realize who's in the community and how they perceive some of this stuff.

February 26, 1996
Great Barrington, Massachusetts

15

CLEVE JONES

CLEVE JONES IS THE FOUNDER OF THE NAMES PROJECT, *the organization responsible for the creation and exhibition of the AIDS Memorial Quilt. He moved from Phoenix, Arizona, to San Francisco in the early 1970s to become part of the city's gay community. He was befriended by San Francisco Supervisor Harvey Milk, one of the nation's first openly gay elected officials, who convinced Jones to give up film school to pursue community organizing.*

Jones was shaken by the 1978 assassination of Harvey Milk and San Francisco Mayor George Moscone, and by the subsequent explosion of AIDS-related deaths in San Francisco in the early eighties, to which he lost many close friends. When he himself was diagnosed as HIV-positive, he conceived of the AIDS quilt as a symbol of a compassionate response, one that might illustrate the enormity of the crisis. From the beginning, the quilt was aimed "at grandma" to bring awareness of AIDS to mainstream America. "Elitism is really destructive," says Jones, who saw the factionalized, "coastal" politics of the gay community as an obstacle to finding a cure for the illness.

Currently based in Palm Springs, California, Jones continues to serve as an AIDS activist and spokesperson for the NAMES project. He recently published his autobiography, Stitching a Revolution *(Harper SF), with Jeff Dawson. In the following pages, he tells the story of the AIDS quilt and reflects on the process of personal transformation in finding his role as an activist, the danger of cynicism, and the potential for art to carry a message to the larger community.*

◻ ◻ ◻ ◻ ◻

Claire Peeps: Can we begin with what you were doing in the period before you started the quilt? I believe you were involved in the political system in San Francisco at the time, and right out of college.

Cleve Jones: I never finished college. I got to San Francisco in 1972 and enrolled in the film program at the San Francisco State University. I was hired to work in the legislature in late '79. For most of the seventies I was involved with street activism. For most of the eighties I was involved with more establishment mainstream politics.

My family's always been political. When I was a child, my parents were very strong supporters of the civil rights movement and the protest against the war in Vietnam. I've always had a fascination for politics. But in the seventies I was very much a part of the fringe, radical edge of San Francisco living, and I didn't have much patience for traditional politics. I wanted to be an artist, really. I didn't know of what sort. As I kid, I loved writing and I thought maybe I could write screenplays. Maybe even direct films. Back then I was very shy, so whatever I did, it had to be behind the scenes. I didn't enjoy being in front of people at all. I couldn't even give an oral book report when I was in high school. I would vomit in the bathroom beforehand. So I started to study literature and film, and I used to buy my film in Harvey Milk's camera store. I never really got into school, though, because I was trying to be part of the gay liberation movement that was really exploding here in San Francisco.

Dancing every night was my top priority then. Between that and attending or organizing demonstrations, I just didn't really have time for school. And then one day Harvey took me aside and told me that I really had no talent in film.

CP: But you had a knack for organizing.

CJ: Yeah. I'm happy that I've ended up getting to blend the two as much as I have.

CP: How did you make the transition from shy person to front person? Now you're speaking publicly all across the country, often several times a week.

CJ: Well, I really set out to change myself. I was a wimp. I was a very fearful child, because I always knew that I was queer. I was ashamed of it, and I was quite frightened. I thought that I would be killed. It sounds so silly, but when I was 17, I read an article about phobias in some sort of *Reader's Digest*-type magazine. It suggested that you should just make a list of the things that frighten you the most, and then do them until you are no longer frightened. Well, the three scariest things that I could think of were public speaking, hitchhiking, and having sex *[laughter]*. I'm not afraid of any of them anymore!

CP: After Harvey Milk was assassinated, you organized a candlelight vigil to commemorate his death. Could you recount the story of that first march?

CJ: Yes, you know I tell that story at least once a week, and I have been for the past ten years. You see, it was different back then. People died faster. You'd see someone, then you wouldn't see them. Maybe you'd see an obituary, or maybe you wouldn't. You might get invited to the memorial, but usually there wasn't one. The partner was ashamed. The dead weren't buried, they were cremated, so there was no grave to visit. People were just vanishing. I learned that San Francisco had just passed the mark of 1,000 dead. I was standing on the corner of Castro and Market and I knew that of those 1,000, a vast majority had lived and died within a few blocks of there. But there was no evidence. Those nice Victorians and the cafés and the restaurants and the sound of music and the smell of coffee . . . There were always people on the street, and you had no idea you were at ground zero of a terrible tragedy. I was standing at that corner, I said to my friend Joseph Durant, who has since died, that I wished we could bulldoze the neighborhood. I thought, if this were a meadow with a thousand corpses rotting in the sun, then people would look at it. They would see it, they would understand. And if they were human, they would be compelled to respond. But there wasn't any such evidence. So when we organized Harvey's march, I asked people to carry signs—placards inscribed with the names of the dead. I was really looking for visual evidence.

That night, we climbed up the walls of the Federal Building and covered it. I looked at it, and it looked like a quilt. And just at that instant, I got it. I don't usually tell people this, because it sounds so unreal, but it was like a slide fell into place. It's like there was a blank screen that I was looking at, and suddenly, I could just see it—an expanse of multicolored placards covering the national mall. It's the perfect symbol of warm, fuzzy, middle-class, middle–American traditional family values—female art. Which is the perfect symbol to match with this disease that seems to be of nontraditional people—drug users, homosexuals, and what was perceived as a product of aggressive gay male sexuality.

CP: How long was it from then until the start of the quilt?

CJ: It was a year and a half before I made the first panel. I can say this now, because it's been true now for a long time: I have what people call visions. I get an idea, almost full blown. And then I usually talk about it for a year. I make little notes, and I doodle, and I just think about it. And then the trick for me is always finding people to do the work, because I'm very lazy, and I'm very disorganized.

CP: I find that a little hard to believe!

CJ: No, this is absolutely true. In any event, I thought about it, and during that year and a half there were three things that happened in my life that sort of put it forward. The first was that I tested positive. The antibody test finally became available, and I decided that I needed to know. That was very scary for me, and very depressing. The second thing was that *60 Minutes* did a piece on me. I was living in Sacramento at the time, I'd actually gotten a job in politics working for the Friends Committee. I began to get death threats and then was attacked by some Aryan Nation thugs. I was badly beaten and stabbed. I thought that I was a fully self-actualized citizen of the world, and when that happened I discovered that there was this enormous reservoir of hatred within me for straight people, the straight world, and straight men. It's not something I wanted to feel, you know. And then, third, my best friend Marvin Feldman got sick and died. I wanted to say goodbye to him and be with his family. When I got back from that I was so paralyzed, my circle was gone. There was no one left in my life who knew me when I was in my twenties except my mom and dad.

So after grieving, and this horrible hatred, I just decided, well, you can start this thing as an antidote. I knew it was going to be huge. There was no question in my mind. But some things surprised me. I mean, I had it in my head that this would be therapy—working with your hands and sharing anecdotes among families that had been divided by homophobia. I certainly understood the media value of it. But I don't think anything prepared me for what turned out to be the enormous spiritual power of it. The quilt is really like a church, you know. It really is. The people who are linked by it are very much a family. That took me by surprise. I also had the idea that there were enough angry queens with sewing machines out there that we would make something that would be visually startling. But I don't really think I expected the artistry that came out of it.

CP: Can you talk a little bit about the scale of the project today? How big an organization is the NAMES Project Foundation now?

CJ: It started in 1987 with $3,000 that I borrowed from friends. We had a little workshop on Market Street, and we were all volunteer. After about six or seven months, when we got back from our first trip to D.C. we started getting some money. We had about a dozen people who received salaries from $12,000 to $25,000 for the first four years. Today, we have 40-some full-time employees with benefits with a budget that's close to $4 million because of the big display we're doing. We have chapters in about 40 U.S. cities now and about 30 international affiliates. One of the greatest moments in my life was in 1995 during the United Nations Fiftieth Anniversary. We got some funding and we were able to bring our colleagues from many different countries. There were representatives from eight of our African chapters. Those women were just so cool! They have no concept of gay/straight, like we do. AIDS is a heterosexual problem there, a problem of families and villages. To meet these women and to have them show me their photographs of these women and their villages in Central Africa, to sit in a circle sewing with them . . . ! We think of quilting as a particularly American folk art. In fact, there are similar traditions on every continent.

Anyway, I got the ball going in 1987. I got no support from anybody at the beginning, which was frustrating because I had been doing political organizing for so long. During the seventies, and most of the eighties, any time gay and lesbian people were marching in the street, which was frequently, I was usually the organizer. If you walked down Castro Street looking for staples in the telephone poles, I put them there. So I had assumed when I first put out the idea for the NAMES Project that people would help me. Nobody did. Everybody thought it was a bad idea.

CP: Why?

CJ: They thought it was morbid. The militants felt that it was passive. For whatever reason, nobody helped. You know, every time I've done something good, it's been the same way. I've put an idea out there, my friends have turned their backs on it, and then strangers have emerged from out of nowhere to make it happen. When I called the first meeting of the NAMES Project, I rented a hall in San Francisco and put posters up all over town. Only two people showed. But their names were Jack Caster and Cindy McMullen, and they ended up being two of the most important people in the history of the quilt. She had been selling cosmetics at Macy's. He was an antique collector who had retired to take care of his lover as he died.

So early on, I sat down with my friend Joseph and we made a list of 40 of our friends who had died. Over one marathon weekend, we just cranked the panels out. They're ugly now. Most of them are just spray paint with stencil. But we got 40 and I sewed them into the first five 12' x 12' sections. I went to Dianne Feinstein, who was mayor at the time, and got permission to hang those from the mayor's balcony at City Hall during the Gay Pride parade. There were close to 300,000 people there, and I got invited to speak. We set up a booth. It was slow going. That whole summer I kept thinking, God damn it, this is such a good idea, I wish people would do it! We went to Washington on October 11, 1987, a year and a day after

Marvin had died, my birthday. We had 1,920 panels. It went out on the wire services and we were on the front page of most of the big daily papers. Money started coming in. Now the funding—I think it's an important part of the NAMES Project. I am not an "A-Gay." I don't hang with society people. I own three pairs of jeans and now I do have a tuxedo. But I had only one business suit for a long time. I was a hippie and a queen. I am not a cocktail party kind of guy. So from the beginning we have supported ourselves almost entirely through merchandise. We've involved artists to create really high quality T-shirts, buttons, videotapes, books. That was and still is the bulk of our financing.

The way it works is we design and market merchandise that is sold at these displays. We get all of that money. It comes back to the foundation. But the local communities are encouraged to have fundraisers around the quilt. They also have donation bins at the quilt. So if you go to see a quilt and you're moved to put five dollars in the jar, that will stay in that town and go to support people with AIDS in that town. So we have made our alignment with the service providers because we knew in each one of these cities that we were going to have enormous volunteer needs. If we draw on them, then we have to leave them something in exchange.

We have had almost no corporate support until recently, since Anthony Turner has taken over. He comes from a more traditional arts background, and he has definitely expanded the base. And now that we've been nominated for a Nobel Peace Prize and have been the subject of award winning documentaries, it has become much easier. Wealthy gay people are much more supportive now than when I started. But really it's been very grassroots funding that has kept us together.

CP: Has your involvement in politics over the years been a good tool for your activism?

CJ: Well, I guess I see everything from the perspective of a gay man, and I think for gay and lesbian people political activism is very important. Our political movement has been simultaneously an internal and external process, and the quilt reflects this very much. Gay liberation was about healing from the scars of terrible abuse and giving people some dignity, giving them a sense of pride, a sense of worth. All of this is an internal thing. But at the same time, we were also outwardly directed to trying to get people to stop hating. To stop killing us, stop firing us, stop taking our children. The feminist movement was very similar—it involved consciousness-raising and changing the way women felt about themselves and their bodies, and giving them the strength to be outwardly directed. So I think for gay people, for women, and for racial minorities, there has been an internal/external duality of people involving themselves in politics for often intensely personal reasons. I think I involved myself in politics to get over having the shit kicked out of me all through grade school, junior high, and high school. I didn't want to be a weakling anymore. I didn't want to be a victim. I wanted power. So I think, yeah, the political process is important for people both on a personal level and on an outward plane of social change. I don't think we always do it very well, and I think a lot of times we squander opportunities. I am bored with the politics of just winning elections and that sort of thing. But I'm fascinated by politics that really changes people, by political activism that tries to alter the way people look at a situation. That's what I've tried very hard to do with the quilt. I think we've been very, very successful. Not just in terms of dollars raised, or people who've come to see it, but I think we have been one of the main factors in changing the way this country looks at the disease.

CP: In one of your op-ed pieces, you wrote a really eloquent statement: "We have sheltered the homeless, and fed the hungry. We've cared for the sick, comforted the dying, built hospices, joined speaker's bureaus, written checks, signed petitions, demonstrated, testified, been arrested, worn red ribbons, sewn quilts for our dead, and raised our candles against an ever darkening sky. And yet none of these actions will save my life or the life of any other person already infected with HIV. The plain truth is only one thing can, research and more of it." I'd like to ask you about momentum. When you know that you're not going to see the change you're striving for in your lifetime, what keeps you going?

CJ: I *have* seen the change in my lifetime. I was born in 1954, the year that Senator McCarthy was repudiated. There were no gay bars in Phoenix, Arizona, in 1954. There were very few here in San Francisco. Three days ago, I was in Farmington, New Mexico, for an HIV symposium. There was a dance in the Farmington Holiday Inn at the end of the conference. Out on the dance floor were about 400 people! There were young Anglo lesbians dancing together. There were 45-year-old gay men dancing together. There were Navajo Indians, Nez Pierce Indians. There were straight couples, gay couples. I looked at this, and I thought, well, I have lived long enough to see the future and I'm seeing it here in Farmington, New Mexico! Where men and women of different ages and races and sexual orientations are dancing together to the same cool music. I see incredible change, incredible progress. I see it every day.

I construct little rituals in my life to remind me. Since I spend most of my life on airplanes now, I've decided that everybody who sits next to me is going to know that I am gay and that I have HIV. That's one of my rituals. No one has responded badly. I tell everybody—mechanics, nuns, high school kids, whoever's sitting next to me. You know, it's natural, we always talk. "Hi, where are you going? Is this for pleasure or business? What do you do?" I say, "Well, have you ever heard of the AIDS Memorial Quilt?" They say, "Yeah." I say, "Well, when my best friend died and I found I was HIV-positive, I decided to start something. And that's what I do." No one has ever responded with hostility or even indifference. They pause sometimes, or are taken aback by my candor, maybe, but they pause and then they tell me about their son, their brother, the girl across the street.

CP: Do you feel that government and industry are sufficiently engaged in AIDS research now? Are there big breakthroughs on the horizon?

CJ: This is not Pollyanna stuff. I almost died in 1994. I had pneumocystitis for nine months, and I was very, very ill. I was allergic to all the treatments for it. So it was a very frightening time for me, and I've also lost a great many friends just in the last six months. So the horror of it is ongoing and nobody can relax. But in the last two years we have seen such progress that I believe that there's enormous hope, and that it's very, very important for everyone right now to be very tough—very strong, very focused. I have no time for cynicism, I have no time for despair, I have no time for laziness. I only have time for: let's kick butt, because we'll save our lives if we do! If we stall right now, if we allow the momentum to wind down, then we'll die. But I don't think that's going to happen. I'm going to be a very old, blue-haired queen [laughter].

CP: How do you build consensus in such a complex environment? You navigate among several factions, among militant perspectives and more moderate ones. You've obviously been very good at that.

CJ: I don't know if it's this bad in the rest of the world, but in the gay community we are terribly factionalized. I believe much of the political and cultural leadership of the gay community is very removed from the reality of day-to-day life for ordinary gay and lesbian people. The leaders in D.C. and New York City are very clever and very articulate, but I think they're totally irrelevant to the lives of most gay and lesbian people. I came from this fringe, from a tiny minority within a minority. I don't have any college degrees but I consider myself an educated person because I come from a family of educated people—educated, politically progressive, intellectually inclined, artistically inclined. I'm from the extreme left. I'm from the counterculture. That's where I'm from. It's a pretty small circle of people. But I want what I do to be real to real people. And that has been an ongoing source of anxiety and frustration. There are still people who hate the quilt, who see it as passive or something. I think they're just absolutely wrong. I think they're stupid and blind and unwilling to see the power this thing has to move people to action. I've never said, "Make a quilt and you'll feel better and it'll all go away." I've said, "Make a quilt and let us take it to Washington and drape it on the Mall, so these politicians will know the consequence of their stupidity." People want to be politically correct, they want to be more avant-garde. I think that is an elitism that is really destructive. You see people with really good ideas expending enormous energy, but they never reach the people who need the message.

From the beginning of the quilt, I wanted nothing to do with the gay establishment. In fact, I was adamant that we were not going to be affiliated with anybody, that we were going to be independent. I had huge struggles with people about the political/nonpolitical nature of the quilt. People can be so obtuse. I would say, "We are going to be as political as possible, by being nonpolitical." And they would go, "Huh?" I said, "Come on, it's really not that hard." It was things like vocabulary and the words we used. I would go through with a red pen and say "No, that's too California, no, that's too left wing." I had a list of words that I banned from our literature. You will not use *empower*. You will not use any of the words that feminists and politically progressive gay people use all the time. I wish I still had the list; it's funny. *Empower* was at the top, *share, centered, grounded*. No coastal words! *[laughter]*. I did not want us to be seen via vocabulary. We were not a Buddhist group or a feminist group or whatever. It had to be Middle America. Sears shoppers. That meant not aligning us with any other groups.

As time passed, I became frustrated because I don't think people quite understood my saying over and over, "We are not political, we are not political, we are not political." Really what I was saying was, "Keep your mouth shut and be as subversive as possible." I would actually talk to the staff and the board about the subversive quality of the quilt. I said, "We are going in under the radar here. We're endorsed by the Pope and the PTA and the president. We're going to go to every fucking high school in this country, and going in with this powerful symbol of gay love." It's full of gay love. It's about the love gay people have for each other, the love our straight families and friends have for us. And now it is changing and there are more people in there who are not gay, but the message isn't really that different. The message is, all these lives are valued. We hold all these lives to be sacred. We cherish these people, we will defend them. Imagine getting into a high school with these panels filled up with gay male lovers. There's one panel that is a letter from a lesbian woman to her gay brother who has died. At the end there is a letter from her mother saying, "How very sad it was indeed that our family couldn't learn love to love you until you had died. Please, wherever you are, forgive your father and forgive me for our stupidity." There are a lot of people who didn't get the subtlety of that.

We are not a political organization. Our goal is to illustrate the enormity of the crisis, to provide people with a positive and creative means of expression, to give the world a clear and powerful symbol of a compassionate and loving response. We do not endorse candidates or legislation, but we have always intended to have an impact on the political process. We see ourselves as being part of creating a political will. We are in the richest and most powerful nation on earth, we possess everything we need to stop this epidemic; all we lack is the will. Why do we lack the will? Well, let's get into that. Let's talk about homophobia and racism.

From the beginning, the quilt's audience was grandma. Your grandma, my grandma. They vote, they've got money. I didn't feel like I needed to preach to men on Castro Street about it. They knew what was happening. Whether it's art or politics, I think that's the real challenge. I'm not an artist, but if I were I would want my work to be understood and be relevant to ordinary people. I would be very frustrated if I made art and it were only appreciated by the art critic for the *Village Voice*. For me, real art is art that you don't have to go to school to be moved by. You don't have to have a political opinion to appreciate it. It's something that touches, speaks to the commonalty, to the humanness of us in some way. A great many of my friends would disagree with me.

CP: What do you make of the demise of the National Endowment for the Arts and the general attack on the arts in America?

CJ: Well, I don't think you're going to like what I'm going to say. I have many artist friends whose work I find not only disturbing but incomprehensible to most people. And I think that artists have to understand that when they allow themselves to go down certain paths, they will find themselves alone. It may be important for them, for their process and their growth to go down that path, but do not be surprised if at the end of that path you find yourself alone. Because most people will not go there. I believe that political activists and artists who share my values and my view of the world have not been terribly effective in the eighties. We still live in a country that was always conservative, that has always been backwards, that has always celebrated ignorance and embraced ugliness. Look around you; this is America. I think a lot of us lost our way in the eighties and nineties. In the political arena, what you see is this mindless PC vocabulary. This endless mouthing of slogans that mean absolutely nothing to people who are struggling to support their kids. In the art world we've seen some of our best and brightest people walk down that road, and no one can follow. I'm not saying that everybody needs to mass-market their stuff. That's not what I'm about at all. But I've always been very clear that I wanted a broader audience. I did not want to limit myself to people who live in Greenwich Village, or Castro, people who all wear the same clothes, speak the same vocabulary, have the same education. That's boring to me.

CP: Do you think this crisis in the arts could have been averted somehow?

CJ: If people had more of a sense of responsibility to the larger community.

CP: By making different art? Are you saying that it's not so much a question of organizing, but essentially it's what they're creating to begin with?

CJ: Their vision is lacking. Look at economic issues. The left in this country has gone down the tubes. There are millions of people facing poverty, workers trapped in dead-end jobs with no hope for advancement. But the rhetoric of the left does not speak to these people. The women's movement is having the same problem. The women who most need the power of feminism are not being included.

CP: How would you approach this issue in the arts? Your mother was a choreographer, you grew up with the arts in your household. You understand the balance between collective process and individual vision. Are there artworks that you think have been successful in reaching a broader audience?

CJ: First I'd point to the Vietnam Wall. When I first went to see it, I was very suspicious. I'm a Quaker. We tend to be suspicious about war memorials. I didn't lose anyone. I was born in '54. I was among the last men who had to register for the Vietnam draft, but I didn't get a lottery number. So I went there not expecting to be moved by the wall. I think it's a beautiful example of how one artist's vision and the collaboration that goes into making something like that happen really work. I spent a lot of time standing in front of that wall, and watching the way people approached it, their ability to touch it. It cuts through the ground and it also cuts right across all the things that most horribly divided us.

When I talk about my inspiration for the quilt, I usually tell people that I would like to give credit to three artists who encouraged me without meaning to. First would be Maya Lin, who created the wall. Another is Christo, whose *Running Fence* was up here. It was gorgeous. It shimmered.

And it required the involvement of thousands and thousands of people. Christo had to get permission from everybody. He has said that battling bureaucracy is part of the artistic process. I don't think he really said that correctly. I think marshalling the forces is part of the artistic process. It doesn't necessarily have to be butting heads with the enemies.

The third artist I point to is Judy Chicago, for her *Dinner Party.* I was intrigued by it. I liked the idea of one artist coming up with a theme, a format, a frame, and then being free and confident enough to say to other artists, "Okay, there's room for you in this too; let's see what this collaboration does." I loved that. Later I found out that she really auditioned these women and put them through all sorts of paces, that they had to give money to purchase the food, but I didn't know that at the time. I don't like the work now, but I was initially inspired by the *Dinner Party.* The quilt, I think, has a lot of the spirit of collaboration in it. We came up with a framework—3' x 6' panels, sewn together into 12' x 12', and then 24' x 24' sections—but within that framework, we will not censor you, you can do whatever you want.

CP: Where does someone who wants to have this kind of public reach go for training? Do you go it alone? Do you find mentors? Do you align yourselves with institutions? Do you go to school? What do you tell young people who say, "I want to be like you, I want to create something that's going to have an impact on the world."

CJ: I think there's a sort of magical quality about throwing an idea out there and waiting to see who picks up the ball. Everything I've ever done, whether it's organizing demonstrations or doing the quilt or whatever, there's always been a kind of waiting period where I've just had to pause and see who steps forward. I think it might not have happened if I had been affiliated with an institution. I think if you're trying to change the way people think, you need to be kind of pure. You need to be able to say, "I will starve to death if I have to." If I had had corporate sponsors at the beginning, if the quilt had been commissioned or I had gotten some artist-in-residency thing, I don't think this would have happened. The struggle was part of it. I think your motives have to be really clear to yourself and to the people around you. Whether it's art or politics, your motivation is really central to what the outcome's going to be. I was motivated just out of horrendous grief and an urgency that made me want to take people by the throat and scream at them. So I guess I'm in favor of people going on their own and struggling with it.

CP: There are long-term goals and short-term goals. How do you pace yourself? How much do you keep the long view in front of you, and how much of it's the shorter view?

CJ: I guess I'm changing. I'd say that when I was younger, it was very much one project at a time. I was trying to keep in mind the long view, but I just loved it when things came to a head! One of the greatest times I ever had with the quilt was in '88 when all of our permits were denied by the park service. They were not going to let us display the quilt on the Mall. I just laughed and I said, "Oh, we're going to have a party now, we're going to make the park service wish they had never been born!" *[laughter].* We organized, and it was a lot of fun. Those immediate battles are nice because they start and then they end. But I think as I've gotten older and I face illness, it really is the long-term perspective that gives me the most comfort. I think to be an effective activist, one really has to not be operating from a place of sacrifice. I have made no sacrifices in my life. Looking at the circumstances of my life, someone might say, "Well, this is a man who has suffered a great deal and has given up a great deal." I do not view it that way. I miss my friends. I'm frightened sometimes that I'm going to get sick and die, but I've found my role. I found what I'm supposed to do in this life. That is the greatest blessing in the world. When I meet young people who don't know what they're supposed to do, I feel bad for them. I didn't quite always know how I was supposed to go about it, or I almost never knew how I was going to pay the rent, but if nothing else, I always knew what I was supposed to be doing.

CP: How does that balance with what you just said about being willing to starve to death?

CJ: Well, yes, you must be willing to starve to death, but you must know that you are not making a sacrifice. You must not feel oppressed by it. You must not feel, "I am a martyr, I am giving up all these fine things so I can save the world and help my people." Paying the rent probably shouldn't even be on your list of things to think about, because you'll be thinking about the demonstration you're going to organize.

CP: What helps somebody determine what they're supposed to do in the world? Is it happenstance, is it design, is it intelligence, is it luck?

CJ: I think it's all of those things. There are a lot of young people in my life. I say to them, "Just look at yourself as clearly as possible, watch yourself as you go through your days and look for the clues. When do you really feel happy? When are you really just feeling the best, the most awake, most connected, most confident? When do you really feel like, goddamn, this life is good!" For me, it's when I've just come from one meeting and I'm racing to the next, and I've got a great idea, and the people I just told it to dug it, and the people I'm gonna go see are probably gonna pay for it *[laughter]*. Well, when that's happening I believe in God, I believe in my place in the universe. I know that I'm doing what I'm supposed to do. Why do I know it? Because I feel so good. I just feel great! I haven't taken any drugs, I haven't eaten a big meal. It's just me and these other people and the connection we made. I know that I'm supposed to feel that good as much as possible. That's when I feel rich.

CP: Is it all public and personal at the same time? Do you have to reserve room for your private life, for your health, for your energy, for things that aren't in the public domain?

CJ: I spend a lot of time alone, but not too much. The worst thing about 1994 was that I was too sick to go out, and I thought I was dying. I just had an awful hard time accepting that I was through, that I wasn't going to make anything else happen. For me, I need to constantly be connected to other people. I don't have much of a dividing line between public and private. I talk about everything. I've revealed most personal details of my life to strangers and to television cameras. Which may be part of why I'm single *[laughter]*. But it's worth it. There's a trade-off. I'm adored by hundreds of thousands of strangers. I can go into a city, people meet me at the airport, they take me to a civic auditorium, and there may be 7,000 strangers dressed in white, waiting to unfold the quilt. They stand in line for hours to shake my hand and get my autograph. I feel they know enough about me that I can accept this love. I have no complaints. If I ever whine, slap me, because I'm living a privileged life. I am amazed and grateful for every day. I'm not a very religious person, but I thank God every day. At some point during the day, I will just say, thank you—however, whoever, whatever made this happen like this.

CP: Could you talk more about ritual in terms of the quilt?

CJ: It's the most exciting part of the quilt. In the last few weeks I've been to quilt displays in Oxford, Ohio, up in Burke, Texas, at Four Corners, and in Palm Springs. Whenever I go to a quilt display, I always try to go to the volunteer training so I can thank the volunteers for the work that they're doing. I tell them that when they are unfolding the quilts during the opening ceremonies they are participating in a ritual that is being repeated in small towns and big cities across the country, and all around the world. It's like the Vietnam Memorial. It has simplicity. That's another ritual for American people—they get on a plane or a train, they go to the capital, they take pieces of paper, and they do a rubbing of the name they've come to find. They stand and see their reflection in the wall. I think these kinds of rituals, particularly memorial rituals, have no connection to the ordinary aspects of our lives. We create them solely to bring us closer to God, or to help us see our position in the universe. I think those are really the most important evidence of our humanity. The whole process of the quilt is an ongoing ritual that continues to bring people in. I've seen it happen in Sweden. I've seen it happen in Mexico. It just has a unifying effect. While the ritual of the quilt is specific to these pieces of fabric, to certain people, and to this particular virus, ultimately it has nothing to do with homosexuals, with the virus, or with America. It has to do with this sanctity of human life and human love, and this is a message anybody on the planet can understand, can be a part of.

CP: The quilt is a living monument because it continues to grow and change. Will it continue as long as people are dying? Will there be a moment when it becomes finite?

CJ: That's the dream. I assume that the quilt will continue to grow for the duration of the epidemic. As long as people are dying of HIV, their loved ones will make quilts and send them to us. My hope is that I will be here when we declare it over. I don't think that's likely. I'll be very curious to see how it changes over the next few years. Here's my little prediction: I think that in April of 1999, we're going to be calling this a manageable chronic condition in North America. What remains to be seen is whether the technological, medical advances are shared with the rest of the world. I will be very curious to see then what happens to the quilt. Right now in my speeches I say to people, "I know you think an HIV diagnosis is a death sentence. I'm here to tell you it's not anymore. You need to plan on living." One of the things we're trying to shift with the quilt is to transform it from a powerful symbol of death, loss, and grief to a symbol of hope. People have to know that if we fight hard, we can save the lives of millions of people. I'm one of them and I don't want to die. I don't accept it and I don't surrender and don't you dare give up on me!

CP: How do you prioritize where your energies need to be now? You're one person, and there are a lot of little fires raging all the time.

CJ: I'm not interested in most of them. I used to be when I was younger and had more energy and was healthier. But now I don't have any trouble prioritizing. My first priority is the quilt and the NAMES Project. Whatever that organization wants me to do, I will do. To the best of my ability. I intend to be out there for the rest of my life, helping them and raising money and staying out of their way. My second priority right now is to finish my book because I almost died last year. And I was really upset that I was going to croak without having told all these really cool stories that I love to tell. I think that losing focus, getting spread too thin is a real risk for artists and for activists.

CP: Can you talk more about not having time for cynicism or despair?

CJ: The old slogan was "Silence = Death." My slogan for the last half of this decade is "Cynicism = Death." It's hard to face this kind of a struggle that seems endless and where you keep losing. It's really hard to explain to people what it's like to lose somebody you care about every week. I pick up the *Bay Area Reporter,* our local gay paper in San Francisco, and there's always two or three pages of obituary notices. I don't think there's ever been a week when I haven't known one of those people. There's just this great weight of grief and fear. So it's understandable that some people would despair and would give in. My lover didn't die of a disease; he killed himself. He hadn't even been sick. His T-cells dropped down to 100. His doctor was a jerk and told him that he should get his affairs in order. He went home and he paid off all of our credit card bills and he killed himself. So I know that if I despair I will die. I've watched my friends give up, and as soon as they give up, they're dead. You can almost predict how long my friends are gonna live. Because so much of it is attitude. You can understand why people would despair. And then the cynicism. Well, yeah, people are real cynical about this government where three presidents in a row have failed to move the nation forward. The first two wouldn't even say the word. Clinton is the first president in history who said the word *gay* out loud. We've got these pharmaceutical companies, governors, and state legislatures who are continuing a decade and a half later to deny children benefits.

People have every reason to be cynical about the politicians and the AIDS industry. But you can't allow yourself to become so cynical that you no longer feel hope.

I am loved. I know there are people with AIDS whose parents have abandoned them. Mine did not. I know there are people out there who have no one to care for them. But I am not one of them and I am grateful for that. In my little town when I got sick and I was new in town, my neighbors came over every day. The teenage boys brought me wood, the old ladies planted flowers outside my bedroom window. You can be cynical, but if you lose sight of the goodness that's out there, you are denying it to yourself and you'll die.

The other thing that's dangerous is mysticism. When my friend Jonathan told me he was sick, he said he was going to paint his room blue and that was all he was going to do. It's very easy to understand how people would retreat into spirituality and mysticism. It's a way to try to accept that they're going to die by saying, "Well, I'm going to go to a better place" or "I'm going to come back." I say, "No, you don't get to make that decision, that's part of the real mystery. But what you do have is all your instincts that tell you to fight for your life." That's another thing about the quilt. It's simply, "You're cold, you're sick, here's a quilt. Wrap it around your shoulders, you'll feel better." It's a practical kind of thing.

I have felt so much comfort and love from family and from strangers and I want other people to feel that too. I have very few friends who enjoy the kind of relationship that I enjoy with my family. I get very angry with the intelligentsia who say, "This has no value." So many of the queers I encounter today experience a sense of rejection, usually by their families. What's wrong with creating something that allows queers to feel that they *are* a part of the larger community? I've had people try to murder me because I'm gay. But I refuse to allow that hatred that I felt that summer after I got stabbed to be in my life.

CP: What explains that? That you were the object of brutality and hatred in high school, but that you feel such comfort and love from friends and strangers now?

CJ: There was something broken in me and I fixed it. Don't hang onto the injury. Scars are ugly.

CP: But what you're saying is you changed your outlook on the world, and consequently people behave differently to you? That's why they stopped beating you up?

CJ: I guess so, yeah. I changed myself.

CP: But you were gay then and you are gay now, so . . .

CJ: Yes, but I was weak then and now I'm strong. I was ashamed then and now I'm proud! *[laughter].* It was deliberate, systematic. I absolutely believe that every single person has the ability to change his or her life. So I get impatient with whiners. I don't consider myself a victim. When I die you can call me a victim of AIDS if I die of AIDS. But I don't think of myself as a powerless person anymore.

CP: So now you're working on the NAMES Project and on your book. Any other big projects on the horizon? Do you think you might reenter the political arena?

CJ: My last foray into politics was when I lost the election for San Francisco city supervisor in '92. In retrospect, I'm relieved that I lost. I think I ran for office primarily because I wanted to give myself that test. It's not so much about the number of votes you get. Running for supervisor means putting yourself up on every stage in town. You've got every neighborhood group, every block association, every business group, every Democratic club. For six months, you talk to six groups of people a day and you stand and talk for two minutes, then you say any questions and you have to handle everything from "A" to "Z," from asbestos to Alzheimer's to the zoo. I wanted to do that and I also wanted to make a statement about people with AIDS.

CP: How does dealing with asbestos and the zoo fit into your life goal of promoting AIDS awareness?

CJ: Well, I thought it was important for people with HIV to show that they were involved with other issues and all of the other quality-of-life issues that affect normal citizens. "Yes, I have HIV, but I'm going to care about you." Issues that affect senior citizens or truck drivers or firefighters.

CP: Would that have finished your role in the AIDS battle?

CJ: I can't imagine that it would have. It might have distracted me. The part of it that I found really ugly had nothing to do with the campaign or the issues or the deal-making or any of that. I just hate raising money. And I found that I really had trouble raising money for myself. It was one thing to go to corporations and say, "I need money for AIDS, I need money for a hospice, I need money for the quilt or I need money for this education program." But to go back to the same people and say, "I need money for me so I can get this office" comes from a different motivation. I'm not trying to sound like I'm some extremely moral person; I just hate the asking.

CP: So you're not going to pursue any more campaigns?

CJ: I didn't say that *[laughter]*. If there was a cure for AIDS tomorrow and if I sold my book for a million bucks, sure, I might buy myself a seat in Congress! *[laughter]*.

April 19, 1996
Guerneville, California

GETTING IN HISTORY'S WAY

Claire Peeps

WE HOPE THAT THIS BOOK HAS BEEN BOTH cause for celebration and call to action. As filmmaker Barbara Trent observes in the first interview, there's a chance that we can intervene in history if we move fast enough. The many individuals represented here are evidence that this is true. Through their strategic efforts to raise public awareness and marshal social and political forces, they have shown themselves to be effective at getting in history's way.

This book is also about passing wisdom to a next generation. The lessons embedded in these activists' stories resonate across time: insist on justice; believe in the possibility of alternatives; never surrender hope; do not underestimate the strength in numbers or the righteousness of anger; pace yourself, because change may be slow in coming.

The activist's job is largely the building of social capital—the grassroots networks that enable people to move information and ideas to a broader audience and ultimately to make change happen. The networks can be constructed in many forms and among diverse groups of people. Migrant labor camps, parent associations, quilting groups, after-school programs, and radio are among the vehicles that the activists here have tapped into to spread their message. They have engaged bus riders, bank employees, students, grieving survivors, and neighbors as their partners in articulating common goals for social change.

From the long view, the accomplishments of the progressive left during the last 100 years are beyond dispute: the vote for women, the legal ban on segregation, environmental protection laws, the emergence of gay rights policy. Despite their occasional misgivings about taking one step forward and two steps back, activists are pushing ahead. They have seen change.

Esther Kaplan notes in her interview that activism's struggle is to make a particular issue one of widespread public concern. That has been the task of all the activists interviewed here. Among the tools available to them in that endeavor, art has been employed as a primary method by many. Why art? Why have we included such a significant number of artists among the activists represented here?

Co-editor Marie Cieri and I came to this project as arts presenters and curators. We were troubled by what we perceived as the increasing American apathy and outright antagonism toward art. As the public debates about support for the National Endowment for the Arts took shape in the early nineties, we were working in our respective careers with artists who were deeply committed to their communities and to social change. It seemed to us that the arts had an important role to play in community building—as a means for the expression of identity, a catalyst for economic development and academic advancement, and a vehicle for dialogue and conflict mediation.

It was clear that our view wasn't shared by the American public at large. It was also clear that the arts community was unprepared for the battle on Capitol Hill. Our field has been built on specialization that has led to fragmentation, which ultimately has isolated us from one another. We are trained to become experts of visual arts, or theater, or music, but we have largely lost the ability to be both clear and articulate about our shared values. Consequently, we were unable to present a united front during the public debates.

Marie and I thought we might learn from activists working in other fields. How have they achieved consensus among differing groups? How have they achieved public support for their causes? How might the artistic imagination be better merged with an activist agenda, and what civic forces might be unleashed in the process?

There is a broad range of artistic practice that advocates for social change. At one end, the artist may function as observer, mirror, or conscience, offering us a critique of a social or political moment—as in Picasso's great painting *Guernica,* or James Baldwin's collection of essays *Notes of a Native Son.* At the other, the artist may seek to rally audiences directly around a particular issue. Think of Pete Seeger singing "Where Have All the Flowers Gone?" at an antiwar rally on the Washington Mall.

Across this continuum of practice, artists have contributed significantly to social reform movements in America. In the early decades of this century, documentary photographs by Lewis Hine of children working in New York sweatshops galvanized public opinion and sparked child labor laws. Photographs by Walker Evans raised public awareness about poverty in rural America during the Great Depression. Musicians, visual artists, poets, and playwrights brought clarity, focus, and passion to public protest during the civil rights and antiwar movements of the fifties and sixties.

By the late sixties, artists were engaging audiences as collaborators in their work. Bread & Puppet Theater staged antiwar processions on the streets of New York's Lower East Side, enlisting bystanders as performers in large-scale spectacles. El Teatro Campesino, under the direction of Luis Valdez, mounted performances on the back of flatbed trucks in the fields of Salinas, California. Their provocative work rallied Chicano farmworkers around Cesar Chavez's pro-union cause. Visual artists played a key role in the Chicano movement, too, partnering with community members in the design and painting of murals. Judy Baca, Barbara Carrasco, and many others used mural-making as a forum for popular education, chronicling a community's untold history and articulating its vision for the future.

While the catalytic issues have shifted over time, artists have continued to engage nonartists in the production of powerful, change-oriented work during the past decade. Bill T. Jones, a choreographer living with HIV, brought together long-term survivors of HIV infection in his controversial 1994 dance narrative *Still/Here.* In the same year, performance artist Suzanne Lacy created *The Roof Is on Fire,* a performance/media installation in which 200 Oakland teenagers sat in cars on a garage roof and talked about media stereotypes of youth and their troubled relationship with the police.

The artist-activists in this book have chosen to use art as an organizing device, more than just as a slogan or a logo for a cause—but those functions are important, too. I once heard Bernice Johnson Reagon deliver a lecture on the history of the civil rights movement through song. She described how, during a march, the sound of protestors singing preceded them as they walked, so that by the time they reached their destination their voices had already occupied the space in a way the police could not reclaim. It wasn't just the message of the music that was important but its ability to give physical presence and visceral force to the movement.

The power of art to influence public opinion and mobilize dissent is demonstrated by periodic efforts around the world to silence artists. Art is usually among the first forms of expression to be censored under repressive regimes. It gives voice to multiple perspectives, eliciting response in the form of reflection, discussion, debate—the sort of civic discourse and public exchange of ideas that are elemental to a flourishing democracy.

The role of art in American democracy has been complicated by the forces of our market-based economy and by our traditions of arts education. We have trained our artists, by and large, to seek inspiration in isolation rather than in collaboration. This is not true in other parts of the world, where the arts are better integrated into the social and economic fabric of society. When American opera and theater director Peter Sellars traveled to Indonesia in 1998 to meet with musicians and dancers there, he asked one of Bali's preeminent choreographers what makes a great dancer. The master artist replied that a good dancer is one who knows all the traditional repertoire and can recall it from memory without error; that a very good dancer is one who knows the traditional repertoire and can infuse its performance with spiritual insight; and that a great dancer is one who knows the traditional repertoire, can perform it with spiritual insight, and who is also a farmer.

We have difficulty, in this country, in accepting multiple identities; witness the ongoing debates over ethnic designation within the U.S. Census. The notion of being both artist and farmer, or artist and activist—like being Latino and Korean, or black and Jewish—runs contrary to our categorical way of thinking. But it is art's ability to be multifaceted, its capacity to communicate a plurality of meanings, that gives it its power in activism. Art may be simultaneously overt and subtle. Its impact may be immediate or may linger in the after-image.

What artmaking nurtures—reflection, and the ability to acknowledge contradiction—may also be a good counterpoint to activism, as Esther Kaplan observes. Activism can be physically and emotionally exhausting, and Kaplan describes a movement's need to care for its members. In addition to being a catalyst for action, art may provide relief from the tyranny of the day-to-day. Artists can transform our dissatisfaction with the world into the image of something better, as artist Amalia Mesa-Bains suggests, and it may be in this imaginative transformation that we find hope and rejuvenation.

You can feed and clothe a person, but to what end? The arts are where we discover and express our humanity, privately or collectively. They provide us the language to share our common joy and grief, to find communion with one another, to pass our stories and wisdom from one generation to the next. If everything is taken from us but life itself, what remains? Our voices, our bodies. With that alone, our humanity may be preserved, and we may carry on the struggle.

APPENDIX

IN ADDITION TO THOSE REPRESENTED in the body of this book, the following individuals graciously shared their time to be interviewed about activism and the pursuit of change in America:

Sue Anderson, lesbian and gay rights, Denver, Colorado

José Artiga, Salvadorean sanctuary movement, San Francisco, California

Judy Baca, art/Chicano movement, Los Angeles, California

Teresa Caudill Bates and Carol Wright, community organizing/environment, Whitesburg, Kentucky

Joe Begley, coal mining and environment, Blackey, Kentucky

Father Gregory Boyle, youth at risk/gang intervention, Los Angeles, California

Bob Brehm, low-income housing development, Chicago, Illinois

Ann Brown, education/race relations, Lexington, Mississippi

Jack Calhoun, crime prevention/community building, Washington, D.C.

Tyree Coleman, youth activism/community building, Indianapolis, Indiana

Ola Cassadore Davis and Mike Davis, Native American land and religious rights, San Carlos Reservation, Arizona

Pat and Tom Gish, newspaper activism, Whitesburg, Kentucky

James Green, legal and prison system reform, Jackson, Mississippi

Jan Hillegas, civil rights/women's issues, Jackson, Mississippi

Judi Jennings, women's rights/race relations, Louisville, Kentucky

Hazel Johnson, urban pollution, Chicago, Illinois

Maxine Kenney, Anne Lewis and Herb E. Smith, media arts/community organizing, Whitesburg, Kentucky

Stewart Kwoh, Asian Pacific American legal advocacy, Los Angeles, California

Abby Leibman, women's rights, Los Angeles, California

Iñigo Manglano-Ovalle, visual arts/ethnic struggles/community building, Chicago, Illinois

Tim McFeeley, lesbian and gay rights, Washington, D.C.

Pam McMichael, lesbian and gay rights/race relations, Louisville, Kentucky

John O'Neal, theater arts/environment/race relations, New Orleans, Louisiana

Angela Oh, legal advocacy/race relations, Los Angeles, California

Pepon Osorio, visual arts/ethnic struggles, New York, New York

Rosanna Perez, Salvadorean immigration, Los Angeles, California

Ada Sanchez; nuclear waste/race relations/community organizing, Amherst, Massachusetts

Peter Schumann, theater and visual arts/human rights/environment/anti-war, Glover, Vermont

Pete Seeger, music/antiwar/environment/social justice, Hudson, New York

Joe Selvaggio, housing/economic justice, Minneapolis, Minnesota

Kasha Songer, women's issues, Denver, Colorado

Joe Szakos, community organizing, Charlottesville, Virginia

Guida West, welfare rights, New York, New York

INDEX